Frommer's

Honolu

day BY day®

5th Edition

by Jeanne Cooper

Contents

Published by:

Frommer Media LLC

ISBN: 978-1-62887-553-9 (print); 978-1-62887-554-6 (ebk)

Editorial Director: Pauline Frommer
Editor: Elizabeth Heath
Production Editor: Erin Geile
Photo Editor: Meghan Lamb
Cartographer: Liz Puhl

Front cover photos, left to right: Tantalus Lookout, Oʻahu © Hawaii Tourism Authority; Hawaiian green sea turtle © Shane Myers Photography/Shutterstock; Hoʻomaluhia Botanical Garden in Kaneohe, Oʻahu © Shane Myers Photography/Shutterstock.

Back cover photo: Snorkeling paradise Hanauma Bay © Juancat/Shutterstock.

For information on our other products and services, please go to Frommers.com/contactus.

Frommer's also publishes its books in a variety of electronic formats. Some content that appears in print may not be available in electronic formats.

About this Guide

Organizing your time. That's what this guide is all about.

Other guides give you long lists of things to see and do and then expect you to fit the pieces together. The Day by Day guides are different. These guides tell you the best of everything, and then they show you how to see it *in the smartest, most time-efficient way*. Our authors have designed detailed itineraries organized by time, neighborhood, or special interest. And each tour comes with a bulleted map that takes you from stop to stop.

Hoping to sunbathe on a secluded beach, pay your respects at the Pearl Harbor Historic Sites, shop for authentic Alohawear or visit a pineapple plantation? Whatever your interest or schedule, the Day by Days give you the smartest routes to follow. Not only do we take you to the top attractions, hotels, and restaurants, but we also help you access those special moments that locals get to experience—those "finds" that turn tourists into travelers.

The Day by Days are also your top choice if you're looking for one complete guide for all your travel needs. The best hotels and restaurants for every budget, the greatest shopping values, the wildest nightlife—it's all here.

Why should you trust our judgment? Because our authors personally visit each place they write about. They're an independent lot who say what they think and would never include places they wouldn't recommend to their best friends. They're also open to suggestions from readers. If you'd like to contact them, please send your comments our way at feedback@frommers.com, and we'll pass them on.

Enjoy your Day by Day guide—the most helpful travel companion you can buy. And have the trip of a lifetime.

About the Author

Jeanne Cooper writes frequently about Hawai'i for U.S. and international newspapers, magazines, and websites. Formerly travel editor at the *San Francisco Chronicle,* she contributed to guidebooks on San Francisco, Boston, and Washington, D.C., for several different publishers before helping Frommer's relaunch its Hawai'i series in 2015. Jeanne lives on Moku o Keawe, the Big Island, with her Ironman triathlete husband, two dogs, and two cats. Her love for Hawai'i comes from her mother, who learned to play ukulele and dance hula as a young teen on O'ahu.

An Additional Note

Please be advised that travel information is subject to change at any time—and this is especially true of prices. We therefore suggest that you write or call ahead for confirmation when making your travel plans. The authors, editors, and publisher cannot be held responsible for the experiences of readers while traveling. Your safety is important to us, however, so we encourage you to stay alert and be aware of your surroundings.

Star Ratings, Icons & Abbreviations

Every hotel, restaurant, and attraction listing in this guide has been ranked for quality, value, service, amenities, and special features using a **star-rating system.** Hotels, restaurants, attractions, shopping, and nightlife are rated on a scale of zero stars (recommended) to three stars (exceptional). In addition to the star-rating system, we also use a **kids icon** to point out the best bets for families. Within each tour, we recommend cafes, bars, or restaurants where you can take a break. Each of these stops appears in a shaded box marked with a coffee-cup-shaped bullet 🍵.

The following **abbreviations** are used for credit cards:

AE	American Express	DISC	Discover	V	Visa
DC	Diners Club	MC	MasterCard		

Frommers.com

Frommer's travel resources don't end with this guide. Frommer's website, **www.frommers.com**, has travel information on more than 4,000 destinations. We update features regularly, giving you access to the most current trip-planning information and the best airfare, lodging, and car-rental bargains. You can also listen to podcasts, connect with other Frommers.com members through our active-reader forums, share your travel photos, read blogs from guidebook editors and fellow travelers, and much more.

A Note on Prices

In the "Take a Break" and "Best Bets" sections of this book, we have used a system of dollar signs to show a range of costs for 1 night in a hotel (the price of a double-occupancy room) or the cost of an entree at a restaurant. Use the following table to decipher the dollar signs:

Cost	Hotels	Restaurants
$	under $150	under $15
$$	$150–$250	$15–$25
$$$	$250–$350	$25–$40
$$$$	$350–$500	$40–$50
$$$$$	over $500	over $50

How to Contact Us

In researching this book, we discovered many wonderful places—hotels, restaurants, shops, and more. We're sure you'll find others. Please tell us about them, so we can share the information with your fellow travelers in upcoming editions. If you were disappointed with a recommendation, we'd love to know that, too. Please write to: Support@FrommerMedia.com

A Note on Hawaiian Words

The Hawaiian language includes the macron (a line over a long vowel) and the 'okina (a single open quotation mark reflecting a glottal stop, similar to the sound in the middle of "uh-oh.") Most street signs use both marks, but many signs and publications may use only the 'okina or neither. For typographical reasons, this guidebook only uses the 'okina except on maps.

15 Favorite
Moments

15 Favorite Moments

Previous page: Waikiki Beach, with the Diamond Head crater in the background.

Honolulu and the island of O'ahu offer many magical moments, enchanting all the senses. Soak up the warm glow on your skin as you watch the sun rise over Diamond Head, then delight in the brilliant colors of tropical fish darting around you in the ocean. Savor the sweet refreshment of shave ice as it melts like a snowflake in your mouth and inhale the scent of a plumeria lei that can perfume your room for days. As the setting sun casts its final rays over the ocean, listen to the *leo nahenahe* (soft, sweet voices) of Hawaiian musicians accompanied by slack key guitar and ukulele. Consider these following favorite moments of mine a jumping-off point for discovering yours.

1 Seeing Waikiki offshore. The wide-angle view of Waikiki from a boat, from Ala Wai Yacht Harbor all the way to Diamond Head, is incomparably beautiful. I prefer a tranquil morning cruise through the clear blue waters, to be greeted perhaps by a green sea turtle, but a sunset cruise can be very romantic, watching the setting sun and the twinkling lights of Waikiki (and fireworks, if it's a Friday) go up. *See p 190.*

2 Experiencing the beginning and end of World War II in the Pacific at Pearl Harbor. A day at Pearl Harbor National Memorial provides an unforgettable opportunity to witness the tragedy and bravery of war. Make reservations early for the shuttle to the USS *Arizona* Memorial, where the sunken ship resting underneath the memorial's open-air white hall exudes oil-like dark teardrops. The Japanese air raid on

December 7, 1941 caused the 608-foot (185m) *Arizona* to sink just 9 minutes after being bombed; more than 900 of the 1,177 men on board who died still remain entombed below. Galleries on land share the context and aftermath of the attack, which claimed 2,341 U.S. service members and sent many more to fight in the Pacific. But your visit is not complete without seeing where that arena of war ended on September 2, 1945: aboard the Battleship *Missouri,* itself a memorial now permanently moored in Pearl Harbor. If stories of heroism, honor, and hard work move you, this is the place to go. *See p 13.*

3 Encountering ancient and modern Hawai'i at the Bishop Museum. To get a sense of what Hawai'i was like before the Europeans landed, and experience the unique worldview of a culture that never

The USS Arizona Memorial at Pearl Harbor.

completely disappeared, head to the Bishop Museum. With a 55-foot (17m) sperm whale hanging above them, the intriguing exhibits in gorgeous Hawaiian Hall tell stories of *wao lani* (the realm of gods and chiefs), *wao kanaka* (the realm of ordinary life) and *kai akea* (the realm of the sea, where all life began) Created by the widower of a Hawaiian princess in 1889, the Bishop Museum also has an interactive science center and planetarium where you can learn about waves, volcanoes, and the stars that Polynesian voyagers used to find these incredibly remote islands. *See p 21.*

❹ **Kayaking at Kailua Beach.** The Windward Side is full of gorgeous, white sand beaches, but Kailua is the easiest for launching a kayak trip to the Mokulua ("two island") islets, ¾ mile (1.2km) offshore. Even easier is paddling to Popoia (nicknamed "Flat Island"), a third of the distance. I love paddling across shimmering turquoise water to Popoia, where I can ogle Mokulua in one direction and the furrowed green Ko'olau mountains in the other. Novices may enjoy taking a guided tour. *See p 190.*

❺ **Touring a royal palace with a painful past.** The grandeur of the Hawaiian monarchy and the shock of its overthrow in 1893 by a

U.S.-backed coup resound in 'Iolani Palace. I love the replicas of royal gowns in the main rooms upstairs and the real jewels and finery in a gallery downstairs, but seeing the bedroom where deposed Queen Lili'uokalani was held under house arrest for a year—unjustly convicted of treason by the new government—is even more moving. *See p 15.*

❻ **Snorkeling among the rainbow-colored fish in the warm waters of Hanauma Bay.** Despite decades of overuse, this underwater park, once a volcanic crater, still teems with tropical fish. Bordered by a 2,000-foot (610m) gold-sand beach, the bay's shallow water (10 ft/3m in places) is perfect for novice snorkelers. A new online permitting system has reduced the crowds to more manageable sizes, but be sure to book an early morning slot if possible. You'll find cheaper snorkel gear rentals offsite. *See p 185.*

❼ **Hiking to the top of Diamond Head for the perfect view of the island.** See Waikiki and Honolulu from the top of Hawai'i's most famous landmark. Nearly everyone in decent shape can handle this 1.4-mile (2.3km) round-trip hike, which goes up to the top of the 750-foot (229m) volcanic cone. There you have a 360-degree view of O'ahu. Online reservations are now required, but it

Calm, shallow Hanauma Bay is a favorite snorkeling spot.

can still get crowded. Allow an hour for the trip up and back, and wear sturdy shoes; the path turns slippery when wet. *See p 173.*

⑧ Watching the North Shore's big waves. When monstrous waves—some 30 feet (9.1m) tall—steamroll into Waimea Bay (Nov–Mar), everyone heads to the North Shore to watch. You can watch the best surfers in the world paddle out to challenge these freight trains—it's shocking to see how small they appear in the lip of the giant waves. My favorite place to observe surfers, though, is from the poolside bar at Turtle Bay Resort, on a bluff above roiling Kawela Bay. *p 145.*

⑨ Buying a lei in Chinatown. There's lots of great shopping in Honolulu's Chinatown, especially for that icon of Hawai'i, the flower lei. Be sure to check out the lei sellers on Maunakea Street (near N. Hotel St.). You'll be intoxicated by the fragrant perfumes of the puakenikeni, pikake (jasmine), tuberose, and other flowers, and the leimakers' artistry of weaving them with other flowers, ferns, and leaves. The simplest leis start around $12. *See p 126.*

⑩ Learning to surf in Waikiki. There are lots of places in the world to learn how to surf, but Hawai'i is where the sport began—and where many of the world's best show off their skills today. Some former pros have opened surf schools in Waikiki or on the North Shore, while the official beachboys of Waikiki have taught generations of visitors how to surf. Take it from me—the first time you ride a wave, even if you're not fully standing or you spill five seconds later, you'll feel a rush like no other. *See p 192.*

⑪ Swimming under a waterfall in a lush, historic valley. Themed botanical gardens with thousands of tropical plants, shrubs, and trees line the paved path in Waimea Valley to a 45-foot (14m) waterfall, where if conditions permit, you're allowed to swim. I enjoy taking my time to learn about the valley's ancient cultural sites well as its indigenous and rare plants before a refreshing dip in the very cool water. *See p 63.*

⑫ Ordering a shave ice on a hot day. You don't need rain to create a rainbow with shave ice. Choose several fruit syrups to cascade over an impossibly large mound of soft, fluffy ice, perhaps drizzled with coconut cream or sitting atop ice cream. My favorite spot is Island X Hawai'i on the North Shore, where the syrups are made with local fruit, such as liliko'i (passionfruit) and mango, and local sugar. *See p 143.*

⑬ Watching a hula dancer at sunset. You'll hear live Hawaiian music in many places throughout the islands, and in many genres, including slack key guitar, reggae-influenced "Jawaiian," falsetto, country, and vintage *hapa haole* (Hawaiian melodies with English lyrics). But there's no better accompaniment to traditional Hawaiian music than a graceful hula dancer. I like to reserve a table at sunset at House Without a Key, the Halekulani's open-air, oceanfront lounge, to enjoy the beautiful hula of a former Miss Hawai'i, backed by a Hawaiian music trio and breathtaking views of Waikiki and Diamond Head. *See p 138.*

Learning to surf in Waikiki.

Finding Your Way Around, O'ahu-Style

Mainlanders sometimes find the directions given by locals a bit confusing. You seldom hear the terms east, west, north, and south; instead, islanders refer to directions as either **makai** (ma-kye), meaning toward the sea, or **mauka** (mow-kah), toward the mountains. In Honolulu, people use **Diamond Head** as a direction meaning to the east (in the direction of the world-famous crater renamed Diamond Head by Westerners), and **'Ewa** (eh-vah, with vowels sounding like "ever") as a direction meaning to the west (toward the town called 'Ewa, on the other side of Pearl Harbor).

So, if you ask a local for directions, this is what you're likely to hear: "Drive 2 blocks makai (toward the sea), then turn Diamond Head (east) at the stoplight. Go 1 block, and turn mauka (toward the mountains). It's on the 'Ewa (western) side of the street."

⑭ Discovering the sport of outrigger canoe paddling. For something uniquely Hawaiian, watch paddlers in six-person outrigger canoes head out to sea from Ala Wai Canal at dawn or dusk. Or try it yourself off Waikiki Beach—with the help of a guide, you can even ride the surf back into shore. *See p 189.*

⑮ Sampling local and Hawaiian food. The diced raw fish dish of poke has spread across the mainland, but have you tried laulau (pork wrapped in taro leaves and then swaddled in ti leaves and steamed), Spam musubi (sushi rice and grilled Spam wrapped in seaweed) or malasadas, deep-fried sweet dough dusted in sugar? These local favorites reflect the "mixed plate" that is modern Hawai'i. Asian and European plantation laborers brought to work in the sugar and pineapple fields added their cuisine and culture to that of Native Hawaiians. Don't leave without having tried the delicious results. *See p 99.* ●

Sweet, fruity shave ice is an O'ahu tradition.

Strategies for Seeing O'ahu

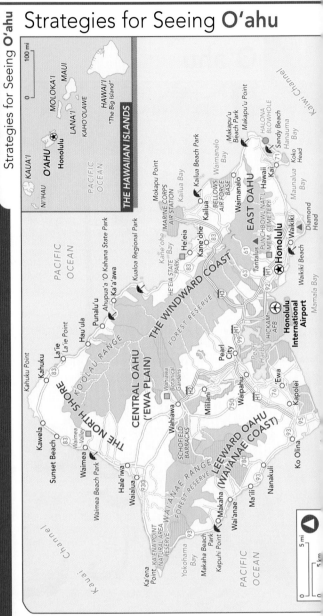

THE HAWAIIAN ISLANDS

KAUA'I

NI'IHAU

O'AHU
Honolulu

MOLOKA'I

MAUI

LANA'I

KAHO'OLAWE

HAWAI'I
"The Big Island"

PACIFIC
OCEAN

0   100 mi

Kaiwi Channel

Makapu'u Point

HALONA
BLOWHOLE
Makapu'u
Beach Park

Makapu'u Point

Sandy Beach

Koko
Head

Hanauma
Bay

Waimanalo

Kai

Hawaii
Kai

Maunalua
Bay

BELLOWS
AIR FORCE
BASE

Kailua

Waimanalo

Kailua Bay

Kailua Beach Park

Mokapu Point

MARINE CORPS
AIR STATION

He'eia

Kane'ohe

Kane'ohe Bay

HE'EIA STATE
PARK

EAST OAHU

Diamond
Head

Waikiki

PUNCHBOWL NAT'L
MEM. CEMETERY

Tantalus

Honolulu

Waikiki Beach

Ahupua'a 'O Kahana State Park

Ka'a'awa

Kualoa Regional Park

THE WINDWARD COAST

KO'OLAU RANGE

FOREST RESERVE

H3

61

83

83

Punalu'u

Hau'ula

La'ie

La'ie Point

PACIFIC
OCEAN

Kahuku Point

Kahuku

THE NORTH SHORE

Waimea
Valley

Waimea
Beach Park

Sunset Beach

Kawela

Wahiawa
Botanical
Gardens

CENTRAL OAHU
('EWA PLAIN')

SCHOFIELD
BARRACKS

Mililani

Wahiawa

Pearl
City

Pearl Harbor

Waipahu

99

750

76

HICKAM
AFB

Honolulu
International
Airport

Mamala Bay

H1

92

H1

Ewa

Kapolei

95

Ko Olina

Waipahu

93

80

Ma'ili

Wai'anae

Nanakuli

Makaha

Makaha Beach
Park

Kepuhi Point

WAI'ANAE RANGE

FOREST RESERVE

LEEWARD OAHU
(WAI'ANAE COAST)

93

93

Ka'ena
Point

KA'ENA POINT
NATURAL
AREA
RESERVE

Yokohama
Bay

Hale'iwa

Waialua

930

83

Kauai Channel

PACIFIC
OCEAN

0   5 mi
0   5 km

Previous page: Surfboards lined up in the rack on Waikiki Beach.

O'ahu may be an island, but it's a good-sized island, and your vacation time is precious. There really is just one cardinal rule: Relax. Don't run yourself ragged trying to see absolutely everything—take the time to experience the magic of the island. In this chapter, I offer several suggestions for making the most of your visit.

Take time to stop and smell the plumeria!

Rule #1. Go in the off season.

Not only will you save a bundle, but there will be fewer people, the beaches will be less crowded, and it'll be easier to get into your favorite restaurants. The "off season," September to November and mid-April through early June, can get hot but is typically not too rainy.

Rule #2. Think about how you want to spend your vacation.

Is this a lie-on-the-beach vacation or a get-up-early-and-go-on-an-adventure-every-day vacation? Or a combination of the two? Whether you are traveling with your sweetie or you're bringing your family, make sure that everyone gets in on the planning—it makes for a vacation that everyone can enjoy.

Rule #3. Don't overschedule.

Don't make your days jam-packed from the time you get up until you drop off to sleep at night. This is Hawai'i: Stop and smell the plumeria. Allow time to just relax. And don't forget that you will most likely arrive jet-lagged, so ease into your vacation. Exposure to sunlight can help reset your internal clock, so hit the beach on your first day (and bring your sunscreen).

Rule #4. Allow plenty of time to get around the island.

If you glance at a map, O'ahu looks deceptively small—as though you could just zip from one side of the island to the other. But you have to

A drive along the North Shore rewards with stunning beaches and numerous historic sites.

Moco from Moke's Bread and Breakfast.

take traffic into consideration; from 6 to 9am and 3 to 6pm, the main roads will be bumper-to-bumper with rush-hour traffic. Plan accordingly: Sleep late and get on the road after the traffic has cleared out. I highly recommend that you rent a car, but don't just "view" the island from the car window. Plan to get out as much as possible to breathe in the tropical aroma, fill up on those views, and listen to the sounds of the tropics.

Rule #5. If your visit is short, stay in one place.

Most places on O'ahu are within easy driving distance of each other, and checking in and out of several hotels can get old fast. There's the schlepping of the luggage, the waiting in line to check in, the unpacking, and more . . . only to repeat the entire process a few days later. Your vacation time is too dear.

Rule #6. Pick the key activity of the day and plan accordingly.

To maximize your time, decide what you really want to do that day, and then plan all other activities in the same geographical area. That way you won't have to track back and forth across the island.

Rule #7. Remember that you are on an island of aloha.

Hawai'i is not the U.S. mainland. Slow down. Smile and say "aloha"; or "Howzit?" (the local expression for "How are you?"). When they ask you, tell 'em, "Couldn't be better—I'm in Hawai'i!" Be patient and laugh a lot, even if things aren't going as planned.

Rule #8. Use this book as a reference, not a concrete plan.

Pick and choose according to your interests—don't feel like you have to follow my suggestions to the letter. Take the weather and surf report into account when choosing outdoor activities and make pit stops whenever a food truck, farm stand, or shave ice place looks good to you.

Rule #9. Eat as the locals do.

The local cuisine tells the history of a place. The food in Hawai'i is the story of waves of immigration: the original Polynesian voyagers; the New England missionaries; the laborers from Japan, China, Korea, the Philippines, and the Azores, among others, who came to work the plantations in the 20th century; the U.S. military. So skip the chain restaurants and head to down-home joints where you can eat popular dishes invented in Hawai'i, like poke (cubes of seasoned raw fish), laulau (pork wrapped in taro leaves), and loco moco (rice topped with a hamburger patty, gravy, and fried egg). (See p 99, "Going Local.") ●

The Best of O'ahu in Three Days

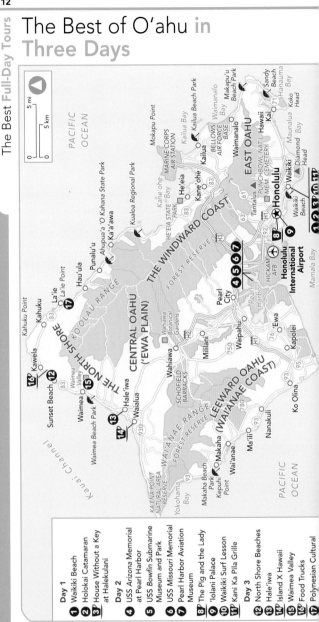

PACIFIC OCEAN

Kahuku Point

Kahuku

Kawela

Waimea Valley

THE NORTH SHORE

Sunset Beach

Waimea

Waimea Beach Park

Hale'iwa

Wai'alua

Kauai Channel

KALENA POINT NATURAL AREA RESERVE

Yokohama Bay

Makaha Beach Park

Kepuhi Point

Wai'anae

Makaha

Ma'ili

Nanakuli

Ko Olina

LEEWARD OAHU (WAI'ANAE COAST)

WAI'ANAE RANGE FOREST RESERVE

PACIFIC OCEAN

Mamala Bay

Kapolei

Ewa

Waipahu

Pearl City

SCHOFIELD BARRACKS

Mililani

Wahiawa

Wahiawa Botanical Gardens

CENTRAL OAHU ('EWA PLAIN)

KO'OLAU RANGE

FOREST RESERVE

La'ie

La'ie Point

Hau'ula

Punalu'u

Ahupua'a 'O Kahana State Park

Ka'a'awa

Kualoa Regional Park

THE WINDWARD COAST

Ka'ne'ohe

He'eia

HE'EIA STATE PARK

Kane'ohe Bay

Mokapu Point

MARINE CORPS AIR STATION

Kailua Bay

Kailua Beach Park

Kailua

Waimanalo

BELLOWS AIR FORCE BASE

Waimanalo Beach Park

Makapu'u Beach Park

Sandy Beach

Koko Head

Hanauma Bay

Maunalua Bay

Koko Kai

Diamond Head

EAST OAHU

Tantalus

PUNCHBOWL NAT'L MEM. CEMETERY

Honolulu

Waikiki Beach

Waikiki

Honolulu International Airport

HICKAM AFB

Pearl Harbor

PACIFIC OCEAN

Day 1

❶ Waikiki Beach
❷ Holokai Catamaran
❸ House Without a Key at Halekulani

Day 2

❹ USS Arizona Memorial at Pearl Harbor
❺ USS Bowfin Submarine Museum and Park
❻ USS Missouri Memorial
❼ Pearl Harbor Aviation Museum
❽ The Pig and the Lady
❾ 'Iolani Palace
❿ Waikiki Surf Lesson
⓫ Kani Ka Pila Grille

Day 3

⓬ North Shore Beaches
⓭ Hale'iwa
⓮ Island X Hawaii
⓯ Waimea Valley
⓰ Food Trucks
⓱ Polynesian Cultural

Previous page: A sunset sail from Waikiki Beach.

Yiou could spend weeks on O'ahu without running out of things to do, but it's possible to see the highlights of this romantic isle in just 3 days. Following this tour will let you see the best of O'ahu, from Waikiki to the North Shore. You'll definitely need to rent a car, so remember to plan for that cost. Each day begins and ends in Waikiki, which, like most urban cities, has traffic congestion, so allow plenty of travel time, especially during rush hour.

Day 1

1 ★★★ Waikiki Beach. You'll never forget your first steps onto the powdery sands of this world-famous beach. If you're just off the plane, plan to spread your towel on the beach, take in the smell of the salt air, feel the warm breeze on your skin, and relax; you're in Hawai'i. *See p 169.*

2 ★★ Holokai Catamaran. One of the most fun and effortless ways to get on the water is a sail off Waikiki. Sign up for the twice-daily Turtle Canyon Adventure Sail (which takes you snorkeling amid green sea turtles and bright, tropical fish) or the mellow Tradewind Sail, on this well-managed catamaran with an admirable selection of adult beverages. ⏱ *11⁄2–21⁄2 hr. Gray's Beach in front of the Halekulani, 2199 Kalia Rd., Waikiki. www. sailholokai.com.* ☎ *808/922-2210. Tradewind Sail $50. Turtle Canyon Adventure Sail $95.*

3 ★★★ House Without a Key. As the sun sinks toward the horizon, toast the day with an expert mai tai or a small-plates dinner at this newly renovated oceanfront lounge and restaurant at Halekulani, the most luxurious hotel on Waikiki Beach. You can watch a former Miss Hawai'i dance hula to the riffs of a virtuoso trio on guitar, ukulele, and stand-up bass. With the sunset and ocean glowing behind her, and Diamond Head visible in the distance, the scene is straight out of a storybook—romantic, evocative, nostalgic. The coconut shrimp and cocktails are fabulous, too. *2199 Kalia Rd., Waikiki. www. halekulani.com.* ☎ *808/923-2311. $$.*

Day 2

Go early to beat the crowds at the sights of Pearl Harbor National Memorial, after reserving your water shuttle to the USS *Arizona* Memorial up to 8 weeks in advance.

4 ★★★ USS *Arizona* Memorial. The top attraction on O'ahu is

First order of business after touch-down in Honolulu? Hit the beach!

this unforgettable memorial. On December 7, 1941, the Japanese launched an air raid on Pearl Harbor that plunged the U.S. into World War II. This 608-foot (185m) battleship sank in 9 minutes without firing a shot, taking 1,177 sailors and Marines to their deaths. The deck of the *Arizona* lies 6 feet (1.8m) below the surface of the sea, with oil still slowly oozing up from the engine room and staining the harbor's calm, blue water. Some say the ship still weeps for its lost crew. A free 23-minute film and thoughtful museums on land help tell the story, including the events leading up to and after the attack. The excellent, 2½-hour ★★★ **audio tour** makes the trip even more meaningful—it's like having your own personal park ranger as a guide. The cost is $9, including a $1 service fee for the otherwise free water shuttle. Book ahead at www.recreation.gov/ticket/facility/233338, which also offers shuttle-only reservations ($1 service fee) and a deluxe tour with virtual reality experience ($19, including service fee). *Note:* Boat rides to the *Arizona* are sometimes suspended because of high winds; check the national monument's website (ww.nps.gov/perl) for updates. For security reasons, visitors also cannot carry purses, handbags, backpacks, or bags of any kind (other than small clutches and wallets) that offer concealment on the boat. Storage is available for $6–$10 near the Visitor Center. ⏱ *3 hr.; book online at www.recreation.gov to be assured a water shuttle reservation ($1), since first-come, first-served ticket distribution has been indefinitely suspended. Arrive early for closer-in parking (free). 1 Arizona Memorial Place, Honolulu. www.nps.gov/perl.* ☎ *808/422-3399. Free admission. Daily 7am–5pm (last water shuttle 3:30pm). Shirts and closed-toe shoes required; no swimsuits or flip-flops allowed. Wheelchairs accommodated.*

If you're a history or military buff, stop in at least one of the next few museums, which are described in the "Wartime Honolulu" tour starting on p 46, and plan on a simple outdoor lunch at the Battleship *Missouri* Memorial's food truck or in the air-conditioned cafe of the Pearl Harbor Aviation Museum. Otherwise, head directly to Chinatown for lunch.

⑤ ★ USS *Bowfin* Submarine Museum & Park. *See p 47,* ❷.

⑥ ★★ Battleship *Missouri* Memorial. *See p 49,* ❺.

⑦ ★ Pearl Harbor Aviation Museum. *See p 48,* ❸.

⑧ ★★★ The Pig and the Lady. You'll want to make reservations in advance for this perennial hot spot, one of the liveliest dining rooms in Chinatown. Chef Andrew Le excels in both classic Vietnamese dishes and modern inspirations, with flavor-packed options for everyone from vegans to meat-lovers. *83 N. King St., Honolulu. www.thepigandthelady.com.* ☎ *808/585-8255. $$*

USS *Arizona* Memorial

Pearl Harbor Without the Drive

Commercial half-day tours (starting at $60 adults, $38 children) provide a water shuttle reservation to the USS *Arizona* Memorial with an air-conditioned bus or van ride to and from Waikiki; the return includes a drive-by tour of the National Memorial Cemetery of the Pacific ("Punchbowl") and historic sites in downtown Honolulu. Longer options (7–10 hr., from $129) add entrance to the Battleship *Missouri* Memorial and other sites. Check out the various options of veteran tour company **Roberts Hawaii** (www.roberts hawaii.com; ☎ **808/539-9400**) and **Pearl Harbor Tours** (www.pearlharbortours.com; ☎ **808/312-3705**); the latter's small-group tours (12 passengers max) include guides enthralled by Pearl Harbor's history.

From the Pig and the Lady, it's only a half-mile (.8 km) south on King St. to 'Iolani Palace, so you may want to leave your car where it is.

⑨ ★★ 'Iolani Palace. Once the site of a *heiau* (temple), 'Iolani Palace took 3 years and $350,000 to complete in 1882, with all the modern conveniences of its time. Royals lived here for 11 years until Queen Lili'uokalani was deposed in a palace coup led by U.S. Marines on January 17, 1893, at the demand of sugar planters and American missionary descendants. She was later tried by a military tribunal in the throne room and sentenced to house arrest in an upstairs bedroom for eight months. Millions of dollars have since been spent to restore it; a more recent initiative has recreated a variety of royal gowns and uniforms. Docent-led and self-guided audio tours (reservations required) reveal both the finery and bravery of the palace's former residents, with an aura of poignant loss and dignified defiance. Online reservations, shirts, footwear, and respectful behavior are required. ① 1–2 hr. 364 S. King St. (at Richards St.; enter off Likelike Mall), Honolulu. www.iolanipalace.org. ☎ 808/522-0832. 90-min. guided tour (including self-guided basement gallery tour afterward) $30 adults, $27 teens 13 to 17, $12 children 5–12; available Wed. 9am–12:30pm, Thu 9am–2:30pm, Sat 3pm. 90-min. audio tour

The Throne Room in the 'Iolani Palace.

Surfing at Waikiki Beach.

$25 adults, $20 teens 13 to 17, $10 children 5–12; available Tues, Fri, Sat 9am–4pm and Wed 1:30–2:30pm, See website for new 45-min. to 1-hr. specialty tours (royal fashion, Chamberlain's Office, Japanese connection), $70 adults, $45 children 5–12, including keepsake.

🔟 **Surf lesson in Waikiki.** If you're not too tired, end the day with a sunset surf session, when the sun is less hot. Waikiki has great waves for learning, and a surf lesson with Hans Hedemann Surf School will have you riding the waves in no time. ⏱ *2 hr. At the Queen Kapi'olani Hotel, 150 Kapahulu Ave., Waikiki. www.hhsurf.com.* ☎ *808/924-7778. $90 for 2-hour group lesson.*

11 ⭐⭐ **Kani Ka Pila Grille.** Nightly entertainment from the best Hawaiian musicians—specializing in slack-key guitar, ukulele, falsetto, traditional, and reggae-inflected ("Jawaiian") genres—plus loyal audiences (split equally among residents and visitors) make this one of the liveliest nightspots in Waikiki. Poolside at the newly renovated Outrigger Reef Waikiki Beach Resort,

it boasts an elevated stage (with room for hula dancers, who often spontaneously join in) and a crowd-pleasing menu with island favorites along with delicious cocktails from locally sourced spirits. *2169 Kalia Rd., Waikiki. www.outrigger.com/landing-pages/services/orf-kkpg.* ☎ *808/924-4990.*

Day 3
Spend your third day on O'ahu on the North Shore, after letting the morning rush hour traffic heading toward downtown and Pearl Harbor subside.

12 ⭐⭐⭐ **North Shore beaches.** Choose any one of the North Shore beaches to spend the morning. If it's winter and the surf's up, you'll want to head to Pipeline or Sunset to watch the surfers on some of the best waves in the world. If it's summer, head to Waimea to swim in the calm, beautiful bay or to Shark's Cove at Pupukea Beach Park for snorkeling. *See p 143.*

13 ⭐⭐⭐ **Hale'iwa.** At lunchtime, explore this famous North Shore surfing town, full of boutiques, art galleries, food trucks, and plenty of surf shops. *See p 144,* ❹.

Waimea Bay Beach Park offers calm waters for summertime swimming.

A famous surfing town, Haleʻiwa is also known for its food trucks.

⑭ ★ Island X Hawaii. After lunch, skip the lines at Matsumoto's Shave Ice, an iconic but always crowded Haleʻiwa tourist hotspot, and head to this family-run coffee bar, shave ice and ice cream stand inside the Old Waialua Sugar Mill. It has my favorite shave ice—Hawaiʻi's rendition of a snow cone, with soft, fluffy shaved ice replacing crunchy, crushed ice—since all the tropical flavors here are natural, including liliʻoi (passionfruit), mango, and pineapple syrups made from local fruit. Even the sugar comes from Oʻahu, and you can order your shave ice more or less sweet. The coffee and cacao beans grown on site are delicious, too; ask for a free sample or quick tour. *67-106 Kealohanui St., Waialua. www.islandxhawaii. com.* ☎ *808-637-2624. Sun–Fri 9:30am–5pm, Sat 8:30am–5pm. $.*

⑮ ★★ Waimea Valley. After lunch and a shave ice, head into this beautiful, 150-acre (61-ha) outdoor cultural park and botanical garden, with more than 5,000 species of tropical plants. Bring a swimsuit in case conditions permit a dip in the pool under the 45-foot-high (14m) waterfall. *See p 63,* ❼. ⏱ *2 hr. Waimea Valley Rd. waimeavalley.net.* ☎ *808-638-7766. Admission $25 adults, $18 seniors and students with ID, $14 children 4–12. Daily 9am–5pm.*

⑯ Food trucks. You'll notice lots of food trucks lining Kamehameha Highway, all the way from Haleʻiwa to Sunset Beach to Kahuku, where the shrimp trucks are famous (p 147). My favorite one for dinner near Sunset Beach is The Elephant Truck, with strands of lights illuminating picnic tables. The specialty here is simple and fresh Thai food: Try the grilled chicken tossed in a tangy lime-cilantro sauce with green papaya. The vegan options are terrific, too. *59-186 Kamehameha Hwy., Pupukea. www. 808elephant.com. Daily 5–9pm. $.*

⑰ ★★ Ha: Breath of Life at the Polynesian Cultural Center. Catch the evening show at the Polynesian Cultural Center, the "living museum" of Polynesia. *Ha: Breath of Life is* a coming-of-age "circle of life" story (reminiscent of "The Lion King") told through the dances of Fiji, New Zealand, Samoa, Tahiti, Tonga, and Hawaiʻi. This long-running production remains one of Oʻahu's best shows. **Note:** You can't book show-only tickets online; reserve by phone to guarantee seating. ⏱ *1½ hr. 55–370 Kamehameha Hwy., Laʻie. www.polynesia. com.* ☎ *800/367-7060, 808/293-3333. $90 adults, $72 children 4–11. Thurs–Sat and Mon–Tues 7:30pm.*

A performance at the Polynesian Cultural Center.

The Best of O'ahu in One Week

If possible, stay on O'ahu for at least 1 week so that you can take in the sights at a leisurely, island-style pace. You'll have time to see all the sights I recommended in the 3-day tour, plus explore the enchanting underwater world at Hanauma Bay, delve into Hawaiian history and culture, visit the art world, do some shopping, and spend more time at the beach.

Malasadas (hole-less doughnuts) from Leonard's Bakery.

Days 1–3

For your first 3 days on O'ahu, follow the itinerary for "The Best of O'ahu in Three Days," starting on p 12, with two exceptions: On Day 2, instead of visiting 'Iolani Palace (don't worry—you'll see it later on this tour), spend more time at Pearl Harbor or Chinatown (see my tour of this neighborhood on p 74) or just relax and wander through Waikiki or shops and spend more time in the waves. On Day 3, skip the evening show—you'll enjoy it after a full afternoon at the Polynesian

Cultural Center on day 7 in this tour—and instead treat yourself to a sunset trail ride or dinner and drinks at Turtle Bay Resort (p 145).

Day 4

1 ★★★ **Malasadas at Leonard's Bakery.** Join the locals and tourists at Leonard's Bakery, which was started in 1952 by Portuguese immigrants. Grab a malasada (a hole-less doughnut), hot and fresh out of the fryer and dipped in sugar. Try the version dusted with sugar and li hing mui ("lee hing moo-ee"), a sweet-and-sour flavoring made from salted dried plums. *933 Kapahulu Ave., Honolulu. www.leonards hawaii.com.* ☎ *808/737-5571. $.*

2 ★★★ **Hanauma Bay Natural Preserve.** You'll need to reserve admission ($25) in advance for O'ahu's best snorkeling site, a spectacular volcanic crater with a beautiful beach; arrive early for the easiest parking and calmest water. *Note:* The preserve is closed Mondays and Tuesdays. *See p 185.*

Tranquil Hanauma Bay is a great place for novice snorkelers.

Hop on a 34-seat, open-air, motorized Waikiki Trolley for a fun way to get around the island. The Red Line's Heroes and Legends tour loops around Waikiki and downtown Honolulu, stopping every hour at 12 sightseeing or shopping destinations (including Honolulu Museum of Art, 'Iolani Palace, Chinatown, Salt at Our Kaka'ako, and Ala Moana Shopping Center) and making a scenic drive through the hillside National Memorial Cemetery of the Pacific ("Punchbowl"). The driver provides commentary along the way. The 10 stops on the fully narrated, 3-hour Blue Line's Coast Line/Diamond Head tour (also a loop from Waikiki) include the Honolulu Zoo, Diamond Head, Halona Blowhole, and Sea Life Park. The Pink Line stops every half-hour at a number of Waikiki hotels en route to Ala Moana Shopping Center and back. All lines permit hop-on, hop-off travel. Book online for the best rates: A 1-day, 1-line Blue or Red Line trolley pass costs $25 ($15 ages 3–11), while the Pink Line is just $5 per person. You can't really take advantage of the Blue and Red lines on the same day, so to sample both, book a 2-day or longer all-lines pass (from $55 adults, $30 ages 3–11). Call ☎ **800/824-8804** or 808/593-2822 for more information, or go to www.waikikitrolley.com.

❸ Halona Blowhole. *See p 150,* **❸**.

❹ ★★ Makapu'u Point Lighthouse Trail. You've seen this famous lighthouse on episodes of *Magnum, P.I.* and *Hawaii Five-O.* No longer staffed by the Coast Guard (it's fully automated now), the lighthouse sits at the end of a precipitous cliff trail on an airy perch looking over the Windward Coast, Manana (Rabbit) Island, and the azure Pacific. The view of the ocean all the way to Moloka'i and Lana'i is often so clear that January through March, if you're lucky, you'll see migrating humpback whales. ⏱ *1 hr. Makapu'u Lighthouse Rd.*

❺ Uncle Clay's House of Pure Aloha. Here's a rare shave ice spot on this side of the island that uses syrups made with local fruit. Unlike other places that rely on artificially colored and flavored syrups, at Uncle Clay's, the pineapple and mango are the real deal. The aloha here is real, too: Co-owners Clayton ("Uncle Clay") Chang and his nephew Bronson Chang also encourage patrons to take their Pure Aloha Pledge to "bring love into the hearts of others and make our world a better place." *820 W. Hind Dr., Honolulu. houseofpurealoha.com.* ☎ *808/373-5111. Daily noon to 6pm. $.*

❻ ★ Pu'u 'Ualaka'a State Wayside. One of the best sunset views in Honolulu is from this 1,048-foot-high (319m) forested cinder cone. Its Hawaiian name means "rolling sweet potato hill," which describes how early planters used gravity to harvest their crop. On a clear day (which is almost always), the majestic, sweeping views stretch from Diamond Head to the

The Waikiki Trolley on Kalakaua avenue in Waikiki.

Wai'anae Range—almost the whole South Shore of O'ahu. At night, several scenic overlooks provide romantic spots for couples to linger with city lights below and stars twinkling above. Arrive before sunset and you can walk off your shave ice and malasada calories on a 1-mile (1.6km) loop trail. ① *20–40 min. At the end of Round Top Dr., Honolulu. dlnr.hawaii.gov/dsp/parks/oahu/puu-ualakaa-state-wayside. Daily (7am–7:45pm in summer).*

Day 5

❼ ★★★ Bishop Museum. If you are the least bit curious about Hawaiian culture, this museum is a must-see. This multi-building museum has the world's greatest collection of natural and cultural artifacts from Hawai'i and the Pacific. Another highlight is the 16,500-square-foot (1,533-sq.-m) Science Adventure Center, which specializes in volcanology and oceanography. In the magnificent Hawaiian Hall, you can see what Hawaiian culture was like before Westerners arrived and how it's being practiced today. Don't miss the shows in the planetarium ($3 each), where you can explore the night sky and learn about

The Bishop Museum presents a vast collection of cultural and natural Hawaiian artifacts.

The mausoleum of King Lunalilo at Kawaiaha'o Church.

8 ★★★ 'Iolani Palace. Book a tour in advance to visit what was once the official residence of Hawai'i's monarchy. It remains a symbol of Hawaiian pride, especially for the islands' sovereignty movement. See p 15, **9**.

9 ★ Kawaiaha'o Church. When the missionaries came to Hawai'i, the first thing they did was build churches. Four thatched grass churches had been built on this site before Rev. Hiram Bingham began building what he considered a "real" church—a New England–style congregational structure with Gothic influences. Between 1837 and 1842, the building of the church required some 14,000 giant coral slabs, some weighing more than 1,000 lb. (454kg), cut from reefs by Hawaiian divers and causing irreparable damage. Kawaiaha'o, the oldest church on O'ahu, has been the site of numerous historical events, such as a speech made by King Kamehameha III in 1843, an excerpt of which became the state motto ("*Ua mau ke ea o ka 'aina i ka pono,*" which translates to "The life of the land is preserved in righteousness"). The clock tower in the church, donated by King Kamehameha III and installed in 1850, continues to tick today. Don't sit in the pews in the back, marked with *kahili* (feather standards) and velvet cushions; they are still reserved for the descendants of royalty. *Tip:* Bring your smartphone and earbuds to take advantage of the church's historical walking tour (including details on King Lunalilo's Tomb and the Princess Ka'iulani bench and plantings outside); you'll download information from QR codes on panels throughout the church campus. *957 Punchbowl St. (at King St.). www.kawaia haochurch.com.* 📞 *808/469-3000. Free admission (donations*

traditional celestial navigation; today, the planetarium helps train new generations of ocean wayfinders. The sunny grounds also host a native Hawaiian botanical garden and family programs. I'm drawn to the somewhat somber gallery with elegant *kahili* (torchlike feather standards) and portraits of the Hawaiian royalty, revered in Hawaiian culture, they represent. Stop by the cafe, operated by local favorite restaurant Highway Inn, for a classic Hawaiian plate lunch. *Tip:* Book online for a $2 discount per ticket and to guarantee your entry time; hourly admissions are limited, but once you're in, you can stay till closing at 5pm. 🕐 *3–4 hr. 1525 Bernice St., just off Kalihi St. (Likelike Hwy.), Honolulu. www.bishop museum.org.* 📞 *808/847-3511. Timed admission $25 adults, $22 seniors, $17 children 4–17, free for children 3 & younger. Daily 9am–5pm.*

A trek to the top of Diamond Head is rewarded with spectacular views.

appreciated). Mon–Fri 8am–4:30pm; Sun services 8:30am.

Between downtown's historic sites and Waikiki Beach are the trendy Kaka'ako and Ward Village neighborhoods, with luxury high-rise condos, modern art murals, boutiques, and popular restaurants like Merriman's Honolulu.

⑩ ★★★ **Merriman's Honolulu.** One of the founders of the Hawai'i Regional Cuisine movement, local farm advocate Peter Merriman has restaurants across the islands, but this newer namesake is my favorite. Elevated above a busy intersection, it offers covered outdoor seating and airy indoor seating in a chic, contemporary dining room. Plan to share an appetizer of tako (octopus), drenched in cognac garlic butter and served escargot-style with country bread, before making the tough decision of which entrée to order. *1108 Auahi St., Honolulu.* ☎ *808/215-0022. Daily 11am–9pm, happy hour 3–5pm. $$$.*

Day 6

⑪ ★★★ **Kailua Beach.** Spend the entire day on the windward side of O'ahu, beginning with a morning kayak at one of the island's most fabulous beaches. *See p 164.*

⑫ ★ **Kailua.** This residential town is seeing more and more tourists who are savvy to the beauty of Kailua Beach. The center is bustling with hamburger joints, antique and vintage shops, and boutiques selling beachy clothes and modern aloha shirts. Kailua is also famous for its pancake and breakfast spots, of which **Moke's Bread and Breakfast** (p 29) is my favorite.

⑬ ★ **Lanikai Pillbox Hike and Lanikai Beach.** Walk from Kailua Beach to take this short, steep hike (p 152) up the Kaiwi ridge to breathtaking views of Kailua, the Ko'olau mountains, and twin Mokulua islands. After you descend, refresh yourself in the crystalline waters of Lanikai, a 1920s developer's bogus Hawaiian name for the area traditionally known as Ka'ohao.

He meant to call it "heavenly ocean," which would be Kailani. At least it is heavenly. ⏱ *1–2 hr. Hike starts at Ka'elepulu Dr.; beach access is along marked paths between homes on Mokulua Dr., Kailua.*

Day 7

Reserve your Diamond Head State Monument entrance and parking permit up to 14 days in advance (online only).

⓮ ★ **Diamond Head.** Get an early start with a bird's-eye view of the island from atop this 760-foot (232m) extinct volcano. Named Le'ahi ("brow of the tuna") by early Hawaiians, it became widely known as Diamond Head after Western sailors admired its sparkling cliffs. A now-classic Hawaiian song, *Kaimana Hila*, takes its title from an English transliteration of the nickname—emblematic of Hawaiians' ability to absorb different cultures and make them their own. *See p 173.*

⓯ ★ **Diamond Head Market and Grill.** Swing by this casual take-out grill and bakery for delicious cream cheese scones for breakfast or a local plate lunch with teriyaki chicken, kalbi short ribs, or 'ahi tuna in a soy-wasabi ginger sauce. A slice of lemon crunch cake or passion orange cheesecake will also help you refuel after a Diamond Head hike. *3158 Monsarrat Ave. www.diamondheadmarket.com.* ☎ *808/732-0077. Market and bakery daily 7:30am–9pm. Lunch and dinner 10am–8pm Wed–Mon. $.*

Enjoy an hourlong scenic drive over the Ko'olau Mountains and past the deep valleys and white-sand beaches of the Windward Side to La'ie.

⓰ ★★★ **Polynesian Cultural Center and Ha: Breath of Life show.** You can buy tickets just for its thrilling Polynesian musical extravaganza, *Ha: Breath of Life* (p 17), but anyone interested in learning more about Polynesia, and families in particular, should try to spend at least half a day at this cultural park. It's staffed by current and former students at nearby Brigham Young University–Hawai'i, many of whom hail from Samoa, Tahiti, New Zealand, Tonga, Fiji, and Hawai'i. Some local families have multiple generations working here, enthusiastically sharing their traditional songs, dances, crafts, and other traditions in outdoor "villages" several times a day. The crowds can be immense at peak periods, but you can always duck into quieter corners like the Rapa Nui (Easter Island) exhibit or

Tahiti Performance at the Polynesian Cultural Center.

Early Hawaiian History

Sailing massive outrigger canoes, the ancestors of today's Hawaiians followed the stars, waves, winds, and birds across the sea to Hawai'i, called "the land of raging fire" in an ancient Tahitian chant. Those first settlers were part of the great Polynesian migration that settled the vast triangle of islands stretching among Aotearoa (New Zealand), Rapa Nui (Easter Island), and Hawai'i. No one knows for sure when they arrived in Hawai'i from Tahiti and the Marquesas Islands, some 2,500 miles to the south, but as early as the 4th century B.C.E. seems plausible.

All we have today are some archaeological finds, some scientific data, and traditional chants to tell the story of Hawai'i's past. The chants, especially the *Kumulipo*, which is the chant of creation and the litany of genealogy of the *ali'i* (high-ranking chiefs) who ruled the islands, discuss the comings and goings between Hawai'i and the islands of the south, presumed to be Tahiti. In fact, the channel between Maui, Kaho'olawe, and Lana'i is called *Kealaika-hiki*, or "the pathway to Tahiti."

Around 1300, the transoceanic voyages stopped for some reason, and Hawai'i began to develop its own culture in earnest. The settlers built temples, fishponds, and aqueducts to irrigate taro fields. Each island was a separate kingdom, and the *ali'i* created a caste system and established taboos (*kapu*); violators could be killed. High priests sought divine guidance from the primary gods Lono, Ku, Kanaloa, and Kane, sometimes performing ritual human sacrifices at temples known as *luakini*.

the Polynesian Football Hall of Fame (honoring an impressive number of NFL stars). Skip the Ali'i Lu'au (a well-done show, but in a cavernous hall with mediocre food) and head to the food stands of **Hukilau Marketplace** (p 147) for a casual, family-friendly outdoor meal before the 7:30pm *Ha: Breath of Life*. **Note:** There's no alcohol at this Mormon-run facility. *55-370 Kamehameha Hwy., La'ie. www. polynesia.com.* ☎ *800/367-7060. Thurs–Sat and Mon–Tues 12:45–9pm.*

The Best of O'ahu in Ten Days

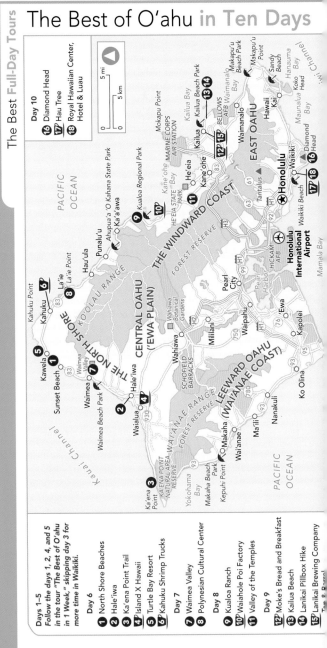

Day 10
- 🟦 Diamond Head
- 🟦 Hau Tree
- 🟦 Royal Hawaiian Center, Hotel & Luau

Days 1–5
Follow the days 1, 2, 4, and 5 in the tour "The Best of O'ahu in 1 Week," skipping day 3 for more time in Waikīkī.

- ❶ North Shore Beaches
- ❷ Hale'iwa
- ❸ Ka'ena Point Trail
- ❹ Island X Hawaii
- ❺ Turtle Bay Resort
- ❻ Kahuku Shrimp Trucks

Day 6
- ❼ Waimea Valley
- ❽ Polynesian Cultural Center

Day 7
- ❾ Kualoa Ranch
- ❿ Waiahole Poi Factory
- ⓫ Valley of the Temples

Day 8
- ⓬ Moke's Bread and Breakfast
- ⓭ Kailua Beach
- ⓮ Lanikai Pillbox Hike
- ⓯ Lanikai Brewing Company

Day 9

Ten days on O'ahu are ideal: They give you enough time to see and experience all the major attractions, with plenty of time left to relax and enjoy the true flavor of Hawai'i. You'll spend two nights on the North Shore, giving you more time to soak in its rural vibe, and then a night in Kailua to marvel at the rugged Windward side.

Days 1–5

For your first 5 days on O'ahu, follow the itinerary for "The Best of O'ahu in One Week," starting on p 18, but skip Day 3 on the North Shore to spend more time enjoying the sights, shops, and surf of Waikiki. This itinerary heads to the North Shore for Day 6.

Day 6

Spend the next two days and nights on O'ahu on the North Shore.

1 ★★★ **North Shore beaches.** Choose any one of the North Shore beaches to spend the morning. If it's winter and the surf's up, you'll want to head to Pipeline or Sunset to watch the surfers on some of the best waves in the world. If it's summer, head to Waimea to swim in the calm, beautiful bay or to Shark's Cove for snorkeling. *See p 143.*

2 ★★ **Hale'iwa.** At lunch time, explore the food trucks, cafes, galleries, and surf shops in this famous North Shore surfing town. *See p 144, 4.*

3 ★★ **Ka'ena Point Trail.** Really get away from it all on this 5-mile (8km) round-trip, mostly flat dirt trail at the end of the road in Mokule'ia. You'll pass tidepools, tranquil coves, and craggy raised limestone reefs en route to Ka'ena Point Natural Area Reserve, traditionally considered a *leina ka 'uhane*, a place where the souls of the recently deceased leap into another dimension. It's also a great site to observe rare nesting seabirds, snoozing Hawaiian monk seals, migrating whales in winter, and practically the entire Wai'anae coast. *See p 144.*

4 ★★ **Island X Hawaii.** A rainbow of tropical, all-natural flavors made from locally sourced fruit and sugar awaits at this shave ice stand inside an old sugar mill. *See p 143.*

5 ★★ **Turtle Bay Resort.** Book a "golden hour" sunset horseback ride on the beach here, or if you're not a fan of horses, sip a cocktail or nibble on *pupu* (appetizers) at any one of the excellent bars and restaurants here. *See p 146.*

6 ★★ **Kahuku Shrimp Trucks.** Some use farmed fresh shrimp, some like the original Giovanni's use frozen, but the cluster of food trucks in Kahuku make a casual dinner here an easy call for seafood lovers. *See p 147.*

Day 7

7 ★★★ **Waimea Valley.** A visit here offers a lush walk around 52 botanical gardens and cultural sites, with the chance for a swim at 45-foot-high Waihi (Waimea) Falls, if conditions permit. *See p 63.*

Horseback riding at Turtle Bay Resort.

ATV tours at Kualoa Ranch, setting for several famous Hollywood films.

❽ ★★★ Polynesian Cultural Center and Ha: Breath of Life show. Spend the afternoon taking in the vibrant, family-friendly cultural demonstrations and performances at the six "island villages" of the Polynesian Cultural Center, browse the eclectic food stalls of adjacent **Hukilau Market** for a casual dinner, and then take in the spectacular evening show (7:30pm), the island's best. *See p 24,* **⓰**.

Day 8
From the North Shore, enjoy the scenic, winding drive down the Windward Side to your Kailua-area lodgings with these stops for adventure and sightseeing along the way.

❾ ★★ Kualoa Ranch. The setting here is stunning, a 4,000-acre private nature reserve and working cattle ranch amid the fluted Koʻolau Mountains. Sign up for one or more activities: Options include riding by horseback, electric bike or ATV through the locations where movies like *Jurassic Park* and *Godzilla* were filmed, as well as farm, beach, and ocean experiences. Get your adrenaline going on the zipline course (p 183), which allows you to fly through the treetops at the ranch. You can even get your feet wet

helping cultivate wetland taro, traditionally revered by Hawaiians as an ancestor as well as a staple food. *Tip:* Book online, since there's a $15 surcharge for phone reservations. ⏱ *2–5 hr. 49-560 Kamehameha Hwy., Kaʻaʻawa. www.kualoa.com.* ☎ *800/231-7321 or 808/237-7321. Single activities $50–$175, packages from $121. Daily 8am–5pm.*

❿ ★ Waiahole Poi Factory. This humble roadside stop in a blink-and-you'll-miss-it hamlet north of Kaneʻohe draws lines of patrons for hearty plate lunches with kalua pig, lomi salmon, squid luʻau, and other classic Hawaiian dishes. Local farmers provide the taro for freshly pounded poi and kulolo, a dense sweet treat served warm with haupia (coconut cream) ice cream. The aloha-filled service and setting—a former poi factory more than a century old—are unmistakably Hawaiian, too. *48-140 Kamehameha Hwy. (at Waiahole Valley Rd.), Kaneʻohe. Entrees $11–$14. Lunch and dinner daily 10am–6pm.*

⓫ ★ Valley of the Temples Memorial Park. This famous cemetery in a cleft of the *pali* (cliffs) is a draw for its 9-foot (2.7m) meditation

The Buddhist temple and gardens at Valley of the Temples.

Lanikai Beach viewed from the Pillbox hike.

Buddha, 2 acres (.8 ha) of ponds full of more than 10,000 Japanese koi fish, and a replica of Japan's 900-year-old Byodo-In Temple. The original, made of wood, stands in the outskirts of Kyoto; the Hawai'i version, made of concrete, was erected in 1968 to commemorate the 100th anniversary of the arrival of the first Japanese immigrants. A 3-ton (2,722kg) brass temple bell brings good luck to those who can ring it. It's also good to stay clear of the wild peacocks. ① 1 hr. 47–200 Kahekili Hwy. (across the street from Temple Valley Shopping Center), Kane'ohe. www.byodo-in.com. ☎ 808/239-8811. $5 adults, $4 seniors 65 & over, $2 ages 2–12. Daily 8:30am–4:30pm.

Spend the night on the Windward side, around Kailua or Kane'ohe.

Day 9

12 ★ **Moke's Bread and Breakfast.** One of the advantages of staying in Kailua is getting to hit its famous breakfast spots before the crowds. Moke's is renowned for its tender, fluffy pancakes; my favorites are topped with a light passionfruit cream sauce. For something savory, try the stuffed hash browns: think omelet fixings sandwiched by crispy potatoes. 27 Ho'olai St., Kailua. www.mokeshawaii.com. ☎ 808/261-5565. Wed–Sun 6am–1pm. $.

13 ★★ **Kailua Beach.** Be as active or relaxed as you want. Lay in the sand or play in the water, rent a kayak and head to the twin Mokulua islands. You'll see why Kailua Beach is one of the island's best. See p 164.

From the beach, walk over to Lanikai.

14 ★ **Lanikai Pillbox Hike.** Start this short hike up to the Ka Iwi ridge around dusk to appreciate the sunset. It's only about 30 minutes each way up the steep, dirt trail, but the payoff is great: picture-perfect views of Kailua, the Ko'olau mountains, and the Mokulua islands. It makes you realize why the pillboxes were built up here in the first place (they were constructed around WWII as observation posts and later abandoned). Take a refreshing dip in Lanikai Beach (p 165) before returning on foot to Kailua. ① 1 hr. Ka'elepulu Dr.

15 ★ **Lanikai Brewing Company Tap & Barrel.** Wash down a wood-fired pizza or Italian-style sandwich with one of many craft beers on tap at this trendy tasting room. The saisons, hazy IPAs, and sour beers (to name a few) feature local ingredients such as honey, strawberries, lemongrass, and cacao. 167 Hamakua St., Kailua. www.lanikaibrewing.com. Mon–Fri noon–10pm, Sat–Sun 11am–10pm. $$.

Lanikai Brewing Company Tap & Barrel.

Aha'aina Luau at the Royal Hawaiian Hotel.

Head back to Waikiki for the night for easier access to your Diamond Head hike in the morning. Be sure to reserve your Diamond Head State Monument entrance and parking permit up to 14 days in advance (online only).

Day 10

⓰ ★ **Diamond Head.** With your online reservation and parking permits in hand, get an early start with a bird's-eye view of the island from atop this 760-foot (232m) extinct volcano, extolled in hula and song. *See p 173.*

⓱ ★★ **Hau Tree.** After your hike, savor eggs benedict or other tasty brunch and lunch dishes under hau trees and hanging lanterns at this hip but casual outdoor restaurant. On the lobby-level lanai at Kaimana Beach Hotel, it overlooks Kaimana (Sans Souci) Beach and also serves expert cocktails and exquisite "bar bites" and dinner entrees, with notable seafood and vegetarian choices. *2863 Kalakaua Ave., Waikiki. www. kaimaina/dining.* ☎ *808/923-1555. Daily brunch 8am–1:30pm, bar menu 3:30–5pm, dinner 5–9pm. $$–$$$.*

⓲ ★★ **Royal Hawaiian Center, Hotel & Luau.** On your last day, pick up souvenirs and gifts—including jewelry, clothing, and specialty foods—exclusively made in Hawai'i by small

businesses, many of them Native Hawaiian owned, at **House of Mana Up** (p 127) in the Royal Hawaiian Center. Browse the open-air mall's other boutiques, including international and national brands with Hawai'i-specific merchandise, before walking through a lush garden to the elegant **Royal Hawaiian** (p 130) a pink Moroccan fantasy opened in 1927 and beautifully restored some 80 years later. If it's a Monday or Thursday, your last dinner on the island will be the hotel's memorable **Aha'aina** ("gathering for a feast") **Luau**, an intimate, oceanfront luau with stories and dances from ancient times to the eras of the19th century monarchy, World War II and Elvis Presley. It's the best luau on the island. But if your last evening falls on another day, take heart: Join the sunset throngs at the hotel's venerable **Mai Tai Bar** for a classic version of the eponymous cocktail ($20) and stick around for a casual island-style dinner. *Royal Hawaiian Center: 2201 Kalakaua Ave., Waikiki. www.royalhawaiiancenter. com.* ☎ *808/922-2299. Aha'aina Luau: Royal Hawaiian Hotel, 2259 Kalakaua Ave., Waikiki. www.royal-hawaiian.com.* ☎ *808/921-4600. $225 adults ($250 for premium seating), $135 children 5 to 12 (any seating), $20 for ages 2 to 4 (seating only, no meal), free lap seating for younger children. Mai Tai Bar: Royal Hawaiian Hotel (see above). Daily 11am–11pm, with live music 6–10pm. $$$.* ●

Mai Tai Bar.

3 The Best Special-Interest Tours

Honolulu & O'ahu with Kids

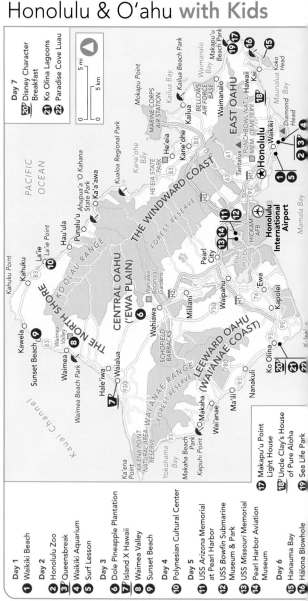

Day 7
20 Disney Character Breakfast
21 Ko Olina Lagoons
22 Paradise Cove Luau

Day 1
1 Waikiki Beach

Day 2
2 Honolulu Zoo
3 Queensbreak
4 Waikiki Aquarium
5 Surf Lesson

Day 3
6 Dole Pineapple Plantation
7 Island X Hawaii
8 Waimea Valley
9 Sunset Beach

Day 4
10 Polynesian Cultural Center

Day 5
11 USS Arizona Memorial at Pearl Harbor
12 USS Bowfin Submarine Museum & Park
13 USS Missouri Memorial
14 Pearl Harbor Aviation Museum

Day 6
15 Hanauma Bay
16 Hālona Blowhole

17 Makapu'u Point Light House
18 Uncle Clay's House of Pure Aloha
19 Sea Life Park

Previous page: The Honolulu Museum of Art.

Families flock to O'ahu not only for the island's breathtaking beauty but also for the abundance of activities. Waikiki is famous for every type of ocean activity you can think of, with the Honolulu Zoo and Waikiki Aquarium nearby. Dotted around the rest of the island are great family outings like the Polynesian Cultural Center, Kualoa Ranch, and the Disney character breakfast and lagoons at Ko Olina. This tour gives families a fun-filled week with something for everyone; it's based out of Waikiki but can be easily adapted for families staying on the North Shore or in Ko Olina.

Day 1

❶ ★★★ **Waikiki Beach.** You've probably arrived midday, so let everyone revive with a splash in the gentle waves of the most famous beach in Hawai'i, up until the golden glow of sunset. *See p 169.*

Day 2

If you're staying on the Diamond Head side of Waikiki, it's an easy, flat walk to the Honolulu Zoo, at the entrance to Kapi'olani Park. If you need to drive, there's free parking across the street in the Waikiki Shell parking lot, and paid parking ($1.50 an hour) at the zoo.

❷ ★ **Honolulu Zoo.** Due to time zone changes, kids typically get up very early their first full day, making it easy to have breakfast and a dip in the ocean or hotel pool before heading to this 43-acre (17-ha) municipal zoo when gates open. Morning is when animals tend to be most

The Honolulu Zoo provides a nice break from the sand and surf.

active, especially in the 10-acre (4-ha) African Savanna habitat, home to black rhinos, cheetahs, giraffes, hippos, and African wild dogs, among other species. The endangered state bird, nene (Hawaiian goose), also has a sanctuary here. ⏱ 2–3 hr. 151 Kapahulu Ave. (btw. Paki & Kalakaua aves.). www.honoluluzoo.org. ☎ 808/971-7171. $19 adults, $11 kids 3–12, free for children 2 & under. Daily 10am–4pm.

From the zoo, it's a 5-minute walk to lunch in Waikiki.

❸ ★★ **Queensbreak.** Everything is elevated at this playful outdoor restaurant at the *Waikiki Beach Marriott Resort & Spa*: the view, the kids' (and adults') menu, and yes, the prices, but they're worth it. Executive Chef Nuño Alves (a dad himself) has taken as much care crafting the mac 'n' cheese, burger, etc., on the keiki menu as he has the fantastic Asian, Mediterranean, island, and American dishes on the adult menu. *2nd floor terrace, Waikiki Beach Marriott Resort & Spa, 2552 Kalakaua Ave. www.queensbreak.com. ☎ 808/922-6611, ext. 7181. Daily 11am–10pm. $$.*

From Queensbreak, it's a 10-minute walk (much of it shaded) to Waikiki Aquarium.

❹ ★ **Waikiki Aquarium.** This jewel box of an aquarium is the closest you can get to snorkeling

More than 420 species are on display at the Waikiki Aquarium.

while still staying dry. Its more than 420 species include all shapes and sizes, from leafy seadragons, colorful moray eels, translucent jellies, and brilliant corals to endemic critters like the Potter's angelfish (named for the aquarium's first director) and a pair of endangered Hawaiian monk seals, both abandoned as pups. My favorite exhibits include the Living Reef, showcasing soft and stony corals from around the Pacific; Giant Clams up to 500 lbs. (227kg); and Northwestern Hawaiian Islands, a 4,000-gallon (15,142-liter) tank with multihued angelfish, triggerfish, and other reef life abundant in the remote islands that are now part of a vast marine preserve. ⏱ 2 hr. 2777 Kalakaua Ave. (in Kapi'olani Park). www. waikikiaquarium.org. ☎ 808/923-9741. $12 adults; $5 seniors and children 4–12. Daily 9am–5pm (last tickets sold at 4:30pm).

Many surf lessons take place near the Waikiki Aquarium and the long-closed War Memorial Natatorium, but you may need to make the short walk back to Waikiki to check in.

❺ **Surf lesson in Waikiki.** End the day with a late afternoon surf session, when the sun is less hot. Waikiki has great waves for learning, and a surf lesson with **Hans Hedemann Surf School** will have your kids riding the waves in no time. ⏱ 2 hr. At the Queen Kapi'olani Hotel, Waikiki. www. hhsurf.com. ☎ 808/924-7778. $90 for 2-hour group lesson (maximum four people) for ages 14 and up; private lesson for ages 5 and up, $170.

Day 3
Spend your second day on O'ahu on the North Shore.

❻ ★ **Dole Pineapple Plantation.** Although very touristy, this is a good place to let kids stretch their legs—for a fee. Amble through gardens and orchards growing coffee, cacao, and tropical flowers and fruit, or wander around the Pineapple Garden Maze. It's touted as the world's largest, covering more than 3 acres (1.2ha) with nearly 2.5 miles (4km) of paths between some 14,000 plants. A single-engine diesel locomotive offers a 22-minute narrated tour (with Hawaiian music) around 2 miles (3.2km) of the plantation. There's no charge to stop at the visitor center (and enormous

Calm waters and ample services make Waikiki Beach a great family beach.

The Pineapple Garden Maze at Dole Plantation.

gift shop), where you can cool down with a Dole Whip, the famously delicious pineapple soft serve. ① *1–2 hr. 64-1550 Kamehameha Hwy.* ☎ *808/621-8408. www.doleplantation.com. Gardens $8 adults, $7 kids 4–12; train tickets $13 adults, $22 kids; pineapple maze $9 adults, $7 kids. Daily 9:30am–5:30pm.*

7 ★ **Island X Hawai'i.** Take time out for a cool, sweet shave ice with syrups made from locally grown fruit and sugar in this former sugar mill. Kids will also enjoy browsing the inexpensive, island-made souvenirs and sampling chocolate from cacao beans grown out the back door. *See p 143,* **2**.

8 ★★ **Waimea Valley.** If conditions permit, you can take a swim below 45-foot Waihi Falls (also known as Waimea Falls) in this botanic garden and cultural center, sheltered in a verdant valley. The water will be chilly, but kids don't seem to mind. Changing rooms with a shower are next to the falls; mandatory life vests will be provided. Call the center at ☎ *808/638-7766 after 9am to find out the current swimming conditions See p 63,* **7**.

9 ★★★ **Sunset Beach.** Spend the rest of the day playing on Sunset Beach. During the summer months, this is a safe beach for swimming. During the winter, it's

best to just sit and watch the big wave surfers. *See p 169.*

Head back to Waikiki or consider spending the night on the North Shore.

Day 4

It's a 75-min. scenic drive from Waikiki to La'ie; pull over at any of the coves or beach parks en route to break up the trip. You can also arrange shuttle service ($25 per person) to and from the Polynesian Cultural Center.

10 ★★ **Polynesian Cultural Center.** Spend the afternoon and evening here—it's great for families, informative and fun. Here you can experience the lifestyles, songs, dances, costumes, and architecture of six Pacific cultures—Fiji, Aotearoa (New Zealand), Samoa, Tahiti, Tonga, and Hawai'i—in the recreated villages dotting the 42-acre lagoon park.

Shave ice makes for a cooling treat on a hot day.

Rainy Days

If it's a rainy day, or your little darlings need a break from being in the sun, take them to the **Hawai'i Children's Discovery Center**, 111 Ohe St. (across from Kaka'ako Waterfront Park), Honolulu (www.discoverycenterhawaii.org; ☎ **808/524-5437**). Perfect for ages 2 to 10, hands-on exhibits, interactive stations, and classes will keep them occupied for hours. Admission is $12, $7 for seniors, and free for kids under 1. Open Tuesday through Friday from 9am to 1pm, Saturday and Sunday from 10am to 3pm.

Another great rainy-day retreat is the **Bishop Museum** (1525 Bernice St., just off the Likelike Hwy.), Honolulu (www.bishop museum.org; ☎ **808/847-3511**). Admission is $25 adults, $22 seniors, $17 kids ages 4 to 17, and free for kids 3 and under. *Tip:* Book online to save $2 per ticket and guarantee your time of admission. Head straight for the Science Adventure Center, where the kids can virtually walk inside an erupting volcano, explore the ocean, and learn about stars and Hawaiian voyagers in the planetarium ($3 additional). There are also kid-friendly interactive exhibits in the impressive Hawaiian Hall. Open daily 9am to 5pm.

Current and former students of Brigham Young University–Hawai'i in La'ie are the "inhabitants" of each village. They engage the audience with spear-throwing competitions, coconut tree–climbing presentations, palm-frond weaving, and invitations to pound Tongan drums. You can also go on a canoe ride in the artificial lagoon. The village experiences end by 5:30pm. Skip the packages with the Ali'i Lu'au or buffet dinner and instead hit the family-friendly food stalls of the center's **Hukilau Marketplace,** which sell fish and chips, hot dogs, Mexican and Thai food, among other options. Then stay for the evening show, *Ha: Breath of Life,* a coming-of-age story told through inventive animation and vibrant music and dance. (Younger children may find some fierce dance moves and plot points a bit scary, but reassure them everything turns out all right in the end, à la Disney's *The Lion King.*) It's one of O'ahu's best shows. *55-370 Kamehameha Hwy., La'ie.*

Children at the Discovery Center.

Afterhours at the Bishop Museum.

www.polynesia.com. ☎ *800/367-7060. Villages and show, $120 adults, $100 children 4–11. Villages only, $70 adults, $56 children 4–11. Mon–Tues and Thurs–Sat 12:45pm–9pm.*

Day 5
Online reservations ($1 fee per person) are required for the water shuttle to the USS *Arizona* Memorial at Pearl Harbor. Try to book an early morning or late afternoon slot, so you can enjoy the other sights listed here before or after, but plan to arrive early for closer-in parking.

⓫ ★★★ **USS *Arizona* Memorial at Pearl Harbor.** This unforgettable memorial is O'ahu's top attraction. Parents should note that strollers and diaper bags are not allowed at the memorial (you can store them for a fee at the visitor center); while aboard the memorial, reached by a reservations-only water shuttle, kids will also need to use their "indoor voices" and respect the reverent atmosphere: They'll be standing above the tomb of more than 1,100 sailors and Marines. Also, there are no restrooms at the memorial, so be sure everyone uses the ones at the visitor center. There are two fascinating museums and other outdoor exhibits to hold their interest while waiting for the water shuttle to the memorial. *See p 13,* ❹.

⓬ ★ **USS *Bowfin* Submarine Museum & Park.** *See p 47,* ❷.

You'll need to take the free shuttle to Ford Island for the next two attractions, which also offer family-friendly lunch options. If younger kids have timed out, head back to the beach at Waikiki.

⓭ ★★ **USS *Missouri* Memorial.** *See p 49,* ❺.

⓮ ★ **Pearl Harbor Aviation Museum.** *See p 48,* ❸.

Day 6
Don't forget to make online reservations and bring $3 cash for parking at your first stop. It opens at 6:45am; arrive early to ensure parking and calmest conditions.

⓯ ★★★ **Hanauma Bay.** Spend the morning at the island's best snorkeling site, a gorgeous natural preserve with free admission for kids 12 and under (adults $25). Everyone must watch a short film about reef safety and conservation before entering the water—make sure the kids know not to stand on coral, a delicate living creature. *Note:* It's closed Monday and Tuesday. *See p 185.*

⓰ **Halona Blowhole.** *See p 150,* ❸.

⓱ ★★ **Makapu'u Point Light House.** Hike out to this 647-foot-high (197m) cliff and functioning lighthouse (not open to the public), where, on winter days, you can often spot whales cavorting in the ocean. *See p 20,* ❹.

Family-Friendly Events

Your trip may be a little more enjoyable with the added attraction of attending a celebration, festival, or party in Honolulu, Waikiki, or other parts of the island. Check out the following events:

- **Chinese New Year,** Chinatown, Honolulu (www.chinese chamber.com; ☎ **808/533-3181**). Late January or early February (depending on the lunar calendar). Chinatown rolls out the red carpet for this important event with a traditional lion dance, firecrackers, food booths, and a host of activities.

- **Punahou School Carnival,** Punahou School, Honolulu (www. punahou.edu; ☎ **808/944-5753**). February. This private school fundraiser is one of the biggest events of the year. It has everything you can imagine in a school carnival, from high-speed rides to homemade goodies.

- **Outrigger Canoe Season,** Ala Wai Canal, Waikiki (www.ohcra. com). Weekends May to September. Canoe paddlers across the state participate in outrigger canoe races.

- **World Fireknife Championships and We Are Samoa Festival,** Polynesian Cultural Center, La'ie (www.polynesia.com; ☎ **808/293-3333**). Mid-May. Fire-knife dancers from around the world gather for this amazing competition. Authentic Samoan food and cultural festivities round out the fun.

- **King Kamehameha Day Celebration,** downtown Honolulu and Waikiki (ags.hawaii.gov/Kamehameha; ☎ **808/586-0300**). Mid-June. A massive floral horseback parade from 'Iolani Palace through Waikiki to Kapi'olani Park, ends in a *ho'olaulea* (celebration) with live entertainment.

- **Aloha Festivals,** Waikiki (www.alohafestivals.com; ☎ **808/ 923-1094**). Second half of September. A huge *ho'olaulea* (celebration) with live entertainment and a floral horseback parade, close Kalakaua Avenue to traffic on two separate days.

18 ★ **Uncle Clay's House of Pure Aloha.** Here's a rare shave ice spot that uses syrups made with local fruit. Unlike other places that rely on artificially colored and flavored syrups, at Uncle Clay's, the pineapple and mango are the real deal—so is the aloha spirit here. *820 W. Hind Dr. Unit 116.* ☎ 808/373-5111. $.

19 ★ **Sea Life Park.** Kids will likely enjoy the large aquarium, interactive exhibits and presentations (including baby shark feeding) and theme park–style sea lion shows here. Despite some hokey aspects, the park is also involved in seabird and marine mammal conservation, native seaweed restoration, and other environmental efforts that the kids can learn about.

The views are quite nice from here, too. *Tip:* Save $5 per ticket by buying them online. *41-202 Kalaniana'ole Hwy., Waimanalo. www.sealifeparkhawaii.com.* ☎ *800/259-2500. Admission $45 ($40 online) ages 3 and older. Dolphin, sea lion, and reef "encounters," $90–$260, including admission. $10 parking (it's also on the Waikiki Trolley Blue Line). Daily 10am–4pm.*

Day 7

For your last full day, head to the typically sunny southwest corner of O'ahu and its manicured Ko Olina Resort. From Waikiki, wait out rush hour traffic (6:30–8:30am) before setting off; you can still make it in plenty of time for breakfast.

⑳ ★ Disney Character Breakfast.
Make your reservations well in advance for this popular experience at Aulani, Disney's first resort outside of its theme parks, in Ko Olina. Mickey, Minnie, and other costumed characters provide entertainment and pose for photo ops during the ample, three-course breakfast at Makahiki restaurant ($45 diners 10 and older, $28 children 9 and younger). Local dishes, classic American fare, and a children's menu are all offered. *92-1185 Ali'inui Dr., Kapolei. www.disney aulani.com/dining/table-service/makahiki-buffet.* ☎ *808/373-5111. Daily 7–11am. $$$.*

㉑ ★ Ko Olina Lagoons.
Spend midday swimming, snorkeling, stand-up paddling, or just splashing around one of these four large sandy, protected lagoons. Created by the developer of the resort through excavation, they feature broad beaches and grassy lawns and well-maintained restrooms and showers. *See p 185.*

㉒ ★★ Paradise Cove Luau.
For your last night, and while you're out in Ko Olina, experience a luau (lu'au in Hawaiian). Don't expect an intimate affair—Paradise Cove generally has some 600 to 800 guests a night—but kids don't seem to mind. In fact, the small thatched village feels a bit like a Hawaiian theme park. But Paradise Cove provides an entire cultural experience, with Hawaiian games, craft demonstrations, Tahitian and hula dancing, canoe rides, and a beautiful shoreline looking out over what is usually a storybook sunset. You'll find typical luau cuisine, plus fried fish, baked chicken, stir-fried veggies, and a variety of salads and desserts. *Note:* Three price levels of packages with various perks and seating are available. There's an optional round-trip shuttle to Waikiki for $35, but a family of three or more would be better off renting a car for the day. ⓛ *3½ hr. Ali'inui Dr., Ko Olina. www.paradisecove.com.* ☎ *808/842-5911. $125–$210 adults, $105–$185 children 13–20, $90–$160 children 12 & under. Daily 5–9pm.*

Kids' surf lessons on Waikiki Beach.

A Week of O'ahu History & Culture

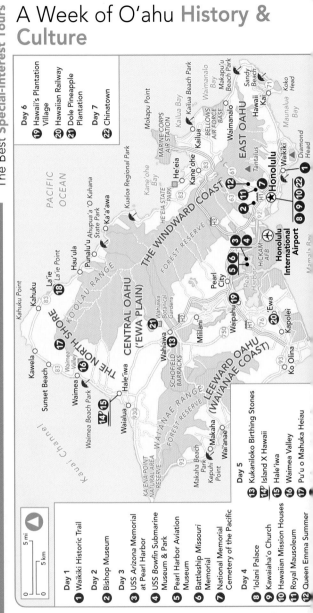

Day 6
19 Hawaii's Plantation Village
20 Hawaiian Railway
21 Dole Pineapple Plantation

Day 7
22 Chinatown

Day 1
1 Waikiki Historic Trail

Day 2
2 Bishop Museum

Day 3
3 USS Arizona Memorial at Pearl Harbor
4 USS Bowfin Submarine Museum & Park
5 Pearl Harbor Aviation Museum
6 Battleship Missouri Memorial
7 National Memorial Cemetery of the Pacific

Day 4
8 'Iolani Palace
9 Kawaiaha'o Church
10 Hawaiian Mission Houses
11 Royal Mausoleum
12 Queen Emma Summer

Day 5
13 Kukaniloko Birthing Stones
14 Island X Hawaii
15 Hale'iwa
16 Waimea Valley
17 Pu'u o Mahuka Heiau

This tour covers O'ahu's most sacred and historically important spots. You'll see ancient sites, visit the birthplaces of Hawaiian royalty, learn about the days of the missionaries and plantations, and reflect on the attack on Pearl Harbor. You'll visit Waikiki, downtown Honolulu, Chinatown, Central O'ahu, and Pearl Harbor.

Day 1

❶ ★★ Waikiki Historic Trail.
To get an overview of Waikiki's history, take this 4.5-mile (7.2km) walk, with stops marked by 6-foot-tall (1.8m) surfboards explaining the history of today's favorite resort area. (Wear a swimsuit and bring a towel so you can take a dip along the way.) For a full description of the trail, see my Historic Waikiki tour starting on p 52.

Day 2

❷ ★★★ Bishop Museum. Take the entire day to visit the Hawaiian and Pacific cultural exhibition halls, art gallery, science center, planetarium, and Highway Inn cafe (a local favorite) at this entrancing museum, which could be the highlight of your trip. *See p 21,* **❼**.

Day 3
See Day 1, p 47.

❸ ★★★ USS *Arizona* Memorial at Pearl Harbor. Start off your day of viewing wartime Honolulu by visiting this somber reminder of how World War II's Pacific theater began. *See p 13,* **❹**.

❹ ★ USS *Bowfin* Submarine Museum & Park. Tour a submarine that conducted nine patrols from 1943 to 1945, then learn more about the underwater war at the adjacent Pacific Fleet Submarine Museum. *See p 47,* **❷**.

Because they're on Ford Island, part of the active naval base, you'll need to take a free shuttle from the Pearl Harbor Visitor Center to the next two attractions, which also have the best on-site options for lunch.

❺ ★ Pearl Harbor Aviation Museum. Some 50 aircraft in two remodeled hangars tell the story of the aerial attack and response on December 7, 1941, and beyond; there's also a pavilion for special exhibitions. The air-conditioned cafe is a good spot to refuel on a hot day. *See p 48,* **❸**.

❻ ★ Battleship *Missouri* Memorial. End your afternoon with where the war in the Pacific ended. Start with the 35-min. guided tour, then explore the rest of the lovingly restored ship that also served in the Korean War, and

Pacific Hall at the Bishop Museum.

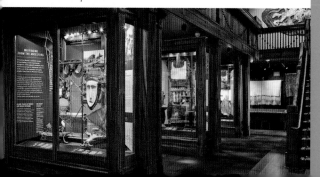

came out of mothballs for the first Gulf War, too. *See p 49,* **5**.

From Pearl Harbor, it's under 10 miles (16km) to the National Memorial Cemetery of the Pacific, but it can take longer than the usual 20 minutes to drive in the afternoon rush hour. If time is tight, you can always visit it at the end of Day 2 or Day 4.

7 National Memorial Cemetery of the Pacific. Twilight is the perfect time to visit this hallowed ground. Nicknamed "Punchbowl" by Westerners, its distinctive cinder cone erupted some 70,000 to 100,000 years ago. Its traditional Hawaiian name of *Puowaina,* or "hill of sacrifice," is actually more in keeping with its present use as a burial ground for 35,000 victims of three American wars in Asia and the Pacific: World War II, Korea, and Vietnam. Among the graves, you'll find many unmarked ones with the date December 7, 1941, carved in the headstone. *See p 51,* **7**.

Passport to Pearl Harbor

You can book guided tours of Pearl Harbor's attractions that include transportation from Waikiki (p 15), but if you prefer to drive yourself, the best value is the Passport to Pearl Harbor ($90 adults, $45 children 4–12). The pass includes an audio

The National Memorial Cemetery of the Pacific.

tour of the USS *Arizona* Memorial; admission to the Battleship *Missouri* Memorial, Pacific Fleet Submarine Museum (including the USS *Bowfin*), and Pearl Harbor Aviation Museum; and the 15-minute air raid simulation at the Pearl Harbor Virtual Reality Center. What it doesn't include is a reservation for the free water shuttle to the *Arizona* memorial, so first book your shuttle seat at www. recreation.gov/ticket/233338/ticket/16 ($1 service fee). Then buy the pass from the nonprofit Pearl Harbor Historic Sites (www.pearlharbor historicsites.org; ☎ 808/454-1435).

Day 4

The first three sights are within walking distance of each other, so plan to park once. There's limited metered street parking and several parking garages, including Ali'i Place, 1099 Alakea St., a 3-min. walk to 'Iolani Palace ($3 for 2 hr., $1.50 every 30 min. after).

8 ★★ 'Iolani Palace. To understand modern Hawai'i, come to this royal palace, built by King David Kalakaua in 1882, and the place of Queen Liliu'okalani's house arrest after her forced abdication in 1893 due to a U.S.-backed coup. Online reservations are required. *See p 15,* **9**.

9 ★ Kawaiaha'o Church. The missionaries' first permanent stone church, complete with bell tower and colonial colonnade, has a long association with Hawaiian royalty. *See p 22,* **9**.

10 Hawaiian Mission Houses. The original buildings of the Sandwich Islands Mission Headquarters still stand, and tours are often led by descendants of the original missionaries to Hawaii. The missionaries brought their own prefab houses along with them when they came around Cape Horn from Boston in

1819. Finished in 1821, the Frame House is Hawai'i's oldest wooden structure. The missionaries' first task was to learn the Hawaiian language, then compose hymns for Hawaiians to sing and print literature for them to read. So it is ironic that the descendants of the missionaries who developed the written Hawaiian language banned it from public education in 1896; Hawaiian only regained status as an official language in 1978. **Note:** It's free to walk around the grounds, which have interpretive signs, and cruise the intriguing gift shop, but it's best to book a small-group (4 max) guided tour in advance. ⏱ *1 hr. 553 S. King St. (at Kawaiaha'o St.). www.missionhouses.org.* ☎ *808/447-3910. Guided tours Tues–Fri 11am and 1pm, Sat 11am, 1pm, 3pm: $12 adults, $10 seniors, $5 students ages 6 through college (with ID). Grounds open Tues–Sat 10am–4pm. Free admission.*

From Ali'i Place parking garage or Hawaiian Mission Houses, it's a less than 10-minute drive uphill into the Nu'uanu neighborhood.

⑪ ★ Royal Mausoleum State Monument (Mauna 'Ala). In the cool uplands of Nu'uanu, on a 3.7-acre (1.5-ha) patch of sacred land dedicated in 1865, is the final resting place of King Kalakaua, Queen Kapi'olani, 16 other Hawaiian royals from the Kamehameha and Kalakaua dynasties, and several Westerners who played key roles during their reigns. Only the Hawaiian flag flies over this gravesite, a reminder of the kingdom's continued significance to contemporary Hawai'i. ⏱ *20 min. 2261 Nu'uanu Ave. dlnr.hawaii.gov/dsp/parks/oahu/royal-mausoleum-state-monument.* ☎ *808/587-2590. Free. Mon–Fri 8am–4:30pm.*

From the Royal Mausoleum, it's only a mile (1.6km) up Nu'uanu Ave., which turns into Pali Hwy. (Hwy. 61), to Queen Emma Summer Palace. If

The Grand Staircase in the 'Iolani Palace.

you run out of time, come back at the start or end of Day 6 or 7.

⑫ ★ Queen Emma Summer Palace. Built in 1847, this gracious home in Nu'uanu Valley served as a cool, tranquil retreat for Queen Emma from 1857 to 1885. Known in Hawaiian as Hanaiakamalama, the home and spacious grounds are now lovingly maintained as a museum by the Daughters of Hawai'i, who offer guided tours (Sat only, reserve in advance) and onsite classes such as hula and Hawaiian quilting. ⏱ *45 min. 2913 Pali Hwy., Honolulu. daughtersofhawaii.org/queen-emma-summer-palace.* ☎ *808/595-3167. Tues, Thurs, Fri, Sat 10am to 3:30pm. Half-hour self-guided tours depart 10am to 3pm; admission $14 adults, $10 seniors 62 and older, $5 children ages 5 to 12, $1 ages 4 and younger. Guided tours Sat 11am and 1:30pm, $20 adults, $16 seniors, $12 children ages 5 to 12, $3 children ages 4 and younger.*

Day 5
From Waikiki it's about a 40-min. drive to Wahiawa. Let the morning commuter traffic heading toward downtown or Pearl Harbor ebb before heading out, after 8:30am or so.

⑬ Kukaniloko Birthstones.
One of the most sacred sites on O'ahu, this is where women of ancient Hawai'i gave birth to *ali'i* (royalty). See p 143, ❶.

Queen Emma Summer Palace.

From the birthstones, it's another 15-minute drive to the old sugar plantation town of Waialua, 2mi (3.2km) west of Hale'iwa.

14 ★ **Island X Hawai'i.** Take time out for a cool, sweet shave ice made from locally grown fruit and sugar at this stand inside the Old Waialua Sugar Mill. *See p 143,* ☕**2**.

15 ★★★ **Hale'iwa.** Meander through the shops and sights of this North Shore surfing town. *See p 144,* **4**.

It's about 4.5 miles (7.2m) along Kamehameha Hwy. (Hwy. 83) to Waimea Valley.

16 ★ **Waimea Valley.** Although perhaps best known for its extensive botanical gardens and 45-foot waterfall (with swimming permitted when conditions allow), this tranquil enclave is also a cultural center with sacred and historic sites like Hale O Lono, a stone *heiau* (temple) built around 1470 A.D.; an ancient fishing shrine made of lava rocks; and Hale Iwi, another large *heiau* that most likely served as a burial temple. Guided history walks are available at 1pm daily. *See p 63,* **7**.

17 ★ **Pu'u o Mahuka Heiau.** Sitting above Waimea Valley as the crow flies, this *heiau* (temple) is the largest ancient religious site on O'ahu, covering nearly 2 acres (.8ha) of a 300-foot (91m) bluff that overlooks Waimea Bay and much of the North Shore. Building of this huge rectangular rock platform likely began in the 1600s, with expansion over time. Its name means "hill of escape," but there was no escape for the victims thought to have been sacrificed here during the late 1700s. Today you're likely to spot flower and fruit *ho'okupu* (ceremonial gifts) on its altar, left by Native Hawaiians. For preservation reasons, avoid the path cut through the temple in the 1960s and just observe it from the outside walls. *Warning:* Never walk on, climb, or even touch the rock walls at a *heiau*. It's not only considered disrespectful and potentially dangerous, but may earn you a fine. ⏱ *30 min. End of Pu'u O Mahuka Rd., Pupukea. dlnr.hawaii.gov/dsp/ parks/oahu/puu-o-mahuka-heiau-state-historic-site. Free. Daily 7am–5pm.*

You'll pass several beach parks—and public access to the beaches inside Turtle Bay resort—perfect for a scenic pit stop along the 13 miles (21km) to La'ie.

18 ★★ **Ha: Breath of Life at the Polynesian Cultural Center.** Catch the dynamic evening show incorporating multiple Pacific cultures at the Polynesian Cultural Center, with a casual food truck dinner from its **Hukilau Marketplace** beforehand. *See p 17,* **17**.

Day 6

From Waikiki, it's about 35 minutes to Waipahu, leaving after morning rush hour (6:30–8:30am).

19 ★ **Hawai'i's Plantation Village.** The self-guided and guided tours of this restored 50-acre (20-ha) village trace the lives and impact of the people who came from around the globe to work on sugar and later pineapple plantations in Hawai'i. From 1852, when the first contract laborers arrived here from China, to 1947, when the plantation immigration era ended, more than 400,000 men, women, and children—primarily from China, Japan (including Okinawa), Portugal, Puerto Rico, Korea, and the Philippines—came to work. With Native Hawaiians, they ultimately created today's "mixed plate" of local culture and cuisine. **Note:** Call ahead to request a 60- to 90-minute guided group tour (available Mon–Sat 10am, 11am, or noon). ⏲ 1½ hr. Waipahu Cultural Garden Park, 94–695 Waipahu St., Waipahu. www.hawaiiplantation village.org. ☎ 808/677-0110. $11 adults, $11 seniors, $8 children 4–17 (only Mastercard and Visa accepted for payment). Mon–Sat 9am–2pm.

From Waipahu, it's a 16-minute drive to 'Ewa Beach.

⑳ ★ Hawaiian Railway. This is a train ride back into history. Between 1890 and 1947, the chief mode of transportation for O'ahu's sugar mills was the O'ahu Railway and Land Co.'s narrow-gauge railroad. The line carried not only equipment, raw sugar, and supplies but also passengers from one side of the island to the other. You can relive those days every Wednesday, Saturday, and Sunday during a 2-hour round-trip narrated ride from 'Ewa Beach to a scenic overlook at Kahe Point. Don't expect ocean views all the way—you're passing through the heart of suburban Honolulu, but the ride is still entertaining. (⏲ 1½ hr. 91–1001 Renton Rd., 'Ewa Beach. www. hawaiianrailway.com. ☎ 808/ 681-5461. Standard ride $18 adults, $13 seniors & children 2–12, free for children 1 & under (they must be held during ride). Second Sunday parlor car rides $30, ages 13 and older only. Departures Wed 1pm, Sat noon and 3 pm and Sun 1 and 3pm.

Afternoon traffic heading towards Central O'ahu gets busy by 4pm, so allow plenty of time if heading to Wahiawa then.

㉑ ★ Dole Pineapple Plantation. If the Hawaiian Railway isn't in operation the day of your visit, consider heading instead to this family-friendly tourist attraction, which includes an informational train ride around its pineapple fields and other gardens. See p 34, ❻.

Day 7

㉒ ★★ Chinatown. Plan to spend the entire day in this vibrant, gritty part of Honolulu. Bustling open markets, Buddhist temples, a waterside walkway, art galleries, and plenty of tempting restaurants (including some of Honolulu's best) will keep you occupied for hours. For complete descriptions, see my Chinatown tour beginning on p 74.

Fruit and flower offerings are still left at the remains of Pu'u o Mahuka Heiau.

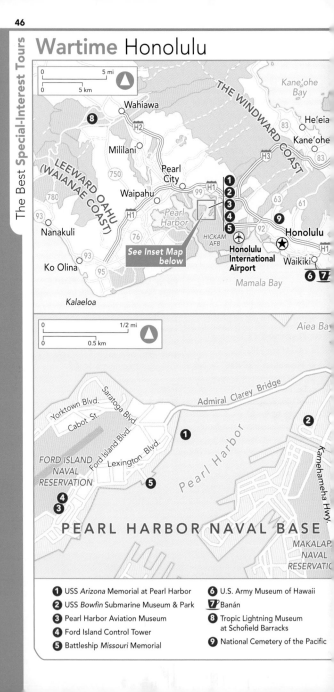

Wartime Honolulu

1 USS *Arizona* Memorial at Pearl Harbor

2 USS *Bowfin* Submarine Museum & Park

3 Pearl Harbor Aviation Museum

4 Ford Island Control Tower

5 Battleship *Missouri* Memorial

6 U.S. Army Museum of Hawaii

7 Banán

8 Tropic Lightning Museum at Schofield Barracks

9 National Cemetery of the Pacific

On December 7, 1941, the historic "day of infamy," Pearl Harbor was bombed by Japanese forces, and the United States entered World War II. Honolulu has a rich history from the war years, and this 2-day tour covers the highlights.

Day 1

Arrive in time for one of the first free morning shuttles to the USS Arizona Memorial, which will also get you closer-in parking.

❶ ★★★ USS Arizona Memorial at Pearl Harbor. No trip to Honolulu would be complete without a visit to this memorial at Pearl Harbor, but make online reservations for the free shuttle well in advance to avoid disappointment. (If necessary, you can also book a shuttle for later in the day and see the remaining sights here out of order.) Two dockside galleries, "Road to War" and "Attack," provide intriguing context, as does a 23-minute documentary analyzing what led to the attack, seen in intense, historical black-and-white footage. **Note:** If planning to see the rest of this day's sights, book the **Passport to Pearl Harbor** (p 42) for the best value. See p 13, **❹**.

❷ ★ USS Bowfin Submarine Museum & Park. This is a great opportunity to see what life was like on a submarine. You can go below deck of this famous vessel—nicknamed the "Pearl Harbor Avenger" after its launch in 1942—and learn how the 80-man crew lived during wartime via an audio tour (with a kid-friendly option for young listeners). The recently expanded Pacific Fleet Submarine Museum has an impressive collection of submarine-related artifacts from World War II through today, while the Waterfront Submarine Memorial honors submariners lost during World War II. ⏱ 1½ hr. 11 Arizona Memorial Dr. (next to the USS Arizona Memorial Visitor Center), Pearl Harbor.

A Pearl Harbor veteran in the Shrine Room of the USS Arizona Memorial.

The USS Bowfin *Submarine Museum & Park.*

www.bowfin.org. ☎ 808/423-1341. $22 adults, $13 children 4–12; children 3 & under not permitted in submarine for safety reasons, but may tour grounds. Daily 7am–5pm.

You'll need to catch a free shuttle bus near the Pearl Harbor Visitor Center to see the next three sights on Ford Island, an active-duty area.

❸ ★★ **Pearl Harbor Aviation Museum.** A 12-minute documentary, "East Wind Rain," runs every 15 minutes near the entrance to this frequently updated museum, where some 50 aircraft in two remodeled hangars tell the story of the aerial attack on December 7, 1941, the military response to it, and contemporary aviation. Don't miss the tale of the Japanese pilot who crashed on the private island of Ni'ihau and took hostages, prompting a daring rescue by Native Hawaiians who had no idea what had transpired on O'ahu. See if you qualify for "Top Gun" status in one of two Fighter Ace

360 simulators. **Note:** The air-conditioned, WWII-themed Laniakea Café is a good spot to refuel with classic American fare; it's open daily 11am to 3pm. ⏱ 1.5 hr. 319 Lexington Blvd., Ford Island, Pearl Harbor. www.pearlharbor aviationmuseum.org. ☎ 808/441-1000. $26 adults, $15 children 4–12, free for younger children. Simulator $11–$21. Daily 9am–5pm.

❹ ★ **Ford Island Control Tower.** Closed for decades, this newly restored, 15-story tower—a bright red-and-white striped structure easily visible from the USS Arizona Memorial—is now open for guided Top of the Tower tours, limited to 120 people a day (and four in the elevator at one time). The 40-minute tour includes a half-hour on the Observation Deck, which offers sweeping cross-island views, and access to the Operations Building and Firehouse. *Access from Pearl Harbor Aviation Museum, 319 Lexington Blvd., Ford Island, Pearl Harbor. www.pearlharboraviation museum.org.* ☎ 808/441-1000. $35 as independent tour, $25 as add-on to museum admission. Children must be at least 42 in. (1.1m); no infants or toddlers. Tours depart 9:40am–4:20pm.

⑤ ★★ Battleship *Missouri* Memorial. On the deck of this 58,000-ton battleship (the last one built by the U.S. Navy), World War II came to an end with the signing of the Japanese surrender on September 2, 1945. I recommend starting with the 35-minute guided tour (included with admission, and often led by veterans) and then exploring on your own, aided by a map and friendly guides stationed around the ship. Kids will be fascinated by the narrow berths in the enlisted crew's bunkroom and the enormous crew's mess (whose four meals a day included "midrats," or midnight rations.) Military highlights of this massive battleship include the forecastle (or *fo'c's'le*, in Navy talk), where the 30,000-pound anchors are dropped on 1,080 feet (329m) of anchor chain; the 16-inch (41cm) guns, which can fire a 2,700-pound (1,225kg) shell some 23 miles (37km) in 50 seconds; and the spot where the Instrument of Surrender was signed as General Douglas MacArthur, Admiral Chester Nimitz, and Admiral "Bull" Halsey looked on. The Kamikaze Deck commemorates where a Japanese pilot fatally crashed on April 11, 1945, during the Battle of Okinawa. The next day, he was accorded a military burial at sea, complete with "Taps" and a rifle salute. **Note**: There's an elevator for those in wheelchairs or need of special assistance, but otherwise be prepared for steep ladders, steps, and "toe-stubbers" (raised thresholds). ⏱ *1½ hr. Ford Island. Ticket kiosk and shuttle boarding are by Pearl Harbor Visitor Center. www.ussmissouri.org.* ☎ *808/455-1600. $35 adults, $17 children 4–12. Daily 8am–4pm (last entry 3pm, last return shuttle 4:05pm).*

PAM Control Tower & WWII aircraft.

Pearl Harbor's Other Memorials

The USS *Arizona* may be the most renowned of the ships sunk in the attack on Pearl Harbor, but the loss of life on the USS *Oklahoma* (429 sailors and marines, second only to those aboard the USS *Arizona*) and the target ship USS *Utah* (58 killed) was also profound. Their onshore memorials lie on Ford Island, in an area inaccessible without an active military ID. Thanks to new, thrice-weekly tours, you can now pay your respects while learning more about the crews' heroism and visiting nearby historic officer bungalows. Currently offered for free, the 90-minute tours aboard a 25-passenger motor coach depart the Pearl Harbor Visitor Center Monday, Wednesday, and Friday at 3:15pm. Tickets must be reserved in advance for all passengers (including infants in arms) at www.recreation.gov (enter "Pearl Harbor Bus Tours" in the search field). There's a $1 reservation fee per ticket.

Day 2

Your day begins on the west side of Waikiki; walk to Fort DeRussy if you can, then reward yourself at Banán before jumping in the car.

❻ ★ U.S. Army Museum of Hawaii. Closed until early 2023 due to an air conditioning replacement, this free museum lies on the oceanside of leafy Fort DeRussy. It's inside the former Battery Randolph, which once housed the largest guns in the Pacific—two 14-inch (36mm) disappearing rifled guns, luckily never fired in combat. Tracing the history of military operations in Hawai'i from the monarchy to the modern day, its exhibitions on the Nisei (second-generation Japanese American) soldiers and the critical role of Hawai'i in World War II are especially worth seeking out. ⏱ *1 hr. Fort DeRussy, 2131 Kalia Rd., Waikiki. history.army.mil/museums/hawaii/moh.* ☎ *808/438-2819. Free. Tues–Sat 10am–5pm (closed until early 2023).*

❼ ★ Banán. This stand next to Fort DeRussy is named for its signature soft-serve, nondairy treat made from local bananas, which also comes flavored with local chocolate and numerous topping options ($8 cup, $13 bowl.) Order it atop an 'ulu (breadfruit) waffle ($10–$11) for an only-in-Hawai'i experience. You can also get shave ice here, with syrups sourced from local fruits like guava, dragonfruit, and strawberry ($10). *Note:* Banán also has branches in the Royal Hawaiian Center (p 130) and Kailua. *Ocean side of Waikiki Shore condos, 2161 Kalia Ave., Waikiki. https://banan.co.* ☎ *808/773-7231. Daily 10am–8pm. $.*

From Waikiki, it's 26 miles (42km) to Schofield Barracks in Central O'ahu, typically about a 40-minute drive.

❽ ★ Tropic Lightning Museum at Schofield Barracks. With its broad, palm-lined boulevards and Art Deco buildings, the old army cavalry post of

Schofield Barracks is the largest of its kind still operating outside the continental U.S. today. The barracks themselves are off-limits, but the history of Schofield Barracks, the 25th Infantry Division (including combat from World War II through the Vietnam War) and Wheeler Airfield are interpreted in this free museum's three galleries. Displays range from a 1917 bunker exhibit to a replica of Vietnam's infamous Cu Chi tunnels. To get on the base, adults will need a U.S. state or federal photo ID (such as a driver's license or passport), and provide a Social Security number (for a background check). Also have your rental car agreement for your vehicle ready at the gate to get a free visitor pass. ⏱ *1 hr. Bldg. 361, 361 Wai'anae Ave., Schofield Barracks (near Wahiawa). https://home.army. mil/hawaii/index.php/tropic-lightning-museum.* ☎ *808/655-0438. Free. Tues–Fri 10am–4pm.*

This next stop lies en route to Waikiki, just outside of downtown.

❾ ★ National Memorial Cemetery of the Pacific. Nicknamed "Punchbowl" by Westerners, this distinctive crater rises 461 feet high, thanks to a volcanic eruption some 70,000 to 100,000 years ago. Its traditional Hawaiian name of *Puowaina,* or "hill of sacrifice," reflects its ancient use as a place of human sacrifice. King Kamehameha the Great installed cannons here to greet dignitaries, and in the 1930s it served as a rifle range. A cemetery since 1949, it now honors the sacrifices of U.S. armed forces in Asia and the Pacific—and a notable civilian, war correspondent Ernie Pyle. World War II victims account for about 13,000 of the more than 35,000 graves. Bus tours just do drive-by sightseeing here, but walking allows you to browse the gorgeous marble maps detailing various campaigns of the war, and absorb more than 70 memorials and monuments along the terraced memorial pathway. The view from the top of the crater is fabulous, too. ⏱ *1½ hr. 2177 Puowaina Dr., Honolulu. www.cem.va.gov/cems/ nchp/nmcp.asp.* ☎ *808/532-3720. Free. Daily 8am–6pm.*

Historic Waikiki

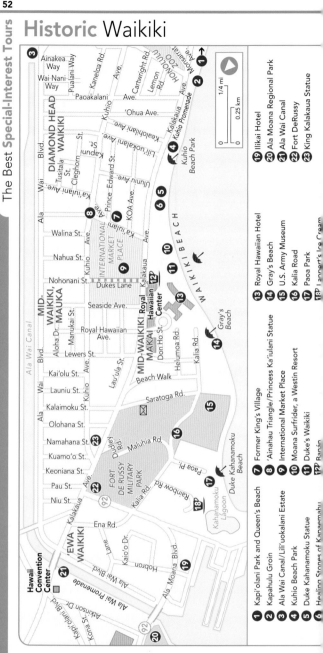

1/4 mi

0.25 km

1. Kapi'olani Park and Queen's Beach
2. Kapahulu Groin
3. Ala Wai Canal/Lili'uokalani Estate
4. Kuhio Beach Park
5. Duke Kahanamoku Statue
6. Healing Stones of Kapaemahu
7. Former King's Village
8. 'Ainahau Triangle/Princess Ka'iulani Statue
9. International Market Place
10. Moana Surfrider, a Westin Resort
11. Duke's Waikiki
12. Banán
13. Royal Hawaiian Hotel
14. Gray's Beach
15. U.S. Army Museum
16. Kalia Road
17. Paoa Park
18. Lappert's Ice Cream
19. Ilikai Hotel
20. Ala Moana Regional Park
21. Fort DeRussy
22. King Kalakaua Statue

Spend a morning strolling through history. Each of the 21 Waikiki Historic Trail Markers, 6-foot-tall (1.8m) surfboards, explains the history of the first and still favorite resort area in Hawai'i, focusing on the time before Westerners came to its shores (I've thrown in a few extra stops along the way). You could probably speed-walk the entire route in a couple of hours, but I recommend taking all morning, stopping at each one and appreciating this culturally rich area.

The Queen Lili'uokalani statue greets guests of the Hawaii State Capitol Building in Honolulu.

❶ ★ Kapi'olani Park and Queen's Beach.

In ancient times, there were two *heiau* (temples) in this area. One was Kupalaha, located on the shoreline at Queen's Beach and thought to be part of the Papa'ena'ena Heiau, where Kamehameha I made the last human sacrifice in Waikiki. The other, Makahuna, near Diamond Head, encompassed all of Kapi'olani Park and was dedicated to Kanaloa, god of the underworld and sea. *Kalakaua Ave., close to Monsarrat Ave.*

❷ ★ Kapahulu Groin.

Waikiki has always been a popular surfing site. Near here, on the slopes of Diamond Head, a *heiau* was dedicated to *he'e nalu*, or surfing, and the priests there were responsible for announcing the surfing conditions to the village below by flying a kite. *Kalakaua & 'Kapahulu aves.*

❸ ★ Ala Wai Canal/Lili'uokalani Estate.

This was the site of the estate of Queen Lili'uokalani, who was overthrown by the U.S. government in 1893. She had two homes here: Paoakalani (royal perfume), located where the canal now stands, and Kealohilani (the brightness of heaven), located opposite Kuhio Beach. *Kapahulu Ave. & Ala Wai Blvd.*

❹ ★ Kuhio Beach Park.

This beach park is named in honor of Prince Jonah Kuhio Kalaniana'ole, *hanai* (adopted) son of King Kalakaua. Jailed for a year for trying to restore Queen Lili'uokalani to the throne in 1895, he later became the

An offshore breakwater at Kuhio Beach creates a calm, shallow swimming area.

territory's second delegate to the U.S. Congress, 1902–22, and is responsible for the Homes Commission Act, which returned some 200,000 acres (80,937 ha) of land to Native Hawaiians. His home, Pualeilani (flower from the wreath of heaven), was located on the beach here and was given to the city when he died. It is no longer there, but you can read about its history. *2453 Kalakaua Ave. (btw. Kealohilani & Lili'uokalani sts.).*

⑤ ★ **Duke Kahanamoku Statue.** Olympic swimming champion, internationally known surfer, movie actor, and ambassador of aloha, Duke Paoa Kahanamoku won three gold medals, two silvers, and a bronze in four Olympics. He introduced surfing to Europe, Australia, and the East Coast of the U.S. and appeared in movies from 1925 to 1933. There's no surfboard marker here, just the imposing bronze sculpture of Duke, typically sporting fresh leis in tribute. *Kalakaua Ave. (btw. Lili'uokalani & Uluniu sts.).*

⑥ ★ **Healing Stones of Kapaemahu.** According to legend, four healers of dual male and female spirit, known as *mahu*, came to Hawai'i from Tahiti, perhaps in the 15th century. Before they left, they transferred their healing powers into these stones, which were located in Kaimuki, 2 miles (3.2km) away. No one knows how the stones, which weigh approximately 8 tons (7 metric tons), got to Waikiki, where they were relocated several times before being mounted in this prominent place with a plaque calling them "The Wizard Stones of Kapaemahu." *Kapaemahu,* an award-winning animated short film from 2020, tells their story and highlights the Hawaiian concept of *mahu,* sometimes called the third gender. *Diamond Head side of the Waikiki Police Sub-Station, 2405 Kalakaua Ave.*

The legendary Wizard Stones of Kapaemahu are said to contain healing powers.

⑦ ★ **Former King's Village.** The home of King Kalakaua (1836–91) once stood here, surrounded by towering coconut trees. The king loved dancing and revived the hula tradition, which the missionaries had just about succeeded in stamping out. He also loved to give parties and earned the nickname "The Merrie Monarch." The area later became a quaint block-long shopping center officially known as King's Village, and widely called King's Alley, but it was razed in 2019 to be replaced by the bane of Waikiki—another high-rise timeshare resort. *131 Ka'iulani Ave. (btw. Koa Ave. & Prince Edward St.).*

⑧ ★ **'Ainahau Triangle/Princess Ka'iulani Statue.** This tiny triangular park was once part of the palm tree–lined grand entrance to the 10-acre (4-ha) estate of Scotland-born Archibald Scott Cleghorn, his wife, Hawaiian *ali'i* (royalty) Miriam Kapili Likelike, and their universally beloved daughter, Princess Ka'iulani. Like her sister, Queen Lili'uokalani, and brothers King Kalakaua and Leleiohoku, Likelike was a gifted composer. She wrote the song "'Ainahau" (land of the hau tree), describing the estate lily ponds, coconut trees, hibiscus, mangos, and a giant banyan tree. The huge, two-story Victorian home stood between what are now Cleghorn and Tusitala streets. The heir to Queen Lili'uokalani, Princess

Mahiku Farmers Market at the International Market Place.

Kaʻiulani joined her aunt in Washington, D.C. in 1897 to protest the imminent annexation of Hawaiʻi; her death in 1899, at just age 23, caused widespread mourning for lost hopes as well as a lost life. *Kaʻiulani & Kuhio aves.*

9 ★ International Market Place. The luxury shopping center that replaced a humble warren of souvenir shops in 2016 kept its massive banyan tree in its courtyard, where you'll find the surfboard historic marker. This area once fronted the ʻApuakehau Stream and was the summer home of King William Charles Lunalilo (1835–74), the first elected king of Hawaiʻi, and later of Queen Emma. The Hawaiians called him *ke aliʻi lokomaikaʻi,* or "the kind chief." His reign was only 1 year and 25 days—he died due to poor health. *Duke's Lane (btw. Kuhio & Kalakaua aves.).*

10 ★ Moana Surfrider, a Westin Resort. The first hotels in Waikiki were just bathhouses that offered rooms for overnight stays. Then the Moana Surfrider Hotel opened its doors on March 11, 1901, with four stories (then the tallest structure in Hawaiʻi) and 75 rooms (with a bathroom and a telephone in each room). Harry Owens and Webley Edwards's radio show *Hawaii Calls,* which started in 1935, was broadcast live from the hotel's banyan Court, named for the large banyan tree where you'll find a historical marker. At the peak of the show's popularity in 1952, it reached 750 stations around the globe. *2365 Kalakaua Ave. (near Kaʻiulani St.).*

11 ★ Duke's Waikiki. The historic marker by the lanai of this popular restaurant at Outrigger Waikiki Beach Resort notes that ʻApuakehau ("basket of dew") Stream once emptied into the ocean here, carving a channel that create a surfbreak. Waikiki's "beach boys," watermen (and women) who guide visitors in all kinds of ocean sports, got their start here in the 1930s. Today they're licensed by the state. *2335 Kalakaua Ave. (across the street from Duke's Lane & Kaʻiulani St.).*

12 ★ Banán. Stop at this stand along the beach access path between Outrigger Waikiki Beach Resort and the Cheesecake Factory for a soft-serve, nondairy treat made from local bananas, which also comes flavored with local chocolate and numerous topping options ($8 cup, $13 bowl). Try it as a float with iced matcha or mac nut mocha coffee ($8–$10). **Note:** There's also a Banán on the ocean side of the Waikiki Shore condos, next to the U.S. Army Museum of Hawaiʻi, which has an expanded menu (see p 80). *2301 Kalakaua Ave., Waikiki.* ☎ *808/200-1640. https://banan.co. Daily 8:30am–8pm. $.*

The coconut grove at the Royal Hawaiian Hotel.

⓭ ★★ Royal Hawaiian Hotel. In the 16th century, a supernatural rooster appeared here and scratched the ground in front of chief Kakuhihewa, who dubbed the area Helumoa ("chicken scratch") and planted a grove of 10,000 coconut trees. Later, Kamehameha I camped here before his conquest of O'ahu. After winning battles in Nu'uanu, he made Waikiki the capital of the Hawaiian Islands. In 1927, the Royal Hawaiian Hotel opened with 400 rooms. The pink Moorish fantasy cost $5 million to build. See p 116. The marker is on the lawn between the Royal Hawaiian Center mall and the hotel. *2259 Kalakaua Ave. (Royal Hawaiian Ave.).*

⓮ ★ Gray's Beach. Waikiki is known today for its incredible beauty, but in the olden days, it was known by the Hawaiians as a powerful place of healing. Very successful *kahuna la'au lapa'au* (medical physicians) lived in this area, and the royal families often came here to convalesce. The beach, stretching from where the Halekulani Hotel is today to the Outrigger Reef (where the marker is found), was called Kawehewehe, "removal," because if you bathed in the waters, your illness would be removed. *2169 Kalia Rd. (at Lewers St.).* ☎ *808/923-3111.*

⓯ ★ U.S. Army Museum of Hawai'i. Now part of Fort DeRussy, the grounds where the museum stands today were once the 3-acre (1.2-ha) estate and villa of Chung Afong, Hawaii's first Chinese millionaire and member of King David Kalakaua's privy council. Afong arrived in Honolulu in 1849 and in just 6 years made a fortune in retail real estate, sugar, rice, and opium (he had the only government license to sell it). In 1904, the U.S. Army Corp of Engineers bought the property for $28,000 to defend Honolulu Harbor. On December 7, 1976, it became a museum (temporarily closed until early 2023; see p 50). *2131 Kalia Rd.*

⓰ ★ Kalia Road. In 1897, Fort DeRussy, from Kalia Road *mauka* some 13 acres (5.3 ha), was the largest fishpond in Waikiki. Called Ka'ihikapu, this pond, like hundreds of others in Waikiki, functioned as "royal iceboxes" where *'ama'ama* (mullet) and *awa* (milkfish) were raised in brackish water. Hawaiians have lots of legends about

Fans of iconic swimmer, surfer, and aloha ambassador Duke Paoa Kahanamoku still drape his statue with leis.

fishponds, which they believed were protected by *mo'o* (lizards) that could grow to some 12 to 30 feet (4–9m). In 1908, it took the U.S. military more than 250,000 cubic yards (191,131 cubic meters) of landfill and 1 year to cover Ka'ihikapu. *Kalia Rd. (btw. Saratoga Rd. & Ala Moana Blvd.) toward Kalakaua Ave.*

⑰ ★ **Paoa Park.** The 20 acres (8 ha) where the Hilton Hawaiian Village stands today was home to Olympic champion Duke Kahanamoku's mother's family, the Paoas. Duke's grandfather, Ho'olae Paoa, was a descendant of royal chiefs and got the land from King Kamehameha III in the Great Mahele of 1848, which allowed the king, chiefs, and commoners to claim private titles to land and for the first time allowed foreigners to own land in Hawai'i. The 5-acre (2 ha) saltwater lagoon, restored in 2007, also bears Duke's name. *Kalia Rd. (bordered by Paoa Rd. & Ala Moana Ave.).*

A protected beach and shady lawns make Ala Moana Regional Park a favorite island playground.

Fort DeRussy Beach Park.

18 ★ **Lappert's Ice Cream.**
Before you leave the Hilton Hawaiian Village, take a break at this yummy local shop with many tropical flavors (my favorite is the white chocolate macadamia nut). If you need a hit of caffeine, try one of the island pour-over coffees (from Kona, Moloka'i, or Maui) or a refreshing iced coffee. *Rainbow Bazaar, Hilton Hawaiian Village, 2005 Kalia Rd. (at Ala Moana Blvd.). www. lappertshawaii.com.* ☎ *808/943-0256. Daily 6am–10pm. $.*

19 ★ **Ilikai Hotel.** Waikiki's third stream, Pi'inaio, once originated here, where the hotel's lanai is today. However, unlike the other two streams (Kuekaunahi and 'Apuakehau), Pi'inaio was a muddy delta area with several smaller streams pouring in. It also was a very productive fishing area filled with reef fish, crabs, shrimp, lobster, octopus, eels, and *limu* (seaweed). However, today, Waikiki is nearly fished out. *1777 Ala Moana Blvd. (at Hobron Lane).*

20 ★★ **Ala Moana Regional Park.** In the late 1800s, Chinese farmers moved into Waikiki and converted the area now occupied by the park and shopping center into duck ponds. In 1931, the city and county of Honolulu wanted to clean up the waterfront and built a park here. In 1959, the 50 acres (20 hectares) across the street opened as one of the largest shopping centers in the U.S. *Diamond Head corner of the entrance to the park, Ala Moana Blvd. (at Atkinson Dr.).*

21 ★ **Ala Wai Canal.** At the turn of the 20th century, people on O'ahu were not very happy with Waikiki, with its smelly duck farms, coupled with the zillions of mosquitoes from the stagnant swamp lands. Work began on the Ala Wai (fresh water) Canal in 1922 and was completed in 1928. Once the canal had drained the wetlands, the taro and rice fields dried up, and the duck farms and fishponds disappeared. Beloved by outrigger canoe paddlers, but unsettlingly murky, the canal is now the subject of a years-long restoration effort using special toxin-eating mud balls (see p 53). *Ala Wai Canal side of the Hawai'i Convention Center, 1801 Kalakaua Ave.*

22 ★ **Fort DeRussy.** This green recreation area was named after Brigadier General Rene E. DeRussy,

The Changing Waters of Waikiki

Waikiki may seem synonymous with high-rise beach hotels, but the meaning of its Hawaiian name, "spouting water," gives a clue to how it looked before Western contact. The drainage basin for the 5 million gallons (18,927 cubic m) of daily rainfall from the Ko'olau Mountains, Waikiki held 2,000 acres (809 ha) of marsh at the time Hawaiians began to settle it, around 600 A.D. They developed vast systems of taro fields, fishponds, orchards, and gardens. When mosquitos arrived with Western ships, starting in the late 18th century, they swarmed swampy Waikiki. The Ala Wai Canal drained the area in 1927, creating dry land that eventually became the resort district. The now-murky Ala Wai is undergoing a years-long restoration effort to make it swimmable and fishable, through the innovative use of "genki balls," mud balls mixed with rice bran and microorganisms that can digest the sludge. Guests at the elegant Ritz-Carlton Residences, Waikiki Beach (p 116) can also book a Malama Hawai'i ("care for Hawai'i") package that supports the project; see genkialawai.org for details on other ways to help.

Corps of Engineers, who served in the American-British War of 1812. All of Fort DeRussy and the land from here to the foothills of Manoa Valley was once planted with taro. By 1870, the demand for taro had diminished, and the Chinese farmers began planting rice in the former taro fields. *Near the corner of Ala Moana Blvd. & Kalakaua Ave.*

㉓ ★ King Kalakaua Statue.
Next to Kamehameha I, King Kalakaua is the best-known Hawaiian king, and certainly lived up to his nickname, "the Merrie Monarch." He was born to royal parents in 1836, raised in the court of King Kamehameha IV, and elected to the position of king in 1874, after King William Lunalilo died. During his 17-year reign, he promoted the traditions of chant and hula (public performances had been banned by the missionaries for years). He was also forced to sign what has been termed the "Bayonet Constitution," which restricted his royal powers, in

1887. In 1890, he sailed to California for medical treatment and died in San Francisco in early 1891, following a mild stroke and kidney failure. *Intersection of Kuhio & Kalakaua aves.*

King David Kalakaua, affectionately remembered as the "Merrie Monarch."

O'ahu's Best Gardens

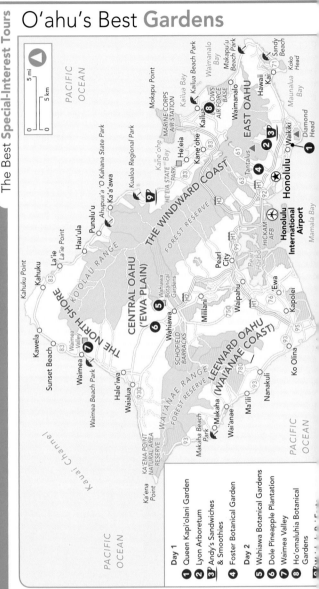

Day 1
1 Queen Kapi'olani Garden
2 Lyon Arboretum
3 Andy's Sandwiches & Smoothies
4 Foster Botanical Garden

Day 2
5 Wahiawa Botanical Gardens
6 Dole Pineapple Plantation
7 Waimea Valley
8 Ho'omaluhia Botanical Gardens

Stop and smell the tuberose, one of the many fragrant nonnative flowers (including plumeria and pikake, or jasmine) that perfume gardens in Hawai'i as well as leis. Spend a couple of days exploring the various gardens of O'ahu, home to endemic plants, i.e. only found in Hawai'i; "canoe plants," brought to the islands by the first Polynesian voyagers; and orchids, palms, tropical fruits, ferns, and flowers from all over the world.

Day 1

You can walk to this first garden from Waikiki, but since you'll need a car for the second stop, take advantage of the free parking around Kapi'olani Park.

❶ ★ Queen Kapi'olani Garden. Wander into this tiny garden at the edge of Waikiki for an array of tropical ornamentals, hibiscus cultivars, and a collection of native plants. ⏲ *20 min. Kapi'olani Park, on Monsarrat Ave. (btw. Paki & Le'ahi aves.). Free. Daily 24 hr.*

From Waikiki, it's a 20-minute drive to Lyon Arboretum.

❷ ★★ Lyon Arboretum. Six-story-tall breadfruit trees. Yellow orchids no bigger than a coin. Ferns with fuzzy buds as big as a human head. At the back of lush Manoa Valley, Lyon Arboretum is 194 budding acres (79 ha) of botanical wonders, managed by the University of Hawai'i. Although admission is free (donations requested), online reservations are required to explore its 7 miles (11m) of hiking trails, including more than 6,000 different species of tropical and subtropical plants. An easy 20-minute loop trail passes many marked plants. 'Aihualama Falls, the destination of a gently rising, 2.2-mile (3.5km) round-trip trail from the visitor center and small gift shop, is often just a trickle, but with fascinating plants and side gardens along the way. ⏲ *2–3 hr. 3860 Manoa Rd. (near the top of the road). manoa.hawaii.edu/lyon.* ☎ *808/988-0456. Suggested donation $10 each. Mon–Fri 9am–3pm.*

A lotus flower at Lyon Arboretum.

☕ ★ **Andy's Sandwiches & Smoothies.** On the way down from Lyon Arboretum, stop at this friendly neighborhood eatery (currently takeout only). The 'ahi tuna melt or hot turkey mushroom sandwiches are favorites. *2904 E. Manoa Rd., opposite Manoa Marketplace. www. andyssandwiches.com. ☎ 808/988-6161. Weekdays 7am–4pm. $.*

A cannonball tree at Foster Botanical Garden.

From Lyon Arboretum, it's another 20-minute drive to Foster Botanical Garden.

❹ ★★ **Foster Botanical Garden.** The giant trees that tower over the main terrace of this leafy oasis were planted in the 1850s by William Hillebrand, a German physician and botanist. Today, this 14-acre (5.7-ha) public garden, on the north side of Chinatown, is a living museum of plants, some rare and endangered, collected from the tropical regions of the world. Of special interest are 26 "Exceptional Trees" protected by state law, a large palm collection, a primitive cycad garden, a butterfly garden, and an orchid conservatory. ⏱ *2–3 hr. 50 N. Vineyard Blvd. (at Nu'uanu Ave.). www.honolulu.gov/ parks/hbg/honolulu-botanical-gardens. ☎ 808/768-7135. $5*

adults, $1 children 6–12, free for children 5 & under. Daily 9am–4pm.

Day 2
From Waikiki, it's about 25 miles (40km) to Wahiawa, typically a 40-minute drive.

❺ ★ **Wahiawa Botanical Garden.** Originally begun as an experimental arboretum by sugar planters in the 1920s, this 27-acre (11-ha) tropical rainforest garden is considered the jewel of Honolulu's botanical gardens. It provides a cool, moist environment for native Hawaiian plants, palms, aroids, tree ferns, heliconias, calatheas, and epiphytic plants. Mosquitos also love the humidity here—bring insect repellent. ⏱ *1½–2 hr. 1396 California Ave., Wahiawa.*

Tropical rainforest plants thrive at Wahiawa Botanical Garden.

www.honolulu.gov/parks/hbg/ honolulu-botanical-gardens. ☎ 808/ 286-7135. Free. Daily 9am–4pm.

From the botanic garden, it's just over 3 miles (5km) to Dole Pineapple Plantation.

6 ★ Dole Pineapple Plantation. This rest stop/retail outlet/ exhibit area also has an interesting self-guided tour through eight mini gardens totaling about 1½ acres (.6 ha). The Pineapple Garden Maze covers more than 2 acres (.8 ha) with a 1.7-mile (2.7km) hibiscus-lined path. See p 34, 6.

From Dole Pineapple Plantation, it's 11.5 miles (18.5km) to Waimea Valley, or about 20 minutes by car.

7 ★ Waimea Valley. About 5,000 species of plants in 52 themed gardens and numerous Hawaiian cultural sites can be found in the 150 acres (61 ha) accessible to the public here. Tours depart at 12:30pm daily. Three large gardens are devoted to Hawaiian plants, 90% of which grow nowhere else, including the endangered *Kokia cookei* hibiscus. The gardens also host the largest public collection of *kalo*, or taro, varieties. Bring a swimsuit, since you're allowed to cool off in the pool of a 45-foot (14m) waterfall, if conditions allow. ◷ 2–3 hr. Waimea Valley Rd., Hale'iwa. www.waimea valley.net. ☎ 808/638-7766. $25

adults, $18 seniors, $14 children 4–12. Daily 9am–5pm.

Day 3
From Waikiki, it takes about 40 minutes to drive the 16 miles (26km) to Ho'omaluhia Botanical Garden.

8 ★ Ho'omaluhia Botanical Garden. This 400-acre (162-ha) botanical garden at the foot of the steepled Ko'olau Mountains is the perfect place for a picnic. Its name means "a peaceful refuge," and that's exactly what the Army Corps of Engineers created when they installed a flood-control project here, which resulted in a 32-acre (13-ha) freshwater lake (no swimming allowed) and garden. You can drive or walk through the gardens featuring geographical groupings of plantings from the major tropical regions around the world, with a special emphasis on native Hawaiian plants. ◷ 2–3 hr. 45–680 Luluku Rd., Kane'ohe. www.honolulu.gov/parks/ hbg/honolulu-botanical-gardens. ☎ 808/233-7323. Free. Daily 9am–4p.

9 ★ Waiahole Poi Factory. After seeing all the different kalo (taro) varieties at Waimea Valley, it's time to eat it as the locals do. Pair poi (the mashed root of kalo) with laulau (pork wrapped with the kalo leaves and then swaddled in ti leaves and steamed). See p 158.

Moku Mo'o (Lizard Islet), in the freshwater lake at Ho'omaluhia Botanical Garden.

Honolulu for Art Lovers

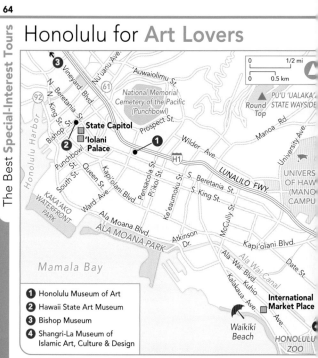

1 Honolulu Museum of Art
2 Hawaii State Art Museum
3 Bishop Museum
4 Shangri-La Museum of Islamic Art, Culture & Design

E ven if you're not a die-hard art lover, you won't regret giving up a day for this tour. Hawai'i's top three cultural galleries aren't just depositories of artwork—each is an incredible edifice in its own right. It's a part of Hawaii you won't want to miss.

Find metered parking or park behind the Honolulu Museum of Art School, 1111 Victoria St., and walk 2 minutes. The lot costs $5 for 5 hours, $2 for each add'l. 30 minutes.

1 ★★★ **Honolulu Museum of Art.** This museum features one of the top Asian art collections in the country. Also on exhibit are American and European masters, contemporary artworks, and prehistoric Mayan, Greek, and Hawaiian art. I love Georgia O'Keeffe's 1939 paintings of Maui's waterfall-laced 'Iao Valley. The gracious indoor-outdoor compound contains tranquil courtyards with lily ponds and a

coffee bar, plus quiet galleries, a 280-seat theater hosting arthouse films and concerts, and a pleasant cafe (reservations suggested). This is also the departure point for tours of Doris Duke's **Shangri La,** her waterfront estate turned museum of Islamic art and culture (see facing box). ⏱ 2–3 hr. 900 S. Beretania St. (at Ward Ave.). www.honolulu museum.org. ☎ 808/532-8700. $20 adults, free for children 18 & under. Thurs 10am–6pm, Fri–Sat 10am–9pm, Sun 10am–6pm.

From the Honolulu Museum of Art, it's a 15-minute walk to the Hawai'i State Art Museum, which does not have onsite parking. Ali'i

A gallery in the Hawaii State Art Museum.

Place parking garage (p 42) is across the street.

❷ ★ Hawai'i State Art Museum.
On the site of a wooden hotel built in 1872, the current Spanish Mission–style structure opened in 1928. There's a cool sculpture garden in the courtyard that once held a large pool and bleachers, with artworks by modern and contemporary Hawaiian artists (including many winners of student art competitions) on the second floor. ⏱ *2–3 hr.* 250 S. Hotel St. (at Richards St.). *hisam.hawaii.gov.* ☎ 808/586-0900. Free. Mon–Sat 10am–4pm.

From downtown Honolulu, it's about 3 miles (5km) to the Bishop Museum.

❸ ★★ Bishop Museum.
Charles Reed Bishop honored the memory of his late wife, Princess Bernice Pauahi, the last descendant of the Kamehameha line, by building an elegant stone museum to house her royal heirlooms and Hawaiian objects. Today it is the definitive repository of Hawaiian and Oceanic cultural artifacts, but also boasts stunning murals by international and Hawai'i street artists and a gallery of gorgeous 19th century Hawaiian art, including oil paintings of royalty and distinctive Hawaiian landscapes, watercolors, rare books, and collectibles. The gift shop is also a treasure trove. *See p 21.*

Shangri La in Hawai'i

In the late 1930s, heiress Doris Duke built her dream home on the exclusive coast southeast of Diamond Head, naming it "Shangri La." The 5-acre (2-ha) estate reflects Duke's love of both Hawai'i and the Middle East by featuring Islamic art and architecture blended with sweeping ocean views, exotic gardens, and water features. Now called Shangri La Museum of Islamic Art, Culture & Design, it's open for self-guided tours by reservation only, Thursday through Saturday from 9am to 3pm. Tickets are $25 for ages 8 and older, including admission to the Honolulu Museum of Art (900 S. Beretania St.), where you pick up tickets and the required shuttle to and from Shangri La (no self-transport allowed). Allow about 2 hours for the tour, including time in transit and about 75 minutes at Shangri La. For more information, visit honolulumuseum.org/shangri-la or call ☎ 808/532-3853.

Romantic Honolulu & O'ahu

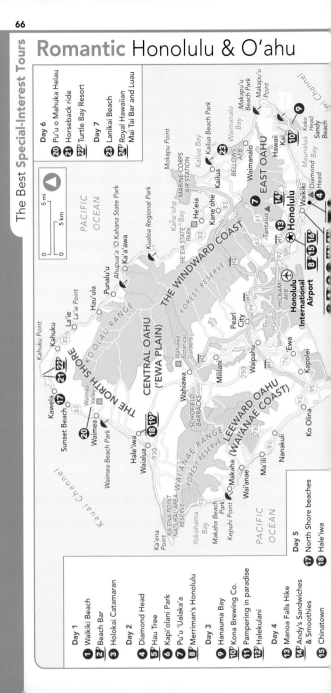

Day 1
1. Waikiki Beach
2. Beach Bar
3. Holokai Catamaran

Day 2
4. Diamond Head
5. Hau Tree
6. Kapi'olani Park
7. Pu'u 'Ualaka'a
8. Merriman's Honolulu

Day 3
9. Hanauma Bay
10. Kona Brewing Co.
11. Pampering in paradise
12. Halekulani

Day 4
13. Manoa Falls Hike
14. Andy's Sandwiches & Smoothies
15. Chinatown

Day 5
17. North Shore beaches
18. Hale'iwa

Day 6
20. Pu'u o Mahuka Heiau
21. Horseback ride
22. Turtle Bay Resort

Day 7
23. Lanikai Beach
24. Royal Hawaiian Mai Tai Bar and Luau

What could be more romantic than a vacation where the gentle breezes caress your skin, the sensuous aroma of tropical flowers wafts through the air, and the relaxing sound of the surf beckons lovers from around the globe? Below is a suggested tour for discovering O'ahu, and each other.

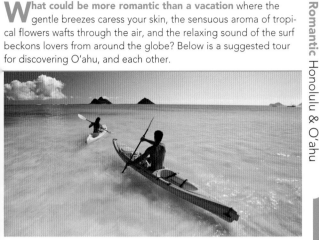

Gentle water conditions make Kailua Beach a great place to kayak.

Day 1

Everything today is in walking distance of Waikiki, so you can stretch your legs after getting off the plane.

① ★★★ **Waikiki Beach.** Your vacation starts when the warm sand covers your toes and the salt air kisses your face. Take a stroll hand-in-hand down this famous beach. *See p 169.*

② ★ **Beach Bar.** Under a spreading banyan tree at the gracious Moana Surfrider, built in 1901, refresh yourself with a late lunch, early dinner, or tropical cocktail. *Moana Surfrider, 2365 Kalakaua Ave. (Ka'iulani St.). www.moana-surfrider. com.* ☎ *808/921-4600. Daily 11am–10:30pm. $$.*

③ ★ **Holokai Catamaran.** Spend your first evening in paradise by sailing into the sunset. If it's Friday night, sign up for the Fireworks Sail and watch the weekly Hilton Hawaiian Village fireworks show from the ocean, where it

seems like the display explodes right above you. ⏱ *1–1½ hr. Gray's Beach in front of the Halekulani. www.sailholokai.com.* ☎ *808/922-2210. Sunset Sail (90 min.) and Fireworks Sail (1 hr.), each $70.*

Day 2

Reserve your hiking and parking permits up to 2 weeks in advance for Diamond Head.

④ ★★ **Diamond Head.** You'll probably be up early on your first few days in Hawai'i before you get

The view from the top of Diamond Head.

Hau Tree Restaurant.

used to the time difference. Greet the sun by hiking up to Waikiki's most famous landmark; you can reserve a permit for as early as 6am. You'll get a bird's-eye view of the island from atop this 760-foot (232m) extinct volcano. *See p 173.*

Park for free or in metered spaces along Kapi'olani Park.

⑤ ★★ **Hau Tree.** After your hike, savor eggs benedict or other tasty brunch dishes under hau trees and hanging lanterns at this hip but casual outdoor restaurant, overlooking Kaimana (Sans Souci) Beach next to Kapi'olani Park. *See p 101.*

⑥ ★★ **Kapi'olani Park.** Explore this tropical park on the east end of Waikiki, which offers some welcome shade as well as dazzling views. It's also home to the fascinating Waikiki Aquarium. See my tour of the park beginning on p 90.

Drive about 6 miles (10km) from Kapi'olani Park into the lush green hills above downtown Honolulu.

⑦ ★ **Pu'u 'Ualaka'a State Wayside.** One of the island's most romantic sunset views is from this 1,048-foot (319m) hill named for sweet potatoes ('uala). Get there before sunset to see the panoramic view of the entire coastline. *See p 20, ⑥.*

⑧ ★★★ **Merriman's Honolulu.** In the heart of Honolulu's trendy Ward Village/Kaka'ako neighborhood is this chic namesake bistro by a cofounder of the Hawai'i Regional Cuisine movement, which began in 1991 and has evolved to include even more locally sourced ingredients, and island- and Asian-inspired flavors. Enjoy the warm night air and vibrant ambience by sitting outside. *See p 105.*

Day 3
To ensure parking, reserve an early-morning arrival, available two days in advance.

⑨ ★★★ **Hanauma Bay Nature Preserve.** Head out to the premiere snorkeling area on O'ahu to discover the incredible beauty of its underwater world. **Note:** The preserve is closed on Mondays and Tuesdays. *See p 185.*

From Hanauma Bay, it's a 5-minute drive to the shops and restaurants of Koko Marina.

⑩ ★ **Kona Brewing Co.** Stop by the waterfront brewing restaurant of this renowned brewing company to sample some of the 48 beers on tap, including seasonal specialties hard to find on the mainland like Lemongrass Luau, Hibiscus Haze, or Mai Time Island Wheat. The casual American menu and tropical hard seltzers are delicious, too. *Koko Marina Center, 7192 Kalani'anaole*

Sampler at Kona Brewing Co waterfront restaurant.

Hwy. (Hwy. 72). www.konabrewingco. com. ☎ 808/396-5662. Daily 11am–9pm. $$.

Trace your route back to Waikiki.

⓫ Pampering in Paradise. Spend the afternoon at a spa getting pampered. For my top picks, see "Pampering in Paradise" on p 114.

Pamper yourself at the aptly named Halekulani ("House Befitting Heaven").

⓬ ★★★ Halekulani. While away the rest of the evening at this exquisitely beautiful resort. Sit outside at its famed House Without a Key and sip a cocktail as a graceful hula dancer performs to beautiful Hawaiian music. After the sun sets, head upstairs to La Mer, O'ahu's most romantic restaurant, where the windows frame intoxicating views of the ocean and Diamond Head. *See p 110.*

Day 4

Start your day early to ensure parking ($5) at the Manoa Falls trailhead, about a 20-minute drive from Waikiki.

⓭ ★★ Manoa Falls Hike. Take this easy, .75-mile (1.2km) one-way hike in a warm, tropical rainforest just minutes from Waikiki. In less than an hour, you'll be at the idyllic Manoa Falls. *See p 175.*

⓮ ★ Andy's Sandwiches & Smoothies. After hiking in the rainforest, stop by this neighborhood eatery. *See p 62,* **⓭**.

From Manoa, it's a 20-minute drive to Chinatown, which has metered parking (free after 6pm).

⓯ ★★ Chinatown. Explore this colorful neighborhood with the help of the tour starting on p 74. Be sure to shop for a lei for your sweetie.

⓰ ★★★ Fête. In 2022 Robynne Mai'i became the first female chef from Hawai'i (and only the second Native Hawaiian) to win a James Beard Award, thanks to her locally sourced, seasonal, New American-meets-the-islands menu at this casual, welcoming restaurant in Chinatown. The cocktails are also superb. *See p 101.*

The Lei

There's no doubt about it: Getting lei'd in Hawaii is a sensual experience, from the visual beauty of interwoven blossoms, vines, kukui nuts, and ferns, to the intoxicating aroma of flowers such as plumeria, pikake (jasmine), and puakenikeni, and the gentle caress of the lei on your neck (or, when draped properly, across your shoulders.) A lei is much more than just a pretty garland: It's the Hawaiian way to express greetings, congratulations, honor, affection, and love. The tradition came to the islands with the first Polynesian voyagers and flourished unabated after Western contact. In 1923, the Territorial Legislature designated an official lei for each island: O'ahu's is made from hundreds of paper-thin, yellow-orange 'ilima blossoms. Whatever lei you receive, it's a wonderful souvenir.

Day 5

Plan to spend nights 5 and 6 on the North Shore.

⓱ ★★★ North Shore beaches. Choose any one of the North Shore beaches to spend the morning. If it's wintertime and the surf's up, you'll want to head to

Shopping for aloha wear in Hale'iwa.

Pipeline or Sunset to watch the surfers in some of the best waves in the world. If it's summer, head to Waimea Bay to swim in typically calm waters, or Shark's Cove for snorkeling. See p 143.

⓲ ★★★ Hale'iwa. Take a break from the beach to explore the shops, cafes, and galleries in this famous North Shore surfing town. See p 144, ➍.

⓳ ★ Maya's Tapas & Wine. Split savory small plates like lamb empanadas, cauliflower ceviche, or shishito peppers with Hawaiian rock salt, and pair them with sangria or the perfect Mediterranean wine at this Spanish-style bistro in Hale'iwa. See p 148.

Day 6

⓴ ★ Pu'u o Mahuka Heiau. Start the day with a quick climb to this sacred heiau and its view overlooking Waimea Bay. See p 44, ⓱.

㉑ Horseback Ride. Explore the North Shore on horseback, from the trails above Pupukea Beach or along the beach and through iron-wood trees at sprawling Turtle Bay Resort. *See p 182.*

㉒ ★★ Turtle Bay Resort. Join the lively throng, from pro surfers to tourists, who gather for cocktail hour at the entrancing open-air lobby bar or cliffside pool bar, watching the waves at sunset. For dinner, head to Roy's Beach House, by beloved local chef Roy Yamaguchi, on the sand of the resort's placid Ku'ilima Cove. Make sure to order Roy's signature chocolate soufflé. *See p 145.*

Every year, tens of thousands of couples travel to O'ahu to say their wedding vows.

Getting Married in Paradise

Honolulu and Waikiki are ideal places for a wedding. Not only does the entire island exude romance and natural beauty, but after the ceremony, you're only a few steps away from the perfect honeymoon.

Most Waikiki resorts and hotels have wedding coordinators who can plan everything from a simple (relatively) low-cost wedding to an extravaganza that people will talk about for years. Planning it on your own? You'll need a permit ($25–$35) for a beach wedding (or similar ceremonies on the shore) if a professional photographer or any vendor is involved; visit dlnr.hawaii.gov/ld/commercial-activities to apply online.

Whoever plans it, you will need a marriage license. Schedule an in-person appointment at the Marriage License Office, Room 101 of the Health Department Building, 1250 Punchbowl St., Honolulu (health.hawaii.gov/vitalrecords/marriage-licenses; ☎ **808/586-4544**); it's open from 8am to 4pm weekdays. You can download an application for a marriage license from the site. Once in Hawai'i, the prospective spouses must go together to the marriage-licensing agent to get a license, which costs $65 and is good for 30 days.

Postcard-perfect Lanikai Beach.

Day 7

After breakfast on the North Shore, allowing time for morning traffic to dissipate, wend your way down the scenic Windward Coast. Look for street parking in Lanikai or walk from Kailua Beach Park, p 164.

23 ★★ **Lanikai Beach.** Spend your last day luxuriating at this narrow beach (p 165) with silky white sand and calm turquoise waters. If you're feeling more active, you can kayak to the Mokulua islands offshore (p 189), or climb up to the pillboxes (p 152, **11**).

24 ★★ **Royal Hawaiian Mai Tai Bar and Luau.** The beachfront setting and leafy grove of the "Pink Palace of Waikiki" have invited romance since 1927. Spend your last evening under the stars here, starting with an eponymous beverage at the Mai Tai Bar. If it's a Monday or Thursday, book a private table for the fabulous Aha'aina Luau, which uses beautiful hula and storytelling to trace the fascinating history of Hawai'i and Waikiki, of which you're now also a part. *See p 138.* ●

Historic Chinatown

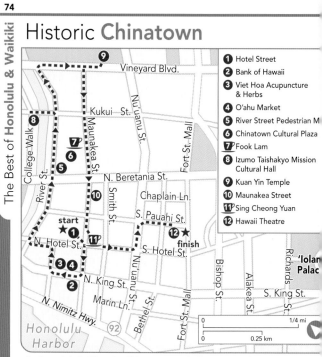

1 Hotel Street
2 Bank of Hawaii
3 Viet Hoa Acupuncture & Herbs
4 Oʻahu Market
5 River Street Pedestrian M
6 Chinatown Cultural Plaza
7 Fook Lam
8 Izumo Taishakyo Mission Cultural Hall
9 Kuan Yin Temple
10 Maunakea Street
11 Sing Cheong Yuan
12 Hawaii Theatre

Honolulu's historic Chinatown includes a mix of Asian cultures, packed into a few blocks of low-rise buildings with vintage architectural ornaments, bustling open-air markets selling produce of every stripe, and lei stands boasting a rainbow of woven flowers. It's also home to hip nightclubs, hot restaurants, cool boutiques, and, sadly, the most urban squalor you're likely to see on Oʻahu—though recent efforts to improve the area, both for residents and visitors, appear to be working. Plan at least 2 hours for a daytime visit, more if you love to browse. At night, it's safest to go directly to your destination by cab, rideshare, or car, rather than wander around, unless it's the first Friday of the month, when art galleries stay open till 9pm amid a festive street scene.

1 ★ **Hotel Street.** During World War II, Hotel Street was synonymous with good times. Pool halls and beer parlors lined the blocks, and prostitutes were plentiful. Nowadays, the more nefarious establishments have been replaced with small shops, from art galleries to specialty boutiques.

Previous page: Kids on Waikiki Beach.

Wander up and down this street and then head to the intersection with Smith Street. On the Diamond Head (east) side of Smith, you'll notice stones in the sidewalk; they were taken from the sandalwood ships, which came to Hawaiʻi empty of cargo except for these stones, which were used as ballast on the trip over. *Hotel St., btw. Maunakea & Bethel sts.*

Fresh tropical flowers at a Chinatown lei shop.

When you've finished exploring Hotel St., head back to Maunakea St. and turn toward the ocean.

❷ Bank of Hawaii. This unusual-looking bank (temporarily closed) is not the conservative edifice you might expect—gilded serpents wind around scarlet columns. *101 N. King St. (Maunakea St.).*

Head mauka on Maunakea St.

❸ Viet Hoa Acupuncture & Herbs. Here, Chinese herbalists act as both doctors and dispensers of herbs. There's a wall of tiny drawers all labeled in Chinese characters; the herbalist pulls out bits and pieces ranging from dried flowers to mashed antelope antler. The patient then takes the concoction home to brew into a strong tea. *1125 Maunakea St.* 📞 *808/523-5499. Mon–Sat 8:45am–5pm, Sun 8:45am–2pm.*

Cross to the south side of King St., where, just west of Kekaulike St., you come to the most-visited part of Chinatown, the open-air market.

❹ ★★ O'ahu Market. Those interested in cooking a variety of Asian cuisines will find all the necessary ingredients here, including pigs' heads, poultry (some still squawking), fresh octopuses, pungent fish sauce, and 1,000-year-old eggs. The friendly vendors are happy to explain their wares and give instructions on how to prepare them. The market has been at this spot since 1904. 🕐 *1 hr. 145 N. King St. Daily 6am–6pm.*

Follow King down to River St. and turn right toward the mountains.

❺ Riverwalk (River Street Pedestrian Mall). The statue of Chinese revolutionary leader Sun Yat-sen marks the beginning of this wide mall, which borders Nu'uanu Stream. It's lined with shade trees, benches, and tables where seniors gather to play mah-jongg and checkers. *N. Beretania St. to Vineyard Blvd.*

❻ Chinatown Cultural Plaza. This modern complex is filled with shops featuring everything from tailors to calligraphers, as well as numerous restaurants and even a small post office for those who want to mail cards home with the "Chinatown" postmark. The best feature of the plaza is the **Moongate Stage** in the center, the site of many cultural presentations around the Chinese New Year. 🕐 *30 min. 100 N. Beretania St. chinatownculturalplaza.com.* 📞 *808/521-4934. Parking garage entrance is on Maunakea St. Day rates are $1 first hr., $3 each add'l. hr.; after 6pm, $1 first hr., $2 each add'l. hr.*

❼ ★ Fook Lam. Stop to refuel at this popular dim sum spot. My favorites here include steamed shrimp dumplings (har gau), Singapore rice noodle and jin dui (fried sesame puffs with red bean inside).

Dragonfruit and other exotic finds at a Chinatown market.

Steaming hot dim sum is a Chinatown specialty.

In Chinatown Cultural Plaza, but enter from River Street pedestrian mall—you can't miss the line waiting outside, which moves quickly. ☎ 808/523-9168. Daily 8am–2pm. $.

Continue mauka (inland) up the Riverwalk and cross Nu'uanu Stream via the bridge at Kukui St.

❽ Izumo Taishakyo Mission Cultural Hall. This small wooden Shinto shrine, built in 1923, houses a male deity (look for the X-shaped crosses on the top). Inside the temple is a 100-pound sack of rice, symbolizing good health. ⏱ *15 min. 215 N. Kukui St.* ☎ *808/538-7778. Daily 8:30am–4pm.*

Walk a block toward the mountains to Vineyard Blvd.; cross back over Nu'uanu Stream, past the entrance of Foster Botanical Gardens (p 62)

❾ ★ Kuan Yin Temple. This Buddhist temple, painted in a

brilliant red with a green ceramic-tile roof, is dedicated to Kuan Yin, often called the "goddess of mercy," but more properly a *bodhisattva*—someone driven by great compassion who attains enlightenment. Her statue towers in the prayer hall. The temple is still a house of worship, not an exhibit, so enter with respect and leave your shoes outside. You may see people burning paper "money" for prosperity and good luck or leaving flowers and fruits at the altar. ⏱ *15 min. 170 N. Vineyard Blvd. (Nu'uanu St.).* ☎ *808/533-6361.*

Continue down Vineyard and then turn right (toward the ocean) on Maunakea St.

❿ ★★ Maunakea Street. Numerous lei shops line this colorful street, which is the best place in all of Hawai'i to get a deal on leis. The size, color, and design of the leis made here are exceptional. *Btw. Beretania & King sts.*

Plan to spend at least a few hours exploring Honolulu's historic Chinatown.

The New Chinatown

Honolulu's Chinatown began to take shape in the second half of the 19th century as many Chinese sugar plantation workers opted not to renew their 5-year contracts and instead moved to Chinatown to open businesses. Chinatown catered to whalers and sailors. and reached its zenith in the 1920s, with restaurants and markets flourishing by day, and prostitutes and opium dens doing brisk business at night. As its reputation as a red-light district began to eclipse everything else, the neighborhood declined.

A turnaround began in the mid-1990s, when restaurants, boutiques, and clubs started filling in abandoned storefronts, many of which still boast turn-of-the-century architectural details. In more recent years, Chinatown also become a haven for unhoused people, drug use, and street crime, while still attracting exciting restaurants like **Senia** (p 107) and **Fête** (p 101) and nightclubs like **Scarlet Honolulu** (p 136). But, the city's new revitalization plan, launched in early 2022, has already seen dramatic decreases in crime and people camping on the Riverwalk, thanks to expanded outreach and police patrols.

Several pioneers among the modern Chinatown merchants include the original location of **Fighting Eel,** 1133 Bethel St. (www.fightingeel.com; ☎ **808/738-9300**). Here you'll find bright, easy-to-wear dresses and shirts with island prints—perfect for Honolulu weather, but chic enough to wear back home. Hunt for vintage treasures of all sorts at **Tin Can Mailman,** 1026 Nu'uanu Ave. (www.tincanmailman.net; ☎ **808/524-3009**) and the funky **Hound & Quail,** 1156 Nu'uanu St. (www.houndandquail.com; ☎ **808/779-8436**). At **Ginger13,** 22 S. Pauahi St. (www.ginger13.com; ☎ **808/531-5311**), you'll find the graceful gemstone beads and baubles of local jewelry designer Cindy Yokoyama, plus a well-curated selection of candles, handbags, home decor, body care products, and other gifts.

Head makai on Maunakea St.

11 ★ **Sing Cheong Yuan Bakery.** Revive yourself with a savory steamed bun or a sweet confection like a silky egg custard or coconut gin dui (a ball of deep-fried mochi rice flour filled with coconut and sprinkled with white sesame seed). There's also a wide selection of dried and sugared candies (ginger, pineapple, and lotus root) that you can eat as you stroll. *1027 Maunakea St.* ☎ *808/531-6688. Daily 7am–5pm. $.*

Head mauka on Maunakea St., turn right onto N. Hotel St. and turn left onto Bethel St.

12 ★★★ **Hawaii Theatre Center.** This restored 1920 Art Deco theater is a work of art in itself. It hosts a variety of programs, from the Hawai'i International Film Festival to Hawaiian concerts. No time for a show? You can take a virtual tour of the ornate interior at hawaiitheatre.dooplikit.com. *1130 Bethel St.* ☎ *808/791-1397. www.hawaiitheatre.com.*

Walking the Beach in Waikiki

start ★

finish ★

1 Ala Wai Yacht Harbor
2 Kahanamoku Beach and Lagoon
3 Duke Paoa Kahanamoku Beach Park
4 Fort DeRussy Beach
5 Banán
Gray's Beach
7 Waikiki Beach Center
8 Kuhio Beach Park
9 Queen's Surf Beach
10 Waikiki Aquarium
11 War Memorial Natatorium
12 Kaimana Beach

Just the name Waikiki conjures images of paradise. Only *ali'i* (royalty) lived on Waikiki Beach in the 1800s. After the overthrow of the Hawaiian monarchy in 1893, accommodations for visitors began to arise. The gracious Moana Hotel was the first to open, in 1901, and still operates today as the expanded Moana Surfrider, a Westin resort. During the 20th century, Waikiki went from wetlands with ducks and taro fields to 3 miles (4.8km) of high-rise hotels, condominiums, restaurants, and shops. The very word "Waikiki" translates into "spouting water," referring to the numerous springs and streams that flowed (and generally flooded) this now-famous destination. In 1922, the Waikiki Reclamation project dredged the Ala Wai Canal to drain the area and also buried the springs, ponds, and marshes. The area you see today is surprisingly nearly all artificially created—even the famous beach is made from sand shipped in from the island of Moloka'i or dredged from offshore. Although most people think of Waikiki Beach as just one long beach, it actually is a series of beaches. Thanks to erosion, they're not all connected by sand, so you may have to take a narrow walkway that can get splashed by surf if you don't want to detour inland a bit. Plan at least 2 to 3 hours to walk this incredible area.

❶ ★ Ala Wai Yacht Harbor. The largest of all the small boat harbors in Hawai'i, this harbor accommodates around 700 boats and one of the longest running ocean yacht races, the biennial Transpac sailing ract, which begins in Los Angeles and ends here.

Find a sunset charter or just enjoy a stroll at Ala Wai Yacht Harbor.

At the ocean end of the harbor, continue down the beach on the sand, just before Hilton Hawaiian Village.

❷ ★ Kahanamoku Beach and Lagoon. The area is named after Duke Paoa Kahanamoku (1890–1968), who spent most of his childhood swimming here and who later became a gold medalist in swimming in the 1912, 1920, and 1924 Olympic Games. He is credited with spreading the sport of surfing to the California coast and to Australia. Offshore is one of Waikiki's surf sites, Kaisers. If the waves are right, you can see the surfers at the west end of the channel leading to the Ala Wai Harbor.

Continue down the beach toward Diamond Head, on the other side of the Hilton Hawaiian Village. At the end of Paoa Place, opposite the catamaran pier, is:

❸ ★ Duke Paoa Kahanamoku Beach Park. This tiny (½-acre/.2-ha) park is also named after

The sheltered waters of Kahanamoku Beach and Lagoon.

Hawai'i's top waterman (see p 54, ⑤). There are restrooms and showers here, and it is a great spot for swimming, and, of course, surfing.

Continue down the beach toward Diamond Head.

④ ★ **Fort DeRussy Beach.** One of the best-kept secrets in Waikiki, this long stretch of sand beach is generally less crowded than other parts of Waikiki. The beach fronts the military reservation of Fort DeRussy Park. The Hale Koa Hotel (for military personnel only) is on the west end of the park, and on the Diamond Head end is the U.S. Army Museum of Hawai'i. Food and beach equipment rentals, concessions, picnic tables, restrooms, and showers are on the ocean side of the park. Another popular surf site, Number Threes, or just Threes, lies offshore.

⑤ ★ **Banán.** This stand next to Fort DeRussy is named for its signature soft-serve, nondairy treat made from local bananas, which also comes flavored with local chocolate and numerous topping options ($8 cup, $13 bowl). Order it atop an 'ulu (breadfruit) waffle ($10–$11) for an only-in-Hawai'i experience. You can also get shave ice here, with syrups sourced from local fruits like guava, dragonfruit, and strawberry ($10). *Ocean side of Waikiki Shore condos, 2161 Kalia Ave., Waikiki. banan.co.* ☎ *808/773-7231. Daily 10am–8pm. $.*

Continue down the beach toward Diamond Head and take the walkway to the sandy cove between Halekulani and the Sheraton Waikiki.

⑥ ★ **Gray's Beach.** Ancient Hawaiians called this area "Kawehewehe" (the removal) and revered the beach and the waters offshore as a sacred healing spot. In 1912, La Vancha Maria Chapin Gray opened a two-story boardinghouse called "Gray's-by-the-Sea," and so the popular swimming area facing it became known as Gray's. By the

Gray's Beach is safe for family swimming and has two popular surfing spots offshore

1920s, the boardinghouse had turned into a hotel named Halekulani ("house befitting heaven"). One of its guests, Earl Derr Biggers, wrote a murder mystery, *The House Without a Key*, based on Honolulu residents who never locked their doors (at that time). The hero of the book was a Chinese detective named Charlie Chan. Today, the House Without a Key is a destination lounge and restaurant in the luxurious Halekulani, while the beach area has sadly shrunk considerably. It's a safe swimming area, but watch out for the occasional catamaran coming ashore. Two surf sites are offshore: Populars and Paradise.

Continue down the beach toward Diamond Head, taking walkways where necessary. You'll pass Sheraton Waikiki, the Royal Hawaiian and Moana Surfrider hotels en route to this beachfront center.

❼ ★ **Waikiki Beach Center.** In addition to the police substation here, you'll find the Stones of Kapaemahu, the Duke Kahanamoku statue, and the Prince Kuhio statue. The massive stones represent four legendary *mahu*, dual-gender healers renowned for their powers and wisdom. Plus the center has restrooms, showers, picnic tables, and ocean equipment rentals.

Continue down the beach toward Diamond Head to:

❽ ★ **Kuhio Beach Park.** In 1951, this large pedestrian pier was built into the ocean and allows visitors to walk out to a great scenic point to view Waikiki. The beach is named after Jonah Kuhio Kalaniana'ole, son of Princess Victoria Kinoiki Kekaulike and High Chief David Kahalepouli Pi'ikoi, born in 1871, on Kaua'i. His mother died

A statue of Jonah Kuhio Kalaniana'ole, namesake of Kuhio Beach Park.

soon after his birth, and he was adopted by Kapi'olani (his mother's sister) and her husband, David Kalakaua. When Kalakaua became king in 1874, Kuhio became prince. He never ruled as Hawaiian royalty, but served 20 years in the U.S. Congress. Kuhio Beach Park fronts the site of Kuhio's home, Pualeilani, where in 1918 he opened the beach to the people of Hawai'i. To the west end of the park are two famous surf sites: Queen's and Canoes. **Pacific Beach Boys** offer surf lessons, board rentals, and other water activities from the two pavilions closest to Diamond Head, while **Grass Shack Bistro** sells cold refreshments in the westernmost pavilion. In between them is the **Queen's Arbor**, where 'Alohilani Resort serves a twice-daily, farm-to-table breakfast and cultural experience ($59) with stories celebrating Queen Lili'uokalani, who also had a home facing this beach (www. alohilaniresort.com/dining; ☎ **808/927-4936**).

Monk seals at the Waikiki Aquarium.

Continue down the beach toward Diamond Head to:

❾ ★ Queen's Surf Beach. King David Kalakaua dedicated this park to his wife, Queen Kapi'olani. Surfing is the most popular activity here, but the area is also great for swimming and fishing. You'll find food stands, picnic tables, restrooms, showers, and ocean equipment concessions here. Surf sites offshore include the Walls, good for bodysurfers and bodyboarders only, no board surfing.

Continue along the pathway toward Diamond Head to:

❿ ★ Waikiki Aquarium. See p 33, ❹.

Continue toward Diamond Head to:

⓫ ★ War Memorial Natatorium. In 1921, Hawai'i (not yet a state at the time) authorized this unique memorial to its some 10,000 residents who served in World War I, including 100 who lost their lives. Although many learned to swim here, over the years it fell into disrepair and was finally closed in 1979. The gorgeous Beaux-Arts facade was restored in 2001, and after many political debates, the city also authorized rebuilding the crumbling pool and bleachers in 2019—not that there are any signs of it yet. Still, good snorkeling, fishing, and swimming can be found offshore.

Continue toward Diamond Head to:

⓬ ★ Kaimana Beach. The latest name for this beach comes from Kaimana Beach Hotel, inspired by the nearby landmark of "Kaimana Hila," the Hawaiian transliteration of Diamond Head. But longtimers also know it as Sans Souci Beach, after an 1880s lodging house here called Sans Souci ("without a care"), or Dig Me Beach, thanks to the well-muscled bodies in often miniscule bathing attire. Many consider this the best family beach in Waikiki: The wide reef offshore protects the shallow, sandy bottom, making it perfect for small children. You may see a parade of open ocean swimmers and one-man canoe paddlers who enter the water here to get through a reef channel leading to deeper waters. Also offshore is a great surf spot called Old Man's.

The beach disappears again, so head back to the sidewalk in Kapi'olani Park and pass Kaimana Beach Hotel and Lotus Honolulu to the parking lot for Michel's at the Colony Surf. Walk through the lot to the sidewalk to the beach.

⓭ ★ Outrigger Canoe Club. This private club (only members and their guests are allowed on the property) was founded in 1908 to "preserve and promote the sports of surfing and canoe paddling." It started as just two grass houses and went through a few iterations before its current structure. This is the birthplace of beach volleyball, and the club continues to host some of O'ahu's most prestigious water races. The tiny public beach fronting the Outrigger marks the end of the Waikiki Beach area. There are no public amenities here, but the waters offshore are good for snorkeling, swimming, and, when the waves are right, surfing.

An outrigger canoe on Waikiki Beach.

Historic Honolulu

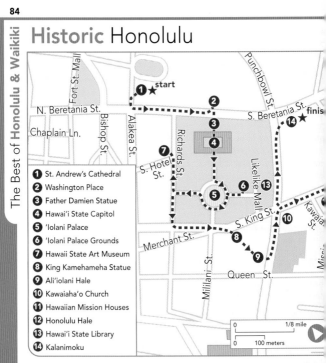

1 St. Andrew's Cathedral
2 Washington Place
3 Father Damien Statue
4 Hawai'i State Capitol
5 'Iolani Palace
6 'Iolani Palace Grounds
7 Hawaii State Art Museum
8 King Kamehameha Statue
9 Ali'iolani Hale
10 Kawaiaha'o Church
11 Hawaiian Mission Houses
12 Honolulu Hale
13 Hawai'i State Library
14 Kalanimoku

The 1800s were a turbulent time in Hawai'i. By the end of the 1790s, Kamehameha the Great had united all the islands. Foreigners began arriving by ship—first explorers, then merchants, and, in 1820, missionaries. By 1873, the monarchy had run through the Kamehameha line, and David Kalakaua was elected to the throne. Known as "the Merrie Monarch," Kalakaua redefined the monarchy by going on a world tour, building 'Iolani Palace, having a European-style coronation, and throwing extravagant parties. By the end of the 1800s, however, the foreign sugar growers and merchants had become extremely powerful in Hawai'i. With the help of the U.S. Marines, they staged the overthrow of Queen Lili'uokalani, Hawai'i's last reigning monarch, in 1893. The United States annexed Hawai'i as a territory in 1898. Much of the history of these turbulent years unfolded within just a few short blocks. Allow 2 to 3 hours for this tour.

1 ★ **St. Andrew's Cathedral.** Educated by Congregationalist missionaries, King Kamehameha IV nevertheless became impressed by Anglican worship during a visit to England as a young man. He invited the Church of England to send its own missionaries, translated its Book of Common Prayer into Hawaiian, and made plans to build

a church in Honolulu. However, he didn't live to see construction begin, dying on St. Andrew's Day, 4 years before his successor Kamehameha V oversaw the laying of the cornerstone in 1867. His widow, Queen Emma, changed the architectural plans to resemble the Gothic cathedrals of Europe, where she raised money for its construction during a trip in 1865. Don't miss the floor-to-eaves hand-blown stained-glass window that faces the setting sun. In the glass is a mural of Reverend Thomas Staley (the first Anglican bishop in Hawai'i), King Kamehameha IV, and his wife Queen Emma. The royal couple, who helped found schools and hospitals, are considered modern saints of the U.S. Episcopal Church, which the diocese of Hawai'i joined after Hawai'i was annexed by the U.S. in 1898. *229 Queen Emma Sq. (btw. Beretania & Alakea sts.).* ☎ *808/524-2822. www.cathedralhawaii.org.*

Walk down Beretania St. in the Diamond Head direction.

② ★ **Washington Place.** This house, the official residence of the governor since 1922, occupies a

A stained-glass window of St. Andrew's Cathedral on Queen Emma Square.

distinguished place in Hawaiian history. The Greek Revival–style home was built in the mid-1840s by a U.S. sea captain named John Dominis, lost at sea in 1846. His widow was forced to take in lodgers, one of whom founded the U.S. Legation here in 1847 and a year later named it after George Washington. The sea captain's son, also named John, married a Hawaiian princess,

Built in the 1840s, Washington Place is now the governor's residence.

who later became Hawai'i's last queen, Lili'uokalani. When the queen was overthrown in 1893 by U.S. businessmen and American missionary-descended sympathizers, she moved out of 'Iolani Palace and into Washington Place. After an attempt led by Native Hawaiians to restore the monarchy failed in 1895, Liliu'okalani spent a total of 13 months under house arrest in the two residences until her pardon in 1896. She then lived in Washington Place until her death in 1917. On the left side of the building, near the sidewalk, is a plaque inscribed with the words to one of the most popular songs Liliu'okalani composed, "Aloha 'Oe" ("Farewell to Thee"). Free tours are held Thursdays at 10am by reservation only. *320 S. Beretania St. (btw. Queen Emma Pl. & Punchbowl St.). washingtonplace.hawaii.gov.* ☎ *808/586-0240.*

Cross the street and walk to the front of the Hawai'i State Capitol.

❸ ★ Father Damien Statue.

The people of Hawai'i have never forgotten the sacrifice this Belgian priest made to help the sufferers of leprosy, now known as Hansen's disease, when he volunteered to work with them in exile on a remote peninsula on the island of Moloka'i. After 16 years of service, Damien died of the disease in 1889, at the age of 49. New York artist Marisol Escobar's bronze sculpture depicts him near the end of his life, his face scarred and one arm in a sling; a duplicate statue stands in the U.S. Capitol, one of two allotted to Hawai'i (the other is of King Kamehameha the Great). Long revered throughout Hawai'i, St. Damien was officially canonized by the Roman Catholic Church in 2009. *415 S. Beretania St. (btw. Queen Emma Pl. & Punchbowl St.).*

Walk behind Father Damien's statue.

❹ ★ Hawai'i State Capitol.

This is where Hawai'i's state legislators work from mid-January to the end of April every year. The building's unusual design has palm tree-shaped pillars, two cone-shaped chambers (representing volcanoes) for the legislative bodies, and, in the inner courtyard, a 600,000-tile mosaic of the sea created by a local artist. A reflecting pool (representing the sea) surrounds the entire structure. On weekdays, you are welcome (after presenting a photo ID) to go into the rotunda and see the woven hangings and murals at the entrance, or take the elevator up to the fifth floor for a spectacular view. *415 S. Beretania St.* ☎ *808/586-0034. www.capitol.hawaii.gov. Entry possible Mon–Fri 7am–5pm.*

Head northwest to Richards St. and turn left toward the ocean.

The architecture of the Hawai'i State Capitol reflects the island's nature and culture.

coronation stand by King Kalakaua. Today, the royal bandstand is still used for concerts, on Fridays from noon to 1pm, by the Royal Hawaiian Band, founded in 1836 by King Kamehameha III and now one of Honolulu's municipal agencies. *364 S. King St. (at Richard St.). www.iolani palace.org.* ☎ *808/522-0822.*

Turn in the 'Ewa (west) direction, cross Richards St., and walk to the corner of Richards and Hotel sts.

⑦ ★ Hawai'i State Art Museum. *See p 64,* ❷.

Walk makai (towards the ocean) down Richards St. and turn left (toward Diamond Head) on S. King St.

⑧ ★ King Kamehameha Statue.

The striking black-and-gold bronze statue in front of Ali'iolani Hale remembers the man who united the Hawaiian Islands. The best day to see the 18-foot (5.5m) statue is on June 11 (King Kamehameha Day), or the Friday closest to it, when admirers drape it in spectacularly long leis to honor the great warrior and statesman. *Juncture of King, Merchant & Mililani sts.*

The Royal Hawaiian Band performs every Friday at noon on the 'Iolani Palace grounds.

⑤ ★★ 'Iolani Palace and ⑥ ★ Palace Grounds. To really

understand Hawai'i's past and present, I suggest taking a tour of this royal palace (see p 15, ❾.) You can wander around the grounds at no charge. The domed pavilion on the grounds was originally built as a

King Kamehameha V Judiciary History Center.

Ali'iolani Hale, or House of the Heavenly King.

⑨ ★ Ali'iolani Hale. Designed by Australian architect Thomas Rowe, this distinctive building with a clock tower has been home of the Hawai'i Supreme Court since 1874. The name translates to "House of Heavenly Kings," one of the names of King Kamehameha V, who laid the cornerstone in 1872 but died the same year. King Kalakaua dedicated the building in 1874. On January 17, 1893, Sanford Dole, backed by other prominent sugar planters and businessmen, stood on the steps of this building to proclaim the overthrow of the Hawaiian monarchy and the establishment of a provisional government. The first floor now houses the **King Kamehameha V Judiciary History Center,** a museum with exhibits and short films about Hawaiian legal history from the ancient *kapu* system through Westernization, the construction of Ali'iolani Hale, martial law after the attack on Pearl Harbor, and the present day. The museum is open for free guided tours by reservation Tuesdays through Thursdays—the only way to go inside without official business. *417 S. King St. (btw. Mililani & Punchbowl sts.). https://www.jhchawaii.net.* ☎ *808/539-4999. King Kamehameha V Judiciary History Center free guided tours Tues–Thurs 9am, 10am & 1:30pm, by reservation only.*

Walk toward Diamond Head on King St. to corner of King and Punchbowl.

⑩ ★ Kawaiaha'o Church. Don't miss this crowning achievement of the first missionaries in Hawai'i—one of the first permanent stone churches, complete with bell tower and colonial colonnade. See p 22, ⑨.

Cross the street.

⑪ ★ Hawaiian Mission Houses. Step into the 1820s and see what life was like for 19th-century Protestant missionaries. See p 42, ⑩.

Cross King St. and walk in the 'Ewa direction to the corner of Punchbowl and King sts.

⑫ ★ Honolulu Hale. The official seat of the City and County of Honolulu (including the entire island of O'ahu) was designed by its most famous architect, C. W. Dickey. Dedicated in 1928, his handsome Spanish Mission–style building includes a courtyard, now covered with a glass ceiling, which is used for art exhibits and concerts. A Japanese garden was added in front of the building in 1968 to commemorate the 100th anniversary of Japanese immigration to the islands. In December, the front lawn also becomes a popular evening destination, illuminated by a massive Christmas tree and lots of island-style holiday decor. **Note:** The second-floor City Council Chambers are currently off-limits to visitors. *530 S. King St. www.honolulucitycouncil. org/visit.* ☎ *808/523-4385. Mon–Fri 7:45am–4:30pm.*

Cross Punchbowl St. and walk *mauka* (inland).

⑬ ★ **Hawai'i State Library.** The main branch of the statewide library system is located in a restored historic building, built in 1913 with financial assistance from Andrew Carnegie. It has an open garden

courtyard in the middle, which is great for stopping for a rest on your walk. *478 S. King St. www.libraries hawaii.org.* ☎ *808/586-3500. Mon–Wed & Sat 9am–4pm, Thurs 9am–7pm, Fri 11am–4pm (closed Sun).*

Head *mauka* up Punchbowl to the corner of Punchbowl and Beretania sts.

⑭ ★ **Kalanimoku.** The name of this ho-hum state office building, opened in 1975, honors an exceptional man nicknamed "Napoleon of the Pacific." Kalanimoku, a high chief and prime minister for King Kamehameha the Great (and the two kings who succeeded him), also adopted the name William Pitt, out of admiration for the British statesman. Here you can find information on hiking and camping in state parks and forests from the Department of Land and Natural Resources, among other agencies in the building. *1151 Punchbowl St. https://dlnr.hawaii.gov.* ☎ *808/587-0400. Mon–Fri 7:45am–4:30pm.*

The rim of Diamondhead Crater.

Kapi'olani Park

1 Honolulu Zoo
2 Kapi'olani Park Bandstand
3 Art on the Zoo Fence
4 Waikiki Shell
5 Queen Kapi'olani Garden
6 People's Open Market
7 Diamond Head Tennis Center
8 Kaimana (Sans Souci) Beach
9 Waikiki Aquarium
10 Queen's Surf Beach

On June 11, 1877 (King Kamehameha Day), King David Kalakaua donated some 140 acres (57 ha) of land for the first official park in Hawai'i. He asked that the park be named after his beloved wife, Queen Kapi'olani, and he celebrated the opening of this vast grassy area with a free concert and "high stakes" horse races (the king loved gambling). The horse racing and the gambling that accompanied it were eventually outlawed, but the park lives on. Just a coconut's throw from the high-rise concrete jungle of Waikiki lies this verdant oasis dotted with spreading banyans, huge monkeypod trees, blooming royal poincianas, and swaying ironwoods. From Waikiki, walk toward Diamond Head on Kalakaua Avenue. If you're coming by car, look for free parking in the lot off Monsarrat Avenue, as well as a handful of free spaces on the ocean side of Kalakaua Avenue next to the park. There's also metered street parking in the area.

is gone now, but the bandstand is still used for concerts—including performances by the historic Royal Hawaiian Band at 1pm Sundays—and special events. *Inside Kapi'olani Park. Royal Hawaiian Band concert schedule: www. rhb-music.com.*

If it's the weekend, back to Monsarrat Ave. and look at the fence facing the zoo.

③ ★ Art on the Zoo Fence. Since 1953, local artists have hung their paintings and photographs on this chain-link fence for the public to view and buy. You get to meet the artists and have an opportunity to purchase their work at a considerable discount from the prices you'll see in galleries. *2760 Monsarrat Ave. www.artonthezoofence.com. Sat–Sun 9am–3pm.*

Cross Monsarrat Ave.

④ ★★ Waikiki Shell. This open-air amphitheater (seating 2,400 in chairs, 6,000 on the lawn) hosts numerous musical shows, from pop acts to traditional Hawaiian music. In 2018 it was officially renamed the Tom Moffatt Waikiki Shell, in honor of Honolulu's late DJ and concert promoter who brought everyone from Jimi Hendrix to Frank Sinatra to the islands. *2805 Monsarrat Ave. blaisdellcenter.com/ venues/tom-moffatt-waikiki-shell.* ☎ *808/768-5488.*

Continue walking down the block to the corner of Monsarrat and Paki aves.

⑤ ★ Queen Kapi'olani Garden. You'll see a range of hibiscus plants and dozens of varieties of

A concert at the Kapi'olani Park Bandstand.

① ★ Honolulu Zoo. The best time to see the city's 42-acre (17-ha) zoo is as soon as the gates open at 10am—the animals seem to be more active, and it's a lot cooler than walking around at mid-day in the hot sun. *Grounds open until 4pm (last admission 3pm) See p 33,* **②**.

Trace your steps back to Kapahulu and Kalakaua aves. and head *mauka* down Monsarrat Ave.

② ★ Kapi'olani Park Bandstand. Once upon a time, from 1937 to 2002, the Kodak Hula Show presented the art of hula to visitors, with some 3,000 people filling bleachers around a grassy stage area every day. The show

The Waikiki Shell entertainment venue.

roses, including the somewhat rare Hawaiian rose. The tranquil, compact garden is always open. *Corner of Monsarrat & Paki aves.*

Walk across the street.

⑥ ★ People's Open Market. These farmer's market stalls are great spots to buy produce and flowers (though not necessarily all grown locally). *Monsarrat & Paki aves. Wed 10–11am.*

Continue in the Diamond Head direction down Paki Ave.

⑦ ★ Diamond Head Tennis Center. Located on the *mauka* side of Paki Avenue, the 10 free tennis courts (and one dedicated pickleball court) are open for play daily during daylight hours. Etiquette suggests that if someone is waiting for a court, limit your play to 45 minutes. *3908 Paki Ave.* ☎ *808/971-2510.*

Turn onto Kalakaua Ave. and begin walking back toward Waikiki.

Open-air farmer's markets are held across the island.

⑧ ★ Kaimana (Sans Souci) Beach. This is one of the best swimming beaches in Waikiki. The shallow reef, which is close to shore, keeps the waters calm. Farther out there's good snorkeling in the coral reef by the Kapua Channel. Facilities include outdoor showers and a lifeguard. *Next to Kaimana Beach Hotel, 2863 Kalakaua Ave.*

Keep walking toward Waikiki.

⑨ ★ Waikiki Aquarium. Try not to miss this tropical aquarium—worth a peek if only to see the rare Hawaiian monk seals and brilliant corals. *See p 33,* ④.

⑩ Queen's Surf Beach. Relax on the grassy lawn alongside the sandy beach, extending to the Kapahulu Groin (also known as the Wall). It's much less crowded than other beaches in Waikiki and has barbecue areas, picnic tables, restrooms, and showers. The swimming is good year-round, there's a surfing spot offshore, and there's always a game going at the volleyball courts. It's part of a Marine Life Conservation District, so you should see colorful fish in the water as well. *2745 Kalakaua Ave.*

Dining Best Bets

Best **Bistro**
★★★ Fête $$ *2 N. Hotel St.*
(p 101)

Best **Breakfast**
★ Koko Head Café $$
1120 12th Ave. (p 103)

Best **Dim Sum**
★ Fook Lam $ *100 N. Beretania St.*
(p 101)

Best for **Families**
★★ Queensbreak $$
2552 Kalakaua Ave. (p 106)

Best **Hamburger**
★ Teddy's Bigger Burgers $
134 Kapahulu Ave. (p 107)

Best **Hawaiian**
★ Helena's Hawaiian Food $
1240 N. School St. (p 102)

Best **Vietnamese**
★★ The Pig and the Lady $$
83 N. King St. (p 106)

Best **Hawai'i Regional Cuisine**
★★★ Merriman's Honolulu $$$
1108 Auahi St. (p 105)

Best **Poke**
★★ Ono Seafood $ *747 Kapahulu Ave. (p 106)*

Best **Seafood**
★★ Azure $$$$ *2259 Kalakaua St.*
(p 99)

Best **Steakhouse**
★ Hy's Steakhouse $$$$
2440 Kuhio Ave. (p 103)

Best **Late-Night Meals**
★ Liliha Bakery $$ *515 N. Kuakini St. & 2330 Kalakaua Ave. (p 104)*

Most **Romantic**
★★★ La Mer $$$$ *2199 Kalia Rd.*
(p 104)

Best **Sunday Brunch**
★★★ Orchids $$$$ *2199 Kalia Rd.*
(p 106)

Best **Sushi**
★★★ Izakaya Gaku $$$$
1329 S. King St. (p 103)

Best **Sunset Views**
★ Duke's Waikiki $$ *2335 Kalakaua Ave. (p 100)*

Best **View of Waikiki**
★ Hau Tree $$$ *2863 Kalakaua Ave. (p 101)*

Waikiki's Best Dining

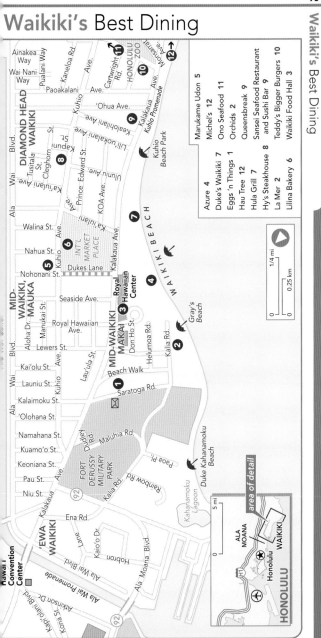

Azure **4**
Duke's Waikiki **7**
Eggs 'n Things **1**
Hau Tree **12**
Hula Grill **7**
Hy's Steakhouse **8**
La Mer **2**
Lilina Bakery **6**

Marukame Udon **5**
Michel's **12**
Ono Seafood **11**
Orchids **2**
Queensbreak **9**
Sansei Seafood Restaurant
and Sushi Bar **9**
Teddy's Bigger Burgers **10**
Waikiki Food Hall **3**

1/4 mi
0.25 km

Honolulu's Best Dining

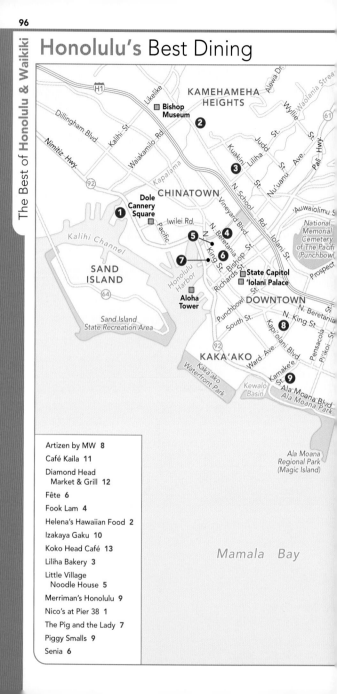

Artizen by MW **8**

Café Kaila **11**

Diamond Head
 Market & Grill **12**

Fête **6**

Fook Lam **4**

Helena's Hawaiian Food **2**

Izakaya Gaku **10**

Koko Head Café **13**

Liliha Bakery **3**

Little Village
 Noodle House **5**

Merriman's Honolulu **9**

Nico's at Pier 38 **1**

The Pig and the Lady **7**

Piggy Smalls **9**

Senia **6**

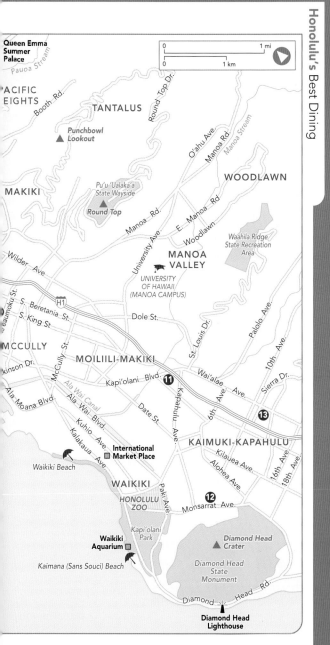

Honolulu & Waikiki
Restaurants A to Z

The Azure Restaurant at The Royal Hawaiian Hotel.

★★ Artizen by MW & MW Restaurant KAKA'AKO HAWAI'I REGIONAL CUISINE

Inside a high-rise above a luxury car dealer on the ground floor seems an unlikely home for this beloved

A daily dose at Waiola Shave Ice.

pair of restaurants. But fans of culinary power couple Wade Ueoka (chef) and Michelle Karr-Ueoka (pastry chef) were just delighted they found a new home after the rocky pandemic years. At the more ambitious **MW,** you can't go wrong with one of the takeout lunch entrees (all $22), but dinner is the best way to explore their multicultural inspirations, such as the mochi crusted Kona kampachi or duck confit with garlic mashed potatoes (both $42). The five-course tasting menu ($110, optional wine pairing $35) is the best value; Karr-Ueoka's desserts, like the Valrhona-chocolate-coated "candy bar" with black sesame ice cream, are justifiably renowned. Formerly a museum cafe, **Artizen by MW** offers a more comfort-based and affordable menu, with dishes like pork tonkatsu, chicken burrito and teri cheeseburger $14-$16. *Both on 2nd floor of Velocity Honolulu, 888 Kapi'olani Blvd. Artizen: www.artizenbymw.com.* ☎ *808/524-0499. Lunch*

Going Local: Uniquely Hawaiian

Poke (pronounced poh-keh, not poh-key) may be ubiquitous on the mainland now, but for locals who move away from Hawai'i, nothing can beat the versions of marinated diced 'ahi tuna and other seafood that originated here. Go to **Ono Seafood ★★** (p 106) and see if you agree. And try these other local favorites, too:

Loco moco Two sunny-side up eggs over a hamburger patty and rice, all doused in brown gravy. Order it at **Liliha Bakery ★★** (p 104), then take some of their renowned cocoa puff pastries home with you.

Spam *musubi* It's true: Hawai'i eats more Spam per capita than any other state, in large part due to delicious Spam *musubi*, a slab of grilled spam on sushi rice wrapped in nori seaweed. For the freshest version, head to **Mana Bu,** 1618 S. King St. (☎ **808/ 358-0287**), where the musubi often sell out by 9am.

Hawaiian plate *Laulau* (pork wrapped in taro leaves), kalua pig (shredded, smoky roasted pork), poi (milled taro), and *haupia* (like coconut Jell-O) are Native Hawaiian staples, now typically served with two scoops of rice and a side of lomi salmon (a salmon-tomato ceviche). Find classic versions at **Helena's Hawaiian Food ★★** (p 102), **Highway Inn ★★** (p 22), and **Da Ono Hawaiian Food,** 726 Kapahulu Ave. (☎ 808/773-0006).

Malasadas Try these sugary hole-less doughnuts, brought to Hawai'i by plantation workers from Portugal's Azores Islands, at **Leonard's Bakery,** 933 Kapahulu Ave. (☎ 808/737-5571), or one of its four Malasadamobiles (check www.leonardsbakery. com for locations).

Shave ice Nothing cools better on a hot day than powdery-soft ice drenched in tropical fruit syrups. Relatively close to Waikiki is **Waiola Shave Ice,** 3113 Mokihana St. (☎ 808/735-8886), but also hit up **Uncle Clay's House of Pure Aloha** (p 20) east of Diamond Head and **Island X Hawai'i** (p 143) on the North Shore for a variety of homemade syrups from real fruit (a rarity).

Mon–Fri 10:30am–5pm, Sat–Sun 10:30am–4pm. Dinner Mon–Fri 4–7pm, Sat & Sun 3–7pm. Brunch Sat–Sun 10am–3pm. Entrees $14– $25. MW: www.mwrestaurant.com. ☎ *808/955-6506. Reservations recommended. Lunch entrees $22, most dinner entrees $42–$58 (ribeye $79, tofu $26). Lunch (takeout only) Tues– Fri 11am–2pm, dinner Tues–Sun 5–9pm. Map p 96.*

★★ Azure Restaurant WAIKIKI *SEAFOOD* This lantern-lit, oceanside restaurant at the Royal Hawaiian Hotel prepares fresh fish with a mixture of French and Hawaiian influences. Dine in plush banquettes with comfy pillows or rent a beachfront cabana and have your own intimate dining area. Hawai'i's fresh fish (most just bought that morning from the

Honolulu Fish Market) is the star of the menu. As at many fine dining establishments in Hawai'i in the post-pandemic lockdown era, a prix-fixe menu ($130 for four courses, including meat options) is the only current offering, but still delicious. *Royal Hawaiian Hotel, 2259 Kalakaua Ave. www.azure waikiki.com.* ☎ *808/923-7311. Reservations recommended. 4-course tasting menu $130 ($185 w/wine pairings). Dinner Wed–Sun 5:30–8:30pm. Map p 95.*

★★ **Café Kaila** KAIMUKI BREAKFAST Hidden in a strip mall next to the freeway is this treasure, where breakfast is always served. Owner/chef Chrissie "Kaila" Castillo serves up all her favorites—do not miss the incredibly fluffy pancakes (get them piled on with fruit)—in a relaxed casual atmosphere. *Warning:* This place is packed at breakfast and lunch. I suggest going late for breakfast (after 9:30am) and lunch (after 1:30pm) so you won't have to wait for a table. Even if you do run into a long line, grab a latte, read a newspaper, and relax—the food is worth the wait. *Market City Shopping Center, 2919 Kapi'olani Rd. www.cafe-kaila-hawaii.com.* ☎ *808/ 732-3330. Entrees $9–$16. Breakfast daily 7am–3:30pm, lunch daily 11am–3:30pm. Map p 96.*

★ **Diamond Head Market & Grill** HONOLULU AMERICAN/ LOCAL Swing by this casual takeout grill and bakery for delicious cream cheese scones for breakfast or a local plate lunch with teriyaki chicken, kalbi short ribs, or 'ahi tuna in a soy-wasabi ginger sauce. A slice of lemon crunch cake or passion orange cheesecake can also help you refuel after a hike up nearby Diamond Head. *3158 Monsarrat Ave. www.diamondheadmarket.com.* ☎ *808/732-0077. Entrees $11–$27*

(most $14–$15). Market and bakery daily 7:30am–9pm. Lunch and dinner 10am–8pm Wed–Mon. Map p 96.

★ **Duke's Waikiki** WAIKIKI STEAK/ SEAFOOD This open-air dining room (outfitted in surfing memorabilia) overlooking Waikiki Beach and its companion Barefoot Bar are the best spots to watch the sunset. Hawaiian musicians serenade diners lingering over a menu ranging from burgers to fresh fish. The best values are the daily lunch buffet with panini ($22) and Tuesday night taco specials ($17–$19) at the Barefoot Bar, although the Thursday night prime rib buffet ($64 adults, $24 children) in the dining room is also a draw. *Outrigger Waikiki Beach Resort, 2335 Kalakaua Ave. www. dukeswaikiki.com.* ☎ *808/922-2268. Breakfast buffet $23, lunch entrees $18–$25 (Barefoot Bar buffet $22), dinner entrees $27–$59. Daily breakfast 7–11am, lunch 11:15am–3pm, dinner 4:45–11pm, Barefoot Bar 11am–close. Map p 95.*

★ **Eggs 'n Things** WAIKIKI BREAKFAST This popular restaurant (one of four locations on the

Surfer nostalgia, oceanside dining, and a kalua pork sandwich at Duke's Waikiki.

island) serves breakfast all day: from pancakes and waffles crowned with a tower of whipped cream to hearty plates of 'ahi and eggs. *343 Saratoga Rd.* ☎ *808/949-0820. www.eggsnthings.com. Entrees $12–$23. Daily 7am–2pm. Map p 95.*

★★★ **Fête** CHINATOWN *NEW AMERICAN / PAN-ASIAN* In 2022 Robynne Mai'i became the first female chef from Hawai'i (and only the second Native Hawaiian) to win a James Beard Award, thanks to her locally sourced and seasonal all-day menu at this casual, welcoming restaurant in Chinatown. This is comfort food with exceptional flair, from Korean fried chicken and a club sandwich with smoked ono salad to the Kualoa pork ragù and veal schnitzel with rose veal from the Big Island's Mahiki Ranch. The cocktails are also superb: Try the Pimm's cup with calamansi lime syrup or the mai tai with mamaki-infused rum and banana jam. Reservations strongly recommended. *2 N. Hotel St. www. fetehawaii.com.* ☎ *808/369-1390. Sandwiches $13–$16, most entrees $22–$29 (ribeye $51.) Mon–Sat 11am–9pm. Map p 96.*

★ **Fook Lam** CHINATOWN *DIM SUM* It's far from fancy, but there's a reason there's always a

Fête Restaurant.

line of visitors and residents spilling out onto the River Street pedestrian mall. The dim sum (including steamed shrimp dumplings, lotus-wrapped sticky rice and fried sesame or taro puffs) that rolls by your table on carts is hot and tasty. *Chinese Cultural Plaza, 100 N. Beretania St. (enter from River St. pedestrian mall).* ☎ *808/523-9168. Dim sum $7–$13. Daily 8am–2pm. Map p 96.*

★ **Hau Tree** WAIKIKI *PACIFIC RIM* Located under a giant hau tree right just a few yards from the waves, this newly chic but still

Hau Tree Lanai serves a casual option on Waikiki Beach.

casual outdoor restaurant has the best view of Waikiki Beach looking west. Long a local favorite, it was recently revamped with a more trendy (and pricier) brunch and cocktail/bar bites menu that attracts cosmopolitan diners. The crab cakes benedict ($35) and breakfast congee with pork belly ($36) are two of the most expensive options at brunch, but will fuel you all day long, if you don't overdo the bloody Marys. At dinner, feta and grapes add complexity to roasted brussels sprouts, while garlic pea foam enhances the savory spring risotto. *Kaimana Beach Hotel, 2863 Kalakaua Ave. (across from Kapi'olani Park). www.kaimana.com/dining. ☎ 808/923-1555. Brunch $20–$46, bar bites $14–$27, most dinner entrees $25–$35 (Wagyu strip loin $55). Daily brunch 8am–1:30pm, bar bites 3:30–5pm, dinner 5–9pm (last order 8:30pm). Map p 95.*

★ Helena's Hawaiian Food

KALIHI *HAWAIIAN* When Chinese immigrant Helen Chock started Helena's in 1946 (she added an "a" at the end to make it sound more "Hawaiian"), she served Chinese and Hawaiian food. Eventually, she pared down the menu to the most popular items—Hawaiian food such as *laulau*, kalua pig, and poi. These days her grandson runs the place, and it's as popular as ever. One reason Helena's won a James Beard Award in 2000: the *pipikaula*, marinated, bone-in short ribs hung above the stove to dry and fried right before they land on your table. *1240 N. School St. www.helenas hawaiianfood.com. ☎ 808/845-8044. À la carte items $6–$27, full meals $15–$37. Tues–Fri 10am–7:30pm. Map p 96.*

★ Hula Grill

WAIKIKI *HAWAIIAN REGIONAL* This second-story bistro has a terrific ocean view (clear to Diamond Head), the food is also fabulous (try the bao bun eggs Benedict with crab and spinach or banana mac pancakes at breakfast), and much is locally sourced, like the grass-fed beef in juicy burgers and the romaine and grape tomatoes in the yummy Hula Caesar salad. Depending where and when you sit, you may also hear the lively music

Locally sourced fare at Hula Grill.

Filet mignon at Hy's Steakhouse.

at Duke's Waikiki below you. *Outrigger Waikiki Beach Resort, 2335 Kalakaua Ave. www.hulagrillwaikiki.com.* 🕿 *808/923-4852. Breakfast entrees $14–$23, brunch $14–$31, lunch $15–$25, dinner $23–$59. Breakfast Mon–Fri 7–10am, brunch Sat–Sun 7am–3pm, lunch Mon–Fri 11am–3pm, "early eats" menu daily 3–6pm, dinner daily 5–10pm. Map p 95.*

★ **Hy's Steakhouse** WAIKIKI *STEAKHOUSE* Bask in the old-school cool of this steakhouse, opened in 1976. Bow-tied waiters carve kiawe-broiled steaks and flambé desserts tableside in a dining room that's all white tablecloths, mahogany, and chocolate brown leather. *2440 Kuhio Ave. www.hyswaikiki.com.* 🕿 *808/922-5555. Steak entrees $66–$130, vegetarian $30–$35, others $49–$97. Dinner daily 5–9pm. Map p 95.*

★★★ **Izakaya Gaku** HONOLULU *JAPANESE* Like Spain's tapas bars, Japan's *izakaya* restaurants create a convivial, casual atmosphere for sharing small plates and drinks. Long a Honolulu favorite, Izakaya Gaku earned a James Beard best restaurant nomination in 2022 for its uncommon seasonal

sushi and seafood, including abalone skewers, uni (sea urchin) jelly, and grilled ray. The servers can help you navigate the frequently changing menu, but save room for desserts like black sesame brûlée or red bean parfait. The compact dining room, which includes tatami and sushi bar seating, fills up quickly, so book reservations well in advance or arrive at opening for seats at the sushi bar. *1329 S. King St.* 🕿 *808/589-1329. Reservations highly recommended. Sashimi $13–$40; other plates $13–$22. Dinner Mon–Sat 5–9:30pm. Map p 96.*

★ **Koko Head Café** KAIMUKI *BRUNCH Top Chef* star Lee Anne Wong's "island-style brunch house" offers inspired takes on breakfast favorites. There's the cornflake French toast, extra crunchy on the outside and custardy on the inside, crowned with frosted flake gelato, and the Don Buri Chen, a rice bowl for carnivores, with miso-smoked pork, five-spice pork belly and eggs ($22). *1120 12th Ave. www.koko headcafe.com.* 🕿 *808/732-8920.*

The casual dining room at Koko Head Café.

Romantic French dining at the acclaimed La Mer restaurant.

Entrees $12–$24. Brunch Wed–Sun 7am–2pm. Map p 96.

★★★ La Mer WAIKIKI FRENCH

This second-floor oceanfront bastion of haute cuisine is the place to go for a romantic evening. Michelin star–winning chef Alexandre Trancher prepares beautifully presented, classically French-inspired dishes with fresh island ingredients (hamachi with pistachio, poached lobster with squid ink gnocchi, calamansi mousse with crème anglaise). Cocktails like the strawberry liliko'i (passionfruit) martini are exquisite, too. *Halekulani, 2199 Kalia Rd. www. halekulani.com.* ☎ *808/923-2311. $180 for 4-course prix fixe menu, $245 for 7-course tasting menu. Dinner Wed–Sat 5:30–8:30pm. Map p 95.*

★ Liliha Bakery LILIHA & WAIKIKI LOCAL/AMERICAN

The original Kuakini St. location in Liliha (across the highway from Chinatown) saw an interior renovation in 2017, but its menu remains that of a classic old-school Hawai'i diner: light and fluffy pancakes, crispy and seriously buttery waffles, and loaded country-style omelets for breakfast, and satisfying dishes like hamburgers, grilled mahi and saimin (noodle soup) for lunch and dinner. If you're staying in Waikiki, the newest branch on the third-floor Grand Lanai of the International Market Place is super convenient and only slightly higher priced. It also offers a pleasant outdoor dining experience and a tempting array of baked goods, including Liliha's signature cocoa puffs and poi mochi doughnuts (plan on taking a box of goodies with you). *515 N. Kuakini St. www.lilihabakeryhawaii.com.* ☎ *808/ 531-1651. Daily 6am–10pm. International Market Place, 2330 Kalakaua Ave.* ☎ *808/922-2488. Daily 7am– 10pm. Entrees $18–$23. Map p 95.*

★★ Little Village Noodle House CHINATOWN CHINESE

For the best Chinese food served "simple and healthy" (its motto), visit this tiny neighborhood restaurant with helpful waitstaff and even parking in the back (unheard of in Chinatown). Try the salt-and-pepper shrimp or the garlic eggplant. The menu includes Northern, Canton, and Hong Kong–style dishes. *1113 Smith St. www.littlevillage hawaii.com.* ☎ *808/545-3008. Most entrees $15–$22, Peking duck $36 half, $65 whole. Mon, Wed & Thurs 3:30–9pm, Fri–Sun 11:30am–9pm. Map p 96.*

★★ Marukame Udon WAIKIKI JAPANESE/UDON

There's always a long line out the door at this cafeteria-style noodle joint, but it moves quickly. Pass the time by watching the cooks roll out and cut the dough for udon right in front of you. Bowls of udon, hot or cold, with toppings such as a soft poached egg or Japanese curry, start at $10. *2310 Kuhio Ave., Waikiki, Honolulu. www.marugameudon.com.* ☎ *808/ 931-6000. Noodles $9–$13. Daily 11am–10pm. Map p 95.*

★★★ **Merriman's Honolulu** WARD *HAWAI'I REGIONAL CUISINE* This indoor-outdoor gem in Honolulu's trendy Ward Village/Kaka'ako neighborhood is the newest and most chic namesake bistro by Peter Merriman, cofounder of the Hawai'i Regional Cuisine movement. The culinary trend began in 1991 and has evolved to include even more locally sourced ingredients, and island- and Asian-inspired flavors. If the prices for standouts like Moroccan spiced Kahua Ranch lamb ($49) and cast iron organic chicken from Puna ($52) are dismaying, know that the grass-fed burgers ($17 at lunch, $23 at dinner) are a worthy alternative, as are the mahi fish tacos ($22, lunch only) and other more affordable options. *1108 Auahi St. www. merrimanshawaii.com/honolulu.* ☎ *808/215-0022. Lunch entrees $17–$28, most dinner entrees $23–$52 (lobster pot pie $69). Daily lunch 11am–3pm, happy hour 3–5pm, dinner 5–9pm. Nightly live music 5:30–7:30pm. Map p 96.*

Beef udon from Marukame Udon.

Nico's at Pier 38.

★★ **Michel's** WAIKIKI *FRENCH/ HAWAI'I REGIONAL* Founded in 1962, this classic French restaurant opens to an ocean view (get there for sunset), but the food is the real draw. Tuxedo-clad waiters serve classic French cuisine with an island infusion (lobster bisque, Hawaiian coffee–rubbed lamb chops, and a Caesar salad made at your table) in an elegantly casual atmosphere. The four-course tasting menu offers the best value at $130 (optional wine pairings $40–$80). *Colony Surf Hotel, 2895 Kalakaua Ave. www. michelshawaii.com.* ☎ *808/923-6552. Entrees $58–$72. Dinner daily 5–9pm, brunch 1st Sun of month 10am–1pm. Map p 95.*

★ **Nico's at Pier 38** IWILEI *SEA-FOOD* This casual spot, on the pier next to the fish auction, serves up, you guessed it, fresh fish. My favorite lunch plate is the furikake-pan-seared ahi with the addicting ginger garlic cilantro dip, served with rice and greens or macaroni salad for $18 ($25 at dinner). Non-fish lovers can opt for pizza, burgers, steak frites, braised short ribs, or the Friday special Hawaiian plate. Nico's also has its own fish market with a great poke bar, and hosts live music most weekdays noon to 2pm and nightly 6 to 8pm. Pier 38, 1129 N. Nimitz Hwy. www.nicospier38.com. ☎ 808/540-1377. *Breakfast $6–$17, lunch $11–$24, dinner $16–$35. Breakfast Mon–Sat 6:30–10am, daily lunch 10am–4pm & daily dinner 5–9pm. Fish Market Mon–Sat 6:30am–5pm (poke counter from 9am), Sun 10am–4pm. Map p 96.*

★★ Ono Seafood WAIKIKI POKE
This little seafood counter serves some of Honolulu's freshest and best poke—cubes of ruby-red 'ahi (tuna) seasoned to order with soy sauce and onions for the *shoyu* poke or *limu* (seaweed) and Hawaiian salt for Hawaiian-style poke. Tako (octopus) poke is another specialty. All poke is sold by weight at market price or in a bowl. **Note:** There's a second location near Koko Head Crater, at 501 Kealahou St. (open Tues–Sat 10am–6pm). *747 Kapahulu Ave.* ☎ *808/732-4806. Bowls $10–$15. Tues–Sat 9am–6pm. Map p 95.*

★★★ Orchids WAIKIKI INTERNATIONAL/SEAFOOD
This is the best Sunday brunch in Hawai'i, with an outstanding array of dishes from popovers to sushi to carving and omelet stations, plus the restaurant's signature fluffy coconut cake. The setting is extraordinary (overlooking the ocean and Waikiki Beach), and the food is excellent. You'll need to book at least a month in advance for brunch reservations. It's also open for casually elegant breakfast, lunch, and dinner (try the exquisite pastas or delicately seasoned curry), with prices to match the high quality and superlative view. *2199 Kalia Rd. www.halekulani.com.* ☎ *808/923-2311. Brunch $89 adults, $45 children 5–12 (higher prices for holiday brunches). Sun 9:30am–2pm. Also available: breakfast & lunch Mon–Sat 7:30–10:30am and 11:30am–1pm,*

daily dinner 5:30–8:30pm. Dinner entrees $36–$64. Map p 95.

★★ The Pig and the Lady CHINATOWN MODERN VIETNAMESE
You'll want to make reservations in advance for this perennial hot spot, one of the liveliest dining rooms in Chinatown. Chef Andrew Le excels in both classic Vietnamese dishes and modern inspirations, including the aromatic vegan pho with kabocha pumpkin, enoki mushrooms, and okra, and the portobello banh mi with chimichurri sauce, crisp baguette, and a side of vegan pho for dipping. Meat lovers will adore the slow-roasted beef brisket in the French dip banh mi, accompanied by Le's signature Pho 75, a garlicky beef broth. ★★ **Piggy Smalls** in Ward Village is Le's more casual version of this restaurant, with a streamlined menu and easier parking (1200 Ala Moana Blvd.; ☎ 808/777-3588); it's open for dinner Tuesday through Saturday and brunch on weekends. *83 N. King St. www.thepigandthelady.com.* ☎ *808/585-8255. Reservations recommended. Entrees $16–$23 lunch, $26–$44 dinner. Lunch Thurs–Sat 11:30am–2:30pm and dinner Tues–Sat 5:30–9:30pm. Map p 96.*

★★ Queensbreak WAIKIKI ISLAND/INTERNATIONAL
Everything is elevated here at this playful outdoor restaurant at the Waikiki Beach Marriott Resort & Spa: the view, the menus, and yes, the prices (relative to the mainland), but they're worth it. Executive Chef Nuño Alves (a dad himself) has taken as much care crafting the mac 'n' cheese, burger, etc., on the keiki menu ($9–$16) as he has the fantastic Asian, Mediterranean, island, and American dishes on the adult menu. Go for the tangy pad thai with Kaua'i prawns, the drunken clams with Portuguese sausage and lobster sauce, or kalua pork tacos. For something light, I love the local

papaya salad with mac nut quinoa. *2nd floor terrace, Waikiki Beach Marriott Resort & Spa, 2552 Kalakaua Ave. www.queensbreak.com.* ☎ *808/922-6611, ext. 7181. Most entrees $18–$30 ($40 strip steak). Daily 11am–10pm. Map p 95.*

★ Sansei Seafood Restaurant & Sushi Bar WAIKIKI *SUSHI/ ASIAN–PACIFIC RIM* Perpetual award-winner D. K. Kodama's Waikiki restaurant is known for its extensive sushi and sashimi menu with spicy additions such as sweet Thai chile sauce, jalapeños, and sambal. Carnivores will love the large plates menu, including dishes such as the chili and porcini mushroom–crusted beef tenderloin and the ginger hoisin smoked duck breast. *Waikiki Beach Marriott Resort, third floor, 2552 Kalakaua Ave. dkrestaurants.com.* ☎ *808/931-6286. Sushi $6–$20, entrees $22–$68. Dinner daily 5:30–9pm. Map p 95.*

★★ Senia CHINATOWN *MODERN AMERICAN* This is one of Honolulu's most exciting restaurants, where something as ordinary as potato gnocchi can surprise and delight. Senia, deriving from "xenia," the Greek word for hospitality, is a rare mesh of the fine dining and comfort food worlds. As in, the food is fancy—bone marrow

Teddy's Bigger Burgers is a local favorite.

custard, citrus cured hamachi, and pretty presentations of smoked salmon with date and cauliflower—but the flavors are accessible, the setting leans casual, and the prices are moderate for such star quality. Chef Anthony Rush changes the menu frequently, but dishes are always eye- and palate-pleasing. *75 N. King St., Honolulu. www.restaurantsenia.com* ☎ *808/200-5412. Reservations recommended. Small plates $18–$36. Dinner Tues–Sat 5:30–9:30pm. Map p 96.*

★ Teddy's Bigger Burgers WAIKIKI *AMERICAN* This casual burger joint has seven outlets on O'ahu and is voted the island's best, year after year. It's deserved: You get juicy patties on buns that are soft, yet sturdy enough to hold the meat and fixin's all together. Get the buttery garlic fries as a side. *134 Kapahulu Ave. www.teddysbb. com.* ☎ *808/926-3444. Sandwiches and burgers $9–$14. Lunch and dinner daily 10am–9pm. Map p 95.*

★ Waikiki Food Hall WAIKIKI *INTERNATIONAL* Escape some of the masses, at least, and graze this intriguing assortment of food stands on the third floor of the Royal Hawaiian Center. You'll pay at a central counter, but get buzzers to notify you when your food is ready to be picked up at each stand where you ordered. I enjoy the gourmet Okinawan varieties of Spam musubi with egg at **Potama** (you can ask them to hold the Spam) and the garlic shrimp at **Five Star Shrimp,** washed down with a local craft brew from **Tap Bar,** but you can also find great burgers, huli (grilled) chicken, and more at the other stands. *At the Royal Hawaiian Center, 2201 Kalakaua Ave., Building C, Level 3. www.royalhawaiiancenter. com/waikiki-food-hall.* ☎ *808/376-0435. Items from $10. Lunch and dinner daily 11am–9pm. Map p 95.*

Lodging Best Bets

Most **Romantic**
★★ Royal Hawaiian $$$$
2259 Kalakaua Ave. (p 116)

Best **Condo Hotel**
★★★ Ritz-Carlton Residences,
Waikiki Beach $$$$
383 Kalaimoku St. (p 116)

Most **Hawaiian Culture**
★ Outrigger Reef Waikiki Beach
2169 Kalia Rd. (p 114)

Most **Historic**
★★ Moana Surfrider, a Westin
Resort $$$$ *2365 Kalakaua Ave.*
(p 113)

Most **Luxurious**
★★★ Halekulani $$$$
2199 Kalia Rd. (p 110)

Best **Moderately Priced**
★ Park Shore Waikiki $$
2586 Kalakaua Ave. (p 115)

Best **Budget Hotel**
★ Royal Grove $ *151 Uluniu Ave.*
(p 116)

Best **for Kids in Waikiki**
★★ Waikiki Beach Marriott $$$
(p 117)

Best **Value**
★ The Breakers $ *250 Beach Walk*
(p 110)

Most **Chic**
★★ Halepuna Waikiki by Haleku-
lani $$$ *2233 Helumoa Rd. (p 111)*

Best **View of Waikiki Beach**
★ Kaimana Beach Hotel $$$
2863 Kalakaua Ave. (p 112)

Best **View of Ala Wai Harbor**
★★ Prince Waikiki $$$$
100 Holomoana St. (p 115)

Best **View of Fort**
DeRussy Park
★ Luana Waikiki $$
2045 Kalakaua Ave. (p 113)

Most **Trendy**
★★ Surfjack Hotel & Swim Club
$$ *412 Lewers St. (p 117)*

Best **Waikiki Beachfront**
★★ Hilton Hawaiian Village
Waikiki Beach Resort $$$
2005 Kalia Rd. (p 111)

Best **View of Diamond Head**
★★ Lotus Honolulu $$$
2885 Kalakaua Ave. (p 112)

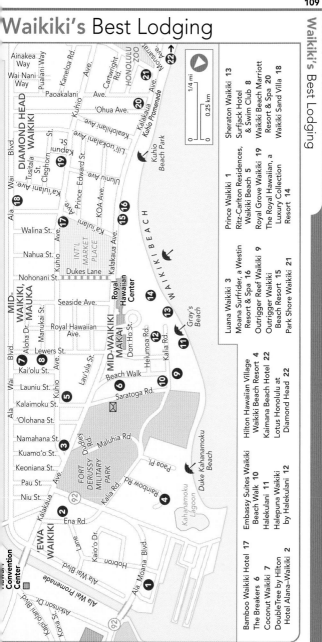

Bamboo Waikiki Hotel **17**
The Breakers **6**
Coconut Waikiki **7**
DoubleTree by Hilton
Hotel Alana–Waikiki **2**

Embassy Suites Waikiki
Beach Walk **10**
Halekulani **11**
Halepuna Waikiki
by Halekulani **12**

Hilton Hawaiian Village
Waikiki Beach Resort **4**
Kaimana Beach Hotel **22**
Lotus Honolulu at
Diamond Head **22**

Luana Waikiki **3**
Moana Surfrider, a Westin
Resort & Spa **16**
Outrigger Reef Waikiki **9**
Outrigger Waikiki
Beach Resort **15**
Park Shore Waikiki **21**

Prince Waikiki **1**
Ritz-Carlton Residences,
Waikiki Beach **5**
Royal Grove Waikiki **19**
The Royal Hawaiian, a
Luxury Collection
Resort **14**

Sheraton Waikiki **13**
Surfjack Hotel
& Swim Club **8**
Waikiki Beach Marriott
Resort & Spa **20**
Waikiki Sand Villa **18**

Waikiki Hotels A to Z

★ Bamboo Waikiki Hotel
MID-WAIKIKI MAUKA Book a studio or suite in this intimate boutique hotel, styled with midcentury modern and Southeast Asian decor, and you can cut your meal costs, thanks to kitchenettes or kitchens. The pool with hot tub, waterfall, and wooden lounge chairs is a pleasant oasis, too, although guest rooms may experience traffic noise and parking can be tight. It's a block from Waikiki Beach. *2425 Kuhio Ave. (at Ka'iulani Ave.). www.castleresorts.com.* ☎ *808/922-7777, reservations 877/367-1912. 96 units. Doubles $169–$260. Map p 109.*

★ The Breakers MID-WAIKIKI MAKAI This two-story 1950s budget hotel is a terrific buy for families (kitchenettes in all rooms) and just 2 minutes' walk to the beach, restaurants, and shopping. Expect comfortable budget accommodations with tropical accents, but limited parking. There's also a Japanese restaurant, **Wasabi Bistro,** by the pool. *250 Beachwalk (btw. Kalakaua Ave. & Kalia Rd.). www.breakers-hawaii.com.* ☎ *800/426-0494 or 808/923-3181. 64 units. Doubles $160–$180; suites $235. Map p 109.*

★ Coconut Waikiki MID-WAIKIKI MAUKA Rooms at this family-friendly, mid-range hotel next to Ala Wai Canal are bright and cheery and come with a small lanai and kitchenette; skip the tiny pool and walk 12 minutes to the beach. Its sister hotel, **Shoreline Hotel Waikiki** (342 Seaside Ave.; shorelinehotel waikiki.com; ☎ **808/931-2444**), is a few minutes closer to the beach, with similar amenities and an Insta-gram-worthy, neon-colored mid-century modern vibe. Check out **Heavenly Island Lifestyle** at the Shoreline, with its surfer-chic decor

and delicious brunch. *450 Lewers St. (at Ala Wai Blvd.). coconutwaikiki hotel.com.* ☎ *808/923-8828. 81 units. Doubles from $169 city view, $199 mountain view; suites from $239. Resort fee $25 (waived for direct bookings). Map p 109.*

★ DoubleTree by Hilton Hotel Alana—Waikiki Beach 'EWA This boutique hotel with a cumbersome name is an oasis of small but comfortable rooms, with amenities of other hotels at more affordable prices. Waikiki Beach is a 10-minute walk away, and the convention center is about a 7-minute walk. *1956 Ala Moana Blvd. (near Kalakaua Ave.). www.hilton.com.* ☎ *808/941-7275. 317 units. Doubles from $228 city view ($194 advance purchase) $253 park/ocean view ($215 advance; suites from $395 ($335 advance). Resort fee $35. Map p 109.*

★★★ Embassy Suites Waikiki Beach Walk MID-WAIKIKI MAKAI This modern high-rise hotel, part of the all-suites brand famous for cooked-to-order breakfast and evening cocktail reception, has a great location just 1 block from the shore (a little farther for wider sand). Downstairs, Waikiki Beach Walk provides plenty of shops and restaurants. Families flock to its spacious one- and two-bedroom suites, and kids enjoy the rooftop pool. *201 Beach Walk (at Kalia Rd.). www.embassy suiteswaikiki.com.* ☎ *808/921-2345. 421 suites. 1-br suites from $354 city view ($290 advance purchase), $505 ocean view ($414 advance); 2-br suites from $795 city view ($659 advance), $884 ocean view ($724 advance). Resort fee $35. Map p 109.*

★★★ Halekulani MID-WAIKIKI MAKAI This is the most serenely luxurious hotel on O'ahu, spread

Halekulani, where 90% of the rooms face the ocean.

over 5 oceanfront acres (2 ha) in Waikiki. Some 90% of the airy, light-toned rooms face the ocean, and all have lanais and top-drawer ameni-ies. Every detail is exquisite, from the orchid mosaic in the beachfront pool to the scent of maile in the spa to dining at Orchids, La Mer, or House Without a Key (see p 106, 104, and 137). The beach has shrunk here but not the hotel's timeless appeal. *2199 Kalia Rd. (at Lewers St.). www.halekulani.com.* ☎ *808/923-2311, reservations 844/873-9424. 455 units. Doubles from $635 courtyard view; $800 ocean view; suites from $1,280. Map p 109.*

★★ Halepuna Waikiki by Halekulani MID-WAIKIKI MAKAI

Recently renamed and renovated with a cool palette of sand and pale blue and enhanced Zen vibe, this "hidden" luxury hotel (formerly the Waikiki Parc, and still operated by the Halekulani) offers lots of pluses. It's just 100 yards (91m) from the beach, has modern high-tech rooms with plush beds and noise-reducing windows (a godsend in Waikiki), and offers great views from the gorgeous infinity-edge rooftop pool and bar. Service is also first-rate. *2233 Helumoa Rd. (at Lewers St.). www.halepuna.com.* ☎ *808/518-2006, reservations 844/873-9424. 297 units. Doubles from $397 city view, from $473 ocean view; suites from $1,076. No resort fee. Map p 109.*

★★ Hilton Hawaiian Village Waikiki Beach Resort 'EWA

This sprawling resort is a micro-cosm of Waikiki—on good days it feels like a lively little beach town, and on bad days it's just an endless traffic jam, with lines everywhere. Its

Cabanas at Halepuna Waikiki.

Waikiki Neighborhoods & West

The neighborhoods in Waikiki can be divided into four districts: **'Ewa** (the western end of Waikiki from Ala Wai Canal to Fort DeRussy Park), **Mid-Waikiki Makai** (from the ocean up to Kalakaua Ave. and from Fort DeRussy Park to Ka'iulani St.), **Mid-Waikiki Mauka** (mountain side of Kalakaua Ave. to Ala Wai Blvd. and from Kalaimoku St. to Ka'iulani St.), and **Diamond Head** (from the ocean to Ala Wai Blvd. and from Ka'iulani to Diamond Head).

The next largest source of lodgings on O'ahu lies about 27 miles (43km) to the west, at the Ko Olina Resort in Kapolei. That's where you'll find family favorite ★★ **Aulani, a Disney Resort & Spa** (www.disneyaulani.com; ☎ **866/443-4763;** doubles from $549, villas with kitchens from $919) and the sybaritic ★★ **Four Seasons Resort O'ahu at Ko Olina** (www.fourseasons.com/oahu; ☎ **808/679-0079;** doubles from $895, suites from $1,955), famed for its multi-story spa, fine dining, and adults-only, sunset-facing pool.

five towers (not counting timeshare units) host a wide range of lodgings from simple hotel rooms to deluxe. The upscale Ali'i Tower is a bit calmer, thanks to private lobby, pool, and other facilities and amenities. The resort's 22 acres (9ha) include tropical gardens, nine restaurant and bars, dozens of shops, six pools (one adults-only), a huge spa and fitness center, and a lovely, wide stretch of Waikiki Beach. (When surf's up, you can always frolic in the tranquil Duke Kahanamoku Lagoon.) However, the $50 resort fee is a real gouge—most of the "amenities" are just discounts on rentals and activities. *2005 Kalia Rd. (at Ala Moana Blvd.). www.hiltonhawaiianvillage.com. ☎ 808/949-4321. Reservations 800/HILTONS (445-8667). 2,860 units. Doubles from $345 resort view ($276 advance purchase), $366 ocean view ($292 advance purchase); suites from $553 ($425 advance purchase). Resort fee $50. Map p 109.*

★ Kaimana Beach Hotel
DIAMOND HEAD   This is one of Waikiki's best-kept secrets: a newly updated, beachfront boutique hotel near Diamond Head, with Kapi'olani Park just across the street. Skip the inexpensive, barely-room-for-two rooms and go for the oceanfront rooms and corner rooms with two balconies (Diamond Head and Waikiki Beach views). Beachfront restaurant **Hau Tree** (p 101) is a casual-chic spot for all-day dining (and rosé), and there's a great coffee bar and gift shop on site too. The $20 resort fee includes e-bike and surfboard rentals, among other amenities. *2863 Kalakaua Ave. (near Waikiki Aquarium, across from Kapiolani Park). www.kaimana.com. ☎ 808/923-1555. 124 units. Doubles from $229 city view, $279 Diamond Head view, $339 ocean view, $419 corner ocean view, $479 oceanfront; 1-bedroom with kitchenette from $319 in park wing (no elevator, sleeps 4). Resort fee $20. Map p 109.*

★★ Lotus Honolulu at Diamond Head
DIAMOND HEAD   On the quiet side of Waikiki, between Kapi'olani Park and Diamond Head, this boutique hotel features calming rooms with dark

A guest room at Kaimana Beach Hotel.

hardwood floors, white bed linens, and shuttered sliding glass doors onto lanais, some of which frame Diamond Head beautifully. The relatively modest resort fee ($30) includes, among other perks, free parking, free use of beach cruiser bikes, daily or hourly car rentals, and complimentary wine tasting five nights a week in the excellent onsite French restaurant and lounge **TBD…by Vikram Garg**, named for the former executive chef at Halekulani. *2885 Kalakaua Ave. www.lotushonoluluhotel.com.* ☎ *808/922-1700. 51 units. Doubles from $279 park view; $319 ocean view. Resort fee $30. Map p 109.*

★ **Luana Waikiki** 'EWA Families take note: This midsize hotel offers studios with kitchenettes and one- and two-bedroom suites with full kitchens. You also get terrific views of Fort DeRussy's green parkland

and the ocean in the distance. *2045 Kalakaua Ave. (at Kuhio Ave.). www.aquaaston.com.* ☎ *808/955-6000, reservations 855/747-0755. 205 units. Doubles from $159; studios from $199 city view, $239 ocean view; 1-bedroom suite from $269 city view, $319 ocean view; 2-bed, 2-bath suite from $529. Resort fee $27. Map p 109.*

★★ **Moana Surfrider, a Westin Resort & Spa** MID-WAIKIKI MAKAI Old Hawai'i reigns here. I recommend staying in the historic Banyan Wing, where rooms are modern replicas of Waikiki's first hotel (built in 1901). Outside is a prime stretch of beach and an oceanfront courtyard with massive banyan tree and live music in the evenings. Moana Lani Spa, a Heavenly Spa by Westin, lives up to that name, too. *2365 Kalakaua Ave. (across from Ka'iulani St.). www.marriott.com.* ☎ *808/922-3111. 793 units. Doubles*

Guestroom at the Moana Surfrider Hotel.

Pampering in Paradise

Just like multicultural modern Hawai'i, the spas on O'ahu draw from Asian, European, and Polynesian traditions, often in settings that celebrate the tropical environment. Beyond traditional Hawaiian massage (lomilomi), you'll find a rich variety of body care, including treatments that feature locally farmed ingredients such as cacao, coconut, coffee, sugar, vanilla, and turmeric.

Of course, all this pampering doesn't come cheap. Massages often cost $175 to $250 for 50 minutes and $250 to $350 for 80 minutes; body treatments may be in the $165 to $275 range; and alternative healthcare treatments can run as high as $200 to $300. But for many, a spa visit is an essential part of a Hawaiian vacation.

For a real getaway within your getaway, spend a day on the North Shore at Nalu Spa at Turtle Bay Resort (p 145), or on the west side at the Four Seasons Resort O'ahu at Ko Olina (p 112). Here are my picks for spas in Waikiki:

- **Most Relaxing: SpaHalekulani**   From the time you step into the elegantly appointed, intimate spa until the last whiff of fragrant maile, the spa's signature scent, you will be transported to nirvana. The Halekulani Massage (60 min. $235, 90 min. $275) combines the gently rolling lomilomi technique with warm stones and maile oil. In Halekulani (p 110; www.halekulani.com/spa; ☎ **808/923-2311**).
- **Best Facial: Abhasa Waikiki Spa**   This contemporary spa, spread out over 7,000 square feet (650 sq. m), concentrates on natural, organic treatments in a soothing, outdoor atmosphere. Try the anti-aging facial (50 min. $200) for an immediately revitalized visage. In the Royal Hawaiian (www.abhasa.com; ☎ **808/922-8200**).
- **Best Day Spa: Moana Lani Spa**   It's hard to beat the ocean views from the elegant, beachfront treatment rooms and the relaxation lounges, where you can indulge in steam rooms and saunas before and after your massage. In Moana Surfrider, a Westin Resort & Spa (www.moanalanispa.com; ☎ **808/237-2535**).

from $388 city view, $445 ocean view; suites from $768 (ocean view). Resort fee $42. Map p 109.

★ **Outrigger Reef Waikiki Beach** MID-WAIKIKI MAKAI   An $80-million renovation of this three-tower megahotel, completed mid-2022, has upgraded rooms and public areas to reflect ancient and modern Hawaiian culture, including lots of prints in handsome rooms and massive artworks in the lobby. Even the standard rooms are large and comfortable, though why linger there—the best Hawaiian music acts play at Kani Ka Pila Grille by the attractive pool; the oceanfront **Monkeypod Kitchen** restaurant (by

A therapeutic massage at SpaHalekulani.

Peter Merriman) is due to open in 2023; and wider sands than the shrunken patch in front of the hotel lie within a short walk to the west. Call in advance to book a free vow renewal ceremony. *2169 Kalia Rd. (at Beach Walk). www.outrigger.com. ☎ 808/923-3111, reservations 866/ 944-1850. 883 units. Doubles from $544 ($354 advance purchase), ocean view from $580 ($371 advance purchase). Resort fee $40. Map p 109.*

★★ **Outrigger Waikiki Beach Resort** MID-WAIKIKI MAKAI   This bustling hotel has an excellent location on a wide part of Waikiki Beach, perfect for catching your first wave. Many rooms have ocean views, including some from oversize Jacuzzi bathtubs. The hotel is known for dining (**Duke's** and **Hula Grill;** see p 100 and 102) and entertainment, including nationally touring music and comedy acts at **Blue Note Hawaii** (p 138). *2335 Kalakaua Ave. (btw. the Royal Hawaiian Shopping Center & the Moana Surfrider). ☎ 808/923-0711, reservations (866) 994-1581. www.outrigger.com. 525 units. Doubles from $539 ($344*

advance purchase), ocean view from $589 ($376 advance), club level from $669 ($428 advance); club-level suites from $1,339 ($888 advance). Resort fee $40. Map p 109.

★ **Park Shore Waikiki** DIA-MOND HEAD   This hotel has a great location, on the quieter end of Waikiki, and yet it's still close to the water. A number of the moderately priced rooms have oceanfront views, while families may appreciate rooms that open right onto the pool deck. *2586 Kalakaua Ave. www. parkshorewaikiki.com. ☎ 808/923-0411. 226 units. Doubles from $194– $209 city view, from $224–$344 ocean view; suites from $394. Resort fee $42. Map p 109.*

★★ **Prince Waikiki** 'EWA   For accommodations with a view and the feel of a high-tech palace, stay in these striking twin 33-story towers, where service is priority. The serenely uncluttered bedrooms face the Ala Wai Yacht Harbor, with floor-to-ceiling windows that open, remote-control blinds, and washlet toilets. The saltwater infinity-edge

An oceanfront king guestroom at Outrigger Reef Waikiki.

pool and stylish wood-planked deck also offers stunning views. The shops of Ala Moana Center and Waikiki Beach are within a 10-minute walk away. Locals know to queue up for the impeccable sushi at **Katsumidori Sushi Tokyo,** the first location outside of Japan, and pastries from **Honolulu Coffee Co.** The mezzanine-level **100 Sails** offers beautiful views and island cuisine, too. *Tip:* Advance purchase and other specials can knock $75 or more off daily rates, while joining Prince Preferred means a waived nightly resort fee and other discounts. *100 Holomoana St. (just across Ala Wai Canal Bridge). www. princewaikiki.com.* ☎ *808/824-5155, reservations 855/622-7557. 521 units. Doubles from $369, club level from $569, suites from $644. Resort fee $37. Map p 109.*

★★★ Ritz-Carlton Residences, Waikiki Beach MID-WAIKIKI

MAUKA Two gleaming 38-story towers just off Kalakaua provide a discreet hideaway for travelers who appreciate posh amenities like Miele kitchen and laundry appliances in spacious suites, Dean & DeLuca downstairs, and infinity-edge pools (one for adults only) on the 7th and 8th floors. All residences face the ocean, many with great views of the Friday night fireworks and Fort DeRussy. *383 Kalaimoku St. www.ritzcarlton.com/ waikiki.* ☎ *808/922-8111. 552 units. Studios (sleep 3) from $610; 1-br suites (sleep 4–6) from $837 2-br, 2-bath suites (sleep 6) from $1,495; 3-br, 3-bath suites (sleep 8) from $2,690. 2-nt. minimum. Map p 109.*

★ Royal Grove Waikiki DIA-

MOND HEAD This is a great bargain for frugal travelers and families; the budget accommodations are no-frill (along the lines of a Motel 6), but studios and 1-bedroom units have kitchens, and the

family-owned hotel shows genuine aloha. Waikiki Beach is a 3-minute walk. *Tip:* Advance purchase shaves $20 to $25 off daily rates. *151 Uluniu Ave. (btw. Prince Edward & Kuhio aves.). www.royalgrovehotel.com.* ☎ *808/923-7691, reservations 888/ 926-7891. 85 units. Doubles from $134–$144; studios from $159–$169, 1-bedroom from $184. Map p 109.*

★★ The Royal Hawaiian, a Luxury Collection Resort MID-

WAIKIKI MAKAI The symbol of Waikiki, this flamingo-pink oasis, nestled in tropical gardens, offers rooms in both the gorgeous 1927 historic wing (my fave, due to carved wooden doors, romantic four-poster canopy beds, and period furniture) and modern oceanfront tower with pink accents. The Mai Tai Bar (p 138), Azure Restaurant (p 99) and Aha'aina Lu'au (p 138) are also excellent here. *2259 Kalakaua Ave. (at Royal Hawaiian Ave.). www.royal-hawaiian.com.* ☎ *808/923-7311. 527 units. Doubles from $417 historic wing ($592 with ocean view), from $630 modern wing, suites from $801 historic wing, $1,329 modern wing. Resort fee $42. Map p 109.*

★ Sheraton Waikiki MID-WAIKIKI

MAKAI It's hard to get a bad room at this hotel sitting right on Waikiki Beach: A whopping 1,200 units have ocean views, and 650 overlook Diamond Head. However, they're in two 30-story towers,

The Royal Hawaiian Hotel's iconic pink building dates to 1927.

The lagoon-style pool at the Sheraton Waikiki.

sharing an immense lobby. A frequent favorite of conventions, the hotel can be noisy and overwhelming, with a long wait at the bank of nearly a dozen elevators. Kids like the large fantasy pool, though. *2255 Kalakaua Ave. (at Royal Hawaiian Ave.). www.marriott.com. ☎ 800/325-3535 or 808/922-4422. 1,852 units. Doubles from $312 city view, $331 ocean view; suites from $597. $42 resort fee. Map p 109.*

★★ Surfjack Hotel & Swim Club MID-WAIKIKI MAKAI

Remade from a 1960s budget hotel, the Surfjack is achingly retro-hip and screams midcentury-beach house cool, from the "Wish You Were Here" mosaic on the swimming pool floor to the vintage headboard upholstery by Tori Richard. It's not close to the beach, and the views are mostly of buildings, but you can get excellent cocktails by the pool and a perfect cup of coffee while you browse the onsite clothing boutique. Book direct and there's no resort fee or parking charge. *412 Lewers St., Honolulu. www.surfjack.com. ☎ 808/923-8882 or reservations 833/330-0130. 112 units. Doubles from $208; 1-br suites from $307, 2-br suites from $507. Map p 109.*

★★ Waikiki Beach Marriott Resort & Spa DIAMOND HEAD

Across the street from the beach, this block-long hotel is newly inviting (once you get past the bustling lobby), thanks to rooms renovated in beach cottage style and the addition of a huge ocean-view pool and activity deck with lawn game and fire pits. It also boasts spacious balconies and great restaurants (notably **Sansei Seafood Restaurant & Sushi Bar ★**, p 107). The nightly $50 resort fee is steep, so make use of the beach chairs and cultural classes it includes. *2552 Kalakaua Ave. (at Ohua Ave.). www.marriott.com. ☎ 800/367-5370 or 808/922-6611. 1,310 units. Doubles from $315 city view, $408 ocean view. Resort fee $50. Map p 109.*

★ Waikiki Sand Villa MID-WAIKIKI MAUKA

Budget travelers, take note: This affordable 10-story hotel is located on the quieter side of Waikiki, with medium-size rooms and a few larger suites that can sleep up to five; some have lovely views of the Ala Wai Canal and Ko'olau Mountains. The $25 resort fee includes daily use of boogie boards and beach chairs and a $25 activity discount, among other perks. It's a 10-minute walk to the beach. *2375 Ala Wai Blvd. (at Kanekapolei Ave.). www.waikikisand villahotel.com. ☎ 808/922-4744. 214 units. Doubles $96–$245, plus nightly $25 resort fee. Map p 109.*

Shopping **Best Bets**

Best **Vintage Aloha Shirts**
★★ Bailey's Antiques & Aloha Shirts, *517 Kapahulu Ave. (p 122)*

Best **Modern Alohawear**
★ Roberta Oaks,
1152 Nu'uanu Ave., (p 122)

Best **Curios**
★ Hound and Quail,
1156 Nu'uanu St. (p 123)

Best **Antiques**
T. Fujii Japanese Antiques,
1016 Kapahulu Ave. (p 123)

Best **Place to Browse**
★★★ Na Mea Hawai'i,
1050 Ala Moana Blvd. (p 127)

Best **Mochi**
Nisshodo Candy Store
1095 Dillingham Blvd. (p 125)

Best **Hawaiian Fashion**
★★ Kealopiko, *3128 Monsarrat Ave. (p 126)*

Best **Locally Made Gifts**
★★★ House of Mana Up,
2201 Kalakaua Ave. (p 127)

Best **Place for Edible Gifts**
Whole Foods, *4211 Wai'alae Ave. and 629 Kailua Rd., Kailua. (p 125)*

Best **Place for a Lei**
★★ Cindy's Lei Shoppe,
1034 Maunakea St. (p 126)

Best **Shopping Center**
★★ Ala Moana Center,
1450 Ala Moana Blvd. (p 128)

Best **Chocolate Truffles**
★ Padovani's Chocolates,
650 Iwilei Rd. (p 125)

Best **Wine & Liquor**
Fujioka's Wine Times,
2919 Kapi'olani Blvd. (p 124)

Best **Contemporary Art**
★★ The Gallery Waikiki
2300 Kalakaua Ave (p 123)

Waikiki's Best Shopping

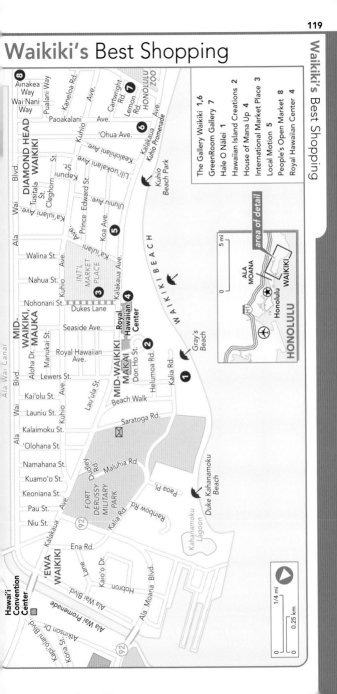

The Gallery Waikiki **1,6**
GreenRoom Gallery **7**
Hale O Nālei **1**
Hawaiian Island Creations **2**
House of Mana Up **4**
International Market Place **3**
Local Motion **5**
People's Open Market **8**
Royal Hawaiian Center **4**

120

Honolulu's Best Shopping

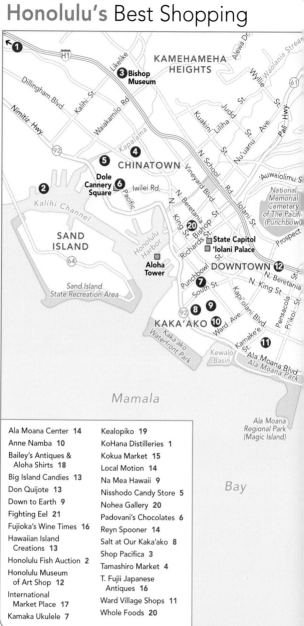

The Best of Honolulu & Waikiki

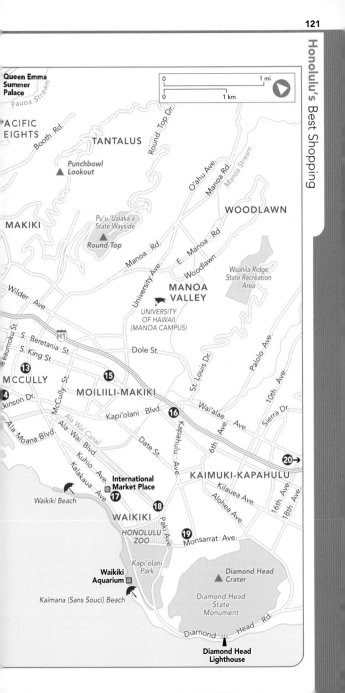

Queen Emma
Summer
Palace

Pauoa Stream

PACIFIC
HEIGHTS

Booth Rd.

TANTALUS

Round Top Dr.

O'ahu Ave.

Manoa Rd.

Manoa Stream

▲ Punchbowl
Lookout

WOODLAWN

Pu'u 'Ualaka'a
State Wayside

MAKIKI

Round Top

Manoa Rd.

E. Manoa Rd.

University Ave.

Woodlawn

Waahila Ridge
State Recreation
Area

MANOA
VALLEY

UNIVERSITY
OF HAWAII
(MANOA CAMPUS)

Wilder Ave.

Seaumoku St.

S. Beretania St.

H1

S. King St

Dole St.

St. Louis Dr.

Palolo Ave.

10th Ave.

MCCULLY

13

kinson Dr.

McCully St.

MOILIILI-MAKIKI

15

Wai'alae Ave.

Sierra Dr.

Ala Moana Blvd.

Ala Wai Canal

Kapi'olani Blvd.

16

Kapahulu Ave.

6th Ave.

Ala Wai Blvd.

Date St.

Kuhio Ave.

International
Market Place

17

Kalakaua Ave.

☂ Waikiki Beach

18

KAIMUKI-KAPAHULU

Kilauea Ave.

16th Ave.

18th Ave.

20→

Alohea Ave.

WAIKIKI

HONOLULU
ZOO

Paki Ave.

19 Monsarrat Ave.

Kapi'olani
Park

Waikiki
Aquarium ☐

▲ Diamond Head
Crater

Diamond Head
State
Monument

Kaimana (Sans Souci) Beach

Diamond Head Rd.

Diamond Head
Lighthouse

0 ——————————— 1 mi
0 ——————————— 1 km

Chinatown's Best Shopping

Cindy's Lei Shoppe 2
Fighting Eel 8
Ginger13 7
Hound & Quail 6
Lin's Lei Shop 3
Maunakea Marketplace Food Court 1
Native Books 6
Roberta Oaks 4
Tin Can Mailman 5

Honolulu & Waikiki Shopping A to Z

Alohawear

★★ Bailey's Antiques & Aloha Shirts KAPAHULU Honolulu's largest selection (thousands) of vintage, secondhand, and nearly new aloha shirts and other collectibles fill this eclectic emporium, as do old ball gowns, feather boas, fur stoles, leather jackets, 1930s dresses, and scads of other garments. *517 Kapahulu Ave. www.alohashirts.com.* ☎ *808/734-7628. Closed Mon. Map p 120.*

Reyn Spooner ALA MOANA Created as a partnership between Waikiki seamstress Ruth Spooner and California menswear retailer Reyn McCullough, the "Brooks Brothers of the Pacific" creates

instantly recognizable aloha shirts for all ages with an inside-out design and lightweight cotton/poly blend. It's the go-to for patterns commemorating everything from Major League Baseball teams and colleges to Stars Wars and Christmas, but has some cool island designs as well. *Ala Moana Center, Diamond Head Wing, Level 2 (near Macy's), 1450 Ala Moana Blvd. www. reyns.com.* ☎ *808/949-5929. Also at the Kahala Mall and Ka Makana Ali'i (Kapolei). Map p 120.*

★ Roberta Oaks CHINATOWN The hippest guys and gals come here. Roberta Oaks ditches the too-big aloha shirt for a more stylish, fitted look, but keeps the vintage

Eclectic offerings at Hound & Quail.

designs. She also has a *keiki* (kids) line, plus table linens, pet bandanas, bags, and even bow ties. *1152 N. Nu'uanu Ave. www.roberta oaks.com.* ☎ *808/526-1111. Closed Sun. Map p 122.*

Antiques & Collectibles
★ Hound and Quail CHINATOWN
A funky collection of antiques and curiosities, from taxidermied mammals and mounted antlers to vintage pens, purses, and prints, make for a fascinating perusal. The bottom floor hosts a gallery of young and local artists. *1156 Nu'uanu St. www.houndandquail.com.* ☎ *808/ 779-8436. Closed Mon & Tues. Map p 122.*

T. Fujii Japanese Antiques
MO'ILI'ILI   This is a long-standing icon in Hawai'i's antiques world and an impeccable source for *ukiyo-e* prints, scrolls, obis, Imari porcelain, *tansu* chests, tea-ceremony bowls, and screens as well as contemporary ceramics, with prices from two to six digits. *Kilohana Square, 1016-B Kapahulu Ave. www.tfujiiantiques. com.* ☎ *808/732-7860. Map p 120.*

Art
★ GreenRoom Gallery WAIKIKI
Stop into this gallery for the best of Hawai'i's surf art and photography. You'll find Clark Little's snaps of pounding beach breaks, Zak Noyle's breathtaking surf photos,

Nick Kuchar's vintage-styled Hawai'i travel posters, Heather Brown's bold and bright prints, and Kris Goto's quirky drawings combing manga sensibilities with Hawai'i beach culture. *Inside Queen Kapi'olani Hotel, 150 Kapahulu Ave. www.greenroomhawaii.com.* ☎ *808/924-4400. Map p 119.*

★★ The Gallery Waikiki
WAIKIKI   Currently wedged between the Waikiki Beachcomber and the International Market Place, this hip coffeehouse gallery may be moving in 2023 to a larger location. For now, it's the most eye-catching and accessible gallery of contemporary art in Hawai'i (with the best waffles, too.) Founded by Hawaiian Aroma Caffe owners Jonathan and

Original Hawaiiana creations at Green-Room Gallery.

Mor Rotmensch, it showcases works from a rotating selection of mostly local artists, including T-shirt designer Rotmensch. Street art, Japanese anime, surfing, and Hawai'i heavily influence the kaleidoscope on display. *2300 Kalakaua Ave. www.hawaiianaromacaffe.com.* ☎ *808/256-2602. Map p 119.*

Food, Wine & Spirits
★ **Big Island Candies** ALA MOANA   There are only two retail outlets for the addictive, chocolate-dipped macadamia nut shortbread cookies and other beautifully packaged goodies from this company, founded in 1977. One is the factory store in Hilo on the Big Island, now a major visitor attraction, and the other is this well-stocked shop at the largest mall in Hawai'i. Purchases come with free samples, too. *Ala Moana Center, Level 1 near Centerstage, 1450 Ala Moana Blvd. www.bigislandcandies.com.* ☎ *808/946-9213. Map p 120.*

Don Quijote KAKA'AKO   You can find everything at this huge emporium, ranging from takeout sushi, Korean *kalbi,* pizza, and Chinese food to Ka'u navel oranges, macadamia nuts, Kona coffee, taro, and other Hawai'i products. (Despite the name, it's part of a Japanese discount chain.) *801 Kaheka St. www.donki.com/en.* ☎ *808/973-4800. Map p 120.*

Take-out sashimi at Don Quijote.

Tasting at KoHana Distillers.

Fujioka's Wine Times MO'ILI'ILI   Oenophiles flock here for the fine selection of wines, single-malt Scotches, craft beers, and cigars—libations for all occasions. *Market City Shopping Center, 2919 Kapi'olani Blvd. (at S. King St.), lower level. www.timessupermarkets.com/store/fujioka's-wine-times.* ☎ *808/739-9463. Map p 120.*

★★ **KoHana Distillers** KUNIA   In the fertile farmland west of Honolulu, heirloom sugarcane (ko) grows, then is pressed into juice and distilled into smooth rum agricole with just a hint of sweetness. You can find KoHana's products in ABC stores and island liquor stores, but it's more fun (for ages 21 and up) to head to the tasting room at the distillery. Drop in to sample the wares, including white and aged rums, for $10 before making your purchase. Tours of the distillery and estate ($25–$45, including tastings) are also available. *92-1770 Kunia Rd., Kunia. www.kohanarum.com.* ☎ *808/649-0830. Map p 120*

Maunakea Marketplace Food Court CHINATOWN   Hungry patrons line up for everything from pizza and plate lunches to quick, authentic, and inexpensive Vietnamese, Thai, Chinese, Japanese, and Filipino dishes. Vendors sell everything from fresh 'ahi, fish heads, and chicken feet to yams

Pan-Asian fare at Maunakea Marketplace Food Court.

and taro, seaweed, and fresh fruits and vegetables. *1120 Maunakea St.* ☎ *808/524-3409. No credit cards. Map p 122.*

Nisshodo Candy Store

IWILEI   Mochi (Japanese sticky rice cake) is so essential to locals' lives that even the drugstores sell it. But for the freshest and widest variety, go straight to the source: Nisshodo, sweetening palates for more than a century. Choose among pink-and-white *chichi dango* (or milk mochi); mochi filled with smooth peanut butter, chocolate-like azuki bean, or coconut; *manju* (treats with fillings like mochi but made with a wheat flour crust); *monaka* (delicate rice wafers sandwiching sweetened lima-bean paste), and much more. *1095 Dillingham Blvd. nisshodomochicandy.com.* ☎ *808/847-1244. Closed Sun. Map p 120.*

★ Padovani's Chocolates IWILEI

Brothers Philippe and Pierre Padovani are two of Hawai'i's best chefs, involved with the Hawai'i Regional Cuisine movement. In recent years, they've been devoting their attention to chocolate truffles. Their edible gems come in delightful flavors such as a calamansi (a small Filipino lime) and pirie mango ganache, flavored with fragrant, local mangoes picked at the height of the season. Other favorites incorporate ginger, Manoa honey, and *liliko'i* (Hawaiian

passionfruit). Temporarily closed in 2022, the store was expected to reopen in 2023. *Dole Cannery, 650 Iwilei Rd., #280. padovanichocolates. com.* ☎ *808/536-4567. Closed Sat–Sun. Map p 120.*

Whole Foods KAHALA   Whole Foods does a great job of sourcing local at its three stores, including specialty items such as honey, jams, hot sauces, coffee, and chocolate. It's also got one of the best selections of locally made soaps, great for gifts to take home. *4211 Wai'alae Ave at Kahala Mall,* ☎ *808/738-0820; 629 Kailua Rd., Kailua,* ☎ *808/263-6800; 388 Kamake'e St., in Ward Village,* ☎ *808/379-1800. www.wholefoodsmarket.com/stores/honolulu. Map p 120.*

Fashion

Anne Namba WARD   Flowing and flattering, this designer's Asian-inspired fashions—often made of printed silk or repurposed vintage kimonos and obis—will add a glamorous splash to any wardrobe. Born in Hawai'i to globetrotting parents, Namba also creates bespoke items and a men's line. *324 Kamani St. www.annenamba.com.* ☎ *808/589-1135. Closed Sun. Map p 120.*

Fighting Eel KAHALA   At this local designer's boutique, you'll find bright, easy-to-wear, rayon and cotton dresses and shirts with island prints that are in every local fashionista's closet—perfect for

Chichi dango candy made from sweet, sticky rice cake at Nisshodo Candy Store.

Fresh fruit at the People's Open Market.

Honolulu weather, but chic enough to wear back home. There are also branches downtown and Kailua (see website for details). *Kahala Mall, 4211 Wai'alae Ave. www.fightingeel. com.* ☎ *808/738-4912. Map p 120 & 122.*

Ginger13 CHINATOWN Local designer Cindy Yokoyama creates eye-catching, asymmetrical earrings and other jewelry with chunky stones such as agate and turquoise. Her airy, plant-filled boutique brims with other artisans' wares, too, including candles, body care products, home decor, baskets, and stationery. *22 S. Pauahi St. www. ginger13.com.* ☎ *808/531-5311. Closed Sun. Map p 122.*

★★ **Kealopiko** DIAMOND HEAD Named for the richest part of a fish, its belly, this fashion line by three friends from Moloka'i is dedicated to sharing the rich cultural heritage of Hawai'i. Designs on dresses, aloha shirts, handbags and T's reflect Hawaiian *mo'olelo* (history and legends) as well as island animals and plants. Many of their distinctive items are still hand-dyed or printed on Moloka'i. *3128 Monsarrat Ave. www.thekealopikoshop.com.* ☎ *808/784-0433. Closed Mon & Tues. Map p 120.*

Fish Markets
★★ **Honolulu Fish Auction**
IWILEI If you want to experience

the high drama of fish buying, hope that the United Fishing Agency has eased its pandemic restrictions to allow the public once again at its early morning auction, modeled on Tokyo's famous market. The auction of individual fish to chefs, wholesalers, and retailers start at 5:30am (sharp) Monday through Saturday. *Pier 38, 1131 N. Nimitz Hwy. www.hawaii-seafood.org.* ☎ *808/536-2148. No credit cards. Map p 120.*

★ **Tamashiro Market** IWILEI Good service and the most extensive selection of fresh fish in Honolulu have made this the granddaddy of fish markets. You'll find everything from live lobsters and crabs to fresh slabs of 'ahi to whole *onaga* and *ehu*, plus a poke counter. *802 N. King St. www.tamashiromarket. com.* ☎ *808/841-8047. Map p 120.*

Leis
★★ **Cindy's Lei Shoppe**
CHINATOWN I love this lei shop because in addition to artistry and variety in designs, it offers less common flowers, such as feather dendrobiums, golden lantern 'ilima, or the spiky red-yellow kukunaokala, plus familiar favorites like ginger, tuberose, orchid, and pikake. "Curb service" allows you to phone in your order and pick up your lei curbside—a great convenience on this busy street. *1034 Maunakea St. www.cindysleishoppe.com.* ☎ *808/536-6538. Map p 122.*

The Honolulu Fish Auction.

A Chinatown lei shop.

★ **Hale O Na Lei** WAIKIKI This tiny lei stand, opened in 2022 inside the gleaming new Outrigger Reef Waikiki Beach lobby, is a convenient place to pick up a simple or stunning lei if you don't have time to go to Chinatown. Call ahead to confirm hours. *Outrigger Reef Waikiki Beach, 2169 Kalia Rd.* ☎ *808/924-4990. Map p 119.*

★ **Lin's Lei Shop** CHINATOWN Features creatively fashioned, unusual leis. *1017 Maunakea St. linsleishop. com.* ☎ *808/537-4112. Map p 122.*

Hawaiiana & Local Gifts
★★★ **House of Mana Up** WAIKIKI Some of the very best shopping in Waikiki—for souvenirs, baby and children's clothes, home decor, jewelry, food gifts, books, stationery, and more—all lies within the confines of this one store in the Royal Hawaiian Center. That's because the founders created it as part of an innovative incubator program for small, artisanal island businesses, including yummy soft-serve producer **Banán** (p 80). The wares of some 63 entrepreneurs are currently represented here, and the sales staff is happy to give you the back story on each. *Royal Hawaiian Center, Bldg. A, ground floor (near P.F. Chang's). houseofmanaup.com.* ☎ *808/425-4028. Map p 119*

★ **Kamaka Ukulele** KAKA'AKO Forget the cheap plastic ukulele found all over the island. Come to this ukulele factory, which began as a one-man shop in 1916, to see these beautiful, locally made instruments. The body is crafted from Hawaiian koa wood, aged for 4 years; the necks are made of mahogany; and the fingerboards and bridges are rosewood. Each one is a work of art, and priced accordingly (upwards of $1,000). *550 South St. www.kamakahawaii. com.* ☎ *808/531-3165. Map p 120.*

★★★ **Na Mea Hawai'i** WARD This is a browser's paradise, featuring a variety of Hawaiian items (the definition of *na mea Hawai'i*) from musical instruments to calabashes, jewelry, leis, books, contemporary Hawaiian clothing, Hawaiian food products, and other high-quality gift items. Regular classes in lauhala weaving, featherwork, the Hawaiian language, and more are also held here; find the schedule online. There's also a sister store, **Native Books,** in Chinatown at 1146 Nu'uanu St. (www.nativebooks hawaii.org; ☎ **808/548-5554**). *Ward Village Shops, 1200 Ala Moana Blvd.* ☎ *808/596-8885. Map p 120.*

★★ **Nohea Gallery** WAIKIKI & KAHALA A fine showcase for

Each handmade instrument from Kamaka Ukulele is a work of art.

contemporary Hawai'i art, Nohea celebrates the islands with thoughtful, attractive selections, such as pit-fired raku (ceramics), finely turned wood vessels, jewelry, handblown glass, paintings, prints, fabrics (including Hawaiian-quilt cushions), and more. *Kahala Mall, 4211 Wai'alae Ave. ☎ 808/762-7407. Hyatt Regency Waikiki, 2424 Kalakaua Ave. ☎ 808/596-0074 (closed Sun). www.nohea gallery.com. Map p 120.*

★ **Tin Can Mailman** CHINATOWN What, not looking for a 1950s hula lamp? Check out this shop anyway. It's packed with vintage Hawaiiana to emulate old-school general stores. The emphasis is on ephemera, such as pinups, postcards, old sheet music and advertisements, and the elusive Betty Boop hula girl bobblehead. *1026 Nu'unau Ave. ☎ 808/524-3009. tincanmailman. net. Closed Sun & Mon. Map p 122.*

Health Food Stores
Down to Earth KAKA'AKO This newer branch of a locally owned shop with four other stores on O'ahu sells organic vegetables, vegetarian bulk foods, herbs and supplements. Grab a drink or lunch from the kombucha bar and deli. *500 Keawe St. www.downtoearth. org. ☎ 808/465-2512. Map p 120.*

Kokua Market HONOLULU The first natural food cooperative in Hawai'i, founded in 1971, is one of Honolulu's best sources for organic vegetables. It also has an excellent variety of cheeses, pastas, bulk grains, sandwiches, salads, prepared foods, organic wines, and vitamins. *2643 S. King St. (at University Ave.). www.kokua.coop. ☎ 808/941-1922. Map p 120.*

Museum Stores
★ **Honolulu Museum of Art Shop** MAKIKI Art books, stationery, prints, and posters reflect the breadth and depth of this

Organic produce at the Kokua Market cooperative.

museum's international collection. *Honolulu Museum of Art, 900 S. Beretania St. (at Ward Ave.). www. honolulumuseum.org. ☎ 808/532-8703. Closed Mon–Wed. Map p 120.*

★★ **Shop Pacifica** KALIHI Plan to spend time browsing through local arts and crafts, including elegantly turned wooden bowls and gourds, *lauhala* (items woven from pandanus leaves), Hawaiian music CDs, and a vast selection of Hawai'i-themed books that anchor this gift shop. *Bishop Museum, 1525 Bernice St. (btw. Kalihi St. & Kapalama Ave.). www.bishopmuseum.org. ☎ 808/848-4158. Map p 120.*

Shopping Centers
★★ **Ala Moana Center** ALA MOANA Nearly 350 shops and

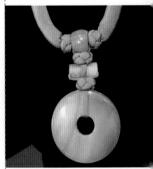

A one-of-a-kind gift at the Honolulu Museum of Art Shop.

There are nearly 400 retailers, from standard to upscale, at the Ala Moana Center.

restaurants sprawl over several blocks, making this Hawai'i's largest shopping center catering to every imaginable need, from upscale (**Neiman Marcus, Tiffany & Co.,** and **Prada**) to mainland chains (**Gap, Lululemon Athletica,** and **Old Navy**), to department stores (**Macy's, Nordstrom, Bloomingdales**), to practical touches, such as banks, a pharmacy (**Longs Drugs**), a U.S. Post Office, several optical companies (including 1-hr. service by **LensCrafters**), and a handful of smaller locally owned stores (**Kahulale'a, Happy Wahine Boutique, Island Slipper**). The **Makai Market food court** is abuzz with dozens of stalls purveying pizza, plate lunches, vegetarian fare, Vietnamese pho, Japanese ramen, and countless other treats. *1450 Ala Moana Blvd. (btw. Kaheka & Pi'ikoi sts.). www.alamoanacenter.com.* ☎ *808/955-9517. Map p 120.*

★ International Market Place

WAIKIKI Not even the spelling of the old International Marketplace—a dark warren of T-shirt and souvenir shops—remains the same as this luxury incarnation with more than 80 stores and restaurants. But now you can revive at **Kona Coffee Purveyors** with excellent espresso and pastries, **Liliha Bakery (p 104)** with local-style lunch plates and baked sweets, or with inspired twists on island plantation-era cuisine at **Roy Yamaguchi's Eating House 1849.** Or just recharge on a rocking chair under the courtyard's giant banyan tree. *2330 Kalakaua Ave. www.shop internationalmarketplace.com.* ☎ *808/921-0536. Map p 120.*

Queen's Court at the International Market Place.

★★ Royal Hawaiian Center

WAIKIKI This block-long, four-level open-air mall boasts 110 stores and restaurants, a cultural heritage room, performance area, and grove of 70 coconut trees. Shops range from the intriguingly homegrown—**House of Mana Up** (p 127), **Lu Koa Collection** (koa wood jewelry, art, and souvenirs) **Lanai Transit** (handbags)—to international luxury brands such as **Fendi, Jimmy Choo,** and **Ferragamo.** *2201 Kalakaua Ave. (at Royal Hawaiian Ave.). www.royal hawaiiancenter.com. ☎ 808/922-2299. Map p 119.*

★ Salt at Our Kaka'ako

KAKA'AKO There are grand plans for Kaka'ako, the neighborhood between Ala Moana and downtown, bordering Ward Village. Mostly, it's a lot of new, high-rise luxury condos, but developers are also trying to create an interesting mix of restaurants and retailers. Among others here, you'll find **Milo,** a hip surf shop that also carries accessories for the home; **Paiko,** an adorable tropical botanical boutique, and **Treehouse,** a must for any photography lover, especially those with a penchant for vintage and film. Get refreshed at Peter Merriman's **Moku Kitchen** or **Lanikai Juice.** *660 Ala Moana Blvd. www.saltatkakaako.com. Map p 120.*

★ Ward Village Shops

WARD Great restaurants (**Piggy Smalls, Goma Tei**) and shops (**Diamond Head Chocolate Co., Na Mea Hawai'i**) make this a popular place, bustling with browsers. The focus at these Ward Village Shops is smaller, independent stores and designers. Its sister **South Shore Market and East Village Shops** complex at 1170 Auahi St. also houses intriguing locally run

Skateboards, surf gear, and beachwear at Hawaiian Island Creations.

boutiques like the graphic design–focused **Rock Candy Hawaii** and **Mori by Art+Flea** gift shops, baby and kids clothing retailer **Hopscotch,** women's fashion vendors **Mahina** and **La Muse,** and Hawaiian sportswear shop **Salvage Public.** *1240 Ala Moana Blvd. www.wardvillage.com. ☎ 808/591-8411. Map p 120.*

T-Shirts

Hawaiian Island Creations ALA MOANA This supercool surf shop with 10 locations on O'ahu offers sunglasses, sun lotions, surf wear, sandals, surfboards, and accessories galore. *Ala Moana Center, 1450 Ala Moana Blvd., Level 1 'Ewa Wing, ☎ 808/973-6780; Level 3 Diamond Head Wing, ☎ 808/941-6363. Inside Sheraton Waikiki, 2255 Kalakaua, ☎ 808/888-8805. www.hicsurf.com. Map p 119 & 120.*

★ Local Motion ALA MOANA

This icon of surfers and

Tropical Farmers' Markets

Have you ever peeled a dragon's eye (a.k.a. longan)? Or kissed a passionfruit or tasted a just-picked mangosteen? Diverse cultures have brought their favorite fruits, vegetables, and other culinary products to Hawai'i, and the best place to taste these interesting and unusual foods is at one of the island's farmers' markets.

- **Kapi'olani Community College**   One of the most popular farmers' markets takes place next door to Waikiki at the Kapi'olani Community College parking lot (4303 Diamond Head Rd.) every Saturday from 7:30 to 11am. Some 8,000 residents and visitors flock to this bountiful market to buy the locally grown produce and to sample the prepared food. The key feature of this market is that the majority of the vendors are actual farmers, so this is a great place to get information about products and the farms themselves. For details on this and other markets organized by the Hawai'i Farm Bureau, including midweek markets at the Blaisdell Arena and in Kailua, see **www.hfbf.org**.
- **Kaka'ako Farmers' Market**   This market takes place on Saturdays from 8am to noon in the trendy Kaka'ako neighborhood, a 10-minute drive from Waikiki. It's filled with local vendors (all produce and products sold have to be grown in Hawai'i) and is a wonderful place to eat at impromptu, temporary cafes, where patrons sit family-style. If you are in town in October, when taro is celebrated, or in January, when cacao is featured, the market turns into a big festival. For more information, including other markets organized by FarmLovers (a local business incubator), see **www.farmloversmarkets.com**.
- **People's Open Market Program**   This is the island's oldest farmers' market program, started in 1973 by the City and County of Honolulu as a way to help people lower their food costs. There are now 23 across the island, with the closest to Waikiki in the Kapi'olani Park parking lot, Monsarrat Ave. and Paki St., open Wed 10–11am. Be aware produce does not have to be grown on island or even in state. Most are only open 45 minutes to an hour; bring bags, small bills, and coins. For details, see **www.honolulu.gov/parks/program/people-s-open-market-program.html**.

kateboarders, both professionals nd wannabes, has everything from urfboards, T-shirts, alohawear, and asual wear, to countless accessores for life in the sun. *Ala Moana enter, 3rd floor, Ewa Wing, 1450*

Ala Moana Blvd. ☎ *808/979-7873. Also inside Hyatt Regency Waikiki, 2424 Kalakaua Ave. www.local motionhawaii.com.* ☎ *808/922-7873. Map p 119 &120.*

Nightlife & Performing Arts
Best Bets

Best Place to **Celebrate St. Patrick's Day**
★ Murphy's Bar & Grill, *2 Merchant St.* (p 135)

Best for **Cocktails**
★ Tchin Tchin, *39 N. Hotel St.* (p 136)

Best **Drag Shows**
Scarlet Honolulu, *80 S. Pauahi St.* (p 136)

Best **Intimate Bar**
★★★ Bar Leather Apron, *mezzanine of Topa Financial Center, 745 Fort St.* (p 135)

Best for **Hawaiian Music**
★★★ Kani Ka Pila Grille, *Outrigger Reef Waikiki Beach, 2169 Kalia Rd.* (p 114)

Best **Club for Jazz**
★★ Lewers Lounge, *Halekulani, 2199 Kalia Rd.* (p 135)

Most **Romantic Place for Sunset**
★★★ House Without a Key, *Halekulani 2199 Kalia Rd.* (p 137)

Best Place to **People-Watch at Sunset**
★★ Duke's Waikiki, *Outrigger Waikiki Beach Resort, 2335 Kalakaua Ave.* (p 137)

Best **Lu'au**
★★ Aha'aina at the Royal Hawaiian, *2259 Kalakaua Ave.* (p 138)

Best **Performing Arts Center**
★★ Neal Blaisdell Center, *777 Ward Ave.* (p 139)

Best for **Outdoor Concerts**
★★ Waikiki Shell, *2805 Monsarrat Ave.* (p 139)

Best for **Film Buffs**
★★ The Movie Museum, *3566 Harding Ave.* (p 137)

Most **Beautiful Theater**
★★★ Hawai'i Theatre, *1130 Bethel St.* (p 139)

Best Place to See **Locally Written and Produced Plays**
★ Kumu Kahua Theatre, *46 Merchant St.* (p 140)

Best Place to See **Stand-up Comedy**
Blue Note Hawai'i, *Outrigger Waikiki Beach Resort (2nd floor), 2335 Kalakaua Ave.* (p 138)

Hawaiian music and a casual dress code at Duke's Waikiki.

Waikiki's Best Nightlife

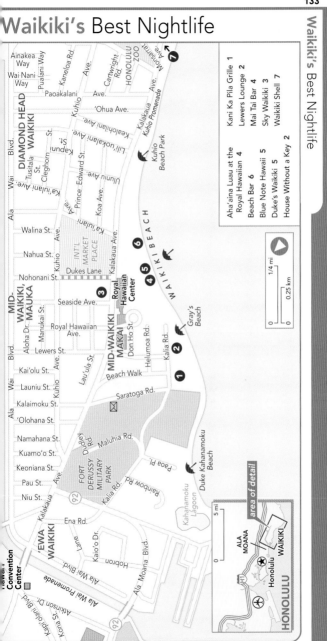

Aha'aina Luau at the Royal Hawaiian **4**
Beach Bar **6**
Blue Note Hawaii **5**
Duke's Waikiki **5**
House Without a Key **2**

Kani Ka Pila Grille **1**
Lewers Lounge **2**
Mai Tai Bar **4**
Sky Waikiki **3**
Waikiki Shell **7**

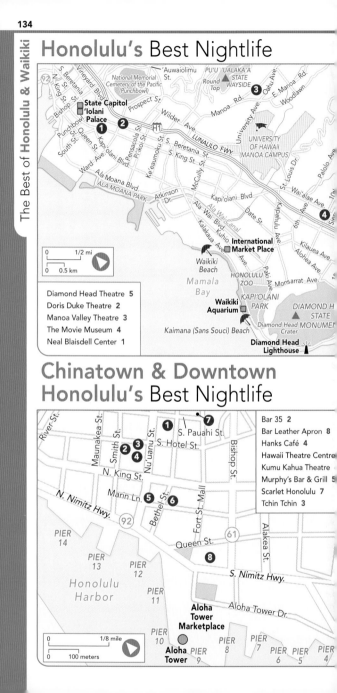

Honolulu's Best Nightlife

Diamond Head Theatre 5
Doris Duke Theatre 2
Manoa Valley Theatre 3
The Movie Museum 4
Neal Blaisdell Center 1

Chinatown & Downtown Honolulu's Best Nightlife

Bar 35 2
Bar Leather Apron 8
Hanks Café 4
Hawaii Theatre Centre
Kumu Kahua Theatre
Murphy's Bar & Grill 5
Scarlet Honolulu 7
Tchin Tchin 3

Nightlife & Performing Arts A to Z

Bartender at Bar Leather Apron.

Bars & Cocktail Lounges

★★★ Bar Leather Apron

DOWNTOWN Award-winning bartender Justin Park and cofounder/leather retailer Tom Park (unrelated) made a big splash in 2015 with this boutique lounge on the mezzanine of a downtown office building. Exquisite cocktails ($14–$20) feature local farm produce and top-shelf spirits, while the whiskey selection is said to be the largest in the state. Don't miss the mai tai, made with unusual ingredients such as kiawe wood smoke, absinthe, and coconut water syrup and served in a tiki box. Reservations strongly recommended. *Topa Financial Center, mezzanine level, 745 Fort St., Honolulu.* ☎ *808/599-4877. $2 validated parking (enter Topa Financial Garage from Nimitz Hwy./Ala Moana Blvd. between Bishop & Fort sts. Tues–Sat 5pm–midnight. Map p 134.*

★ Hanks Café CHINATOWN

This tiny, kitschy, friendly dive bar has live music nightly, open-mic nights, and special events that attract great talent and a supportive crowd, sometimes spilling out into the streets. You can order bar food like chicken wings and waffle fries, or try the new organic juices or Filipino specialties such as lumpia and silog rice. *1038 Nu'uanu Ave. www. hankscafehonolulu.com.* ☎ *808/888-3988. Daily 7am–2am. Map p 134.*

★★ Lewers Lounge WAIKIKI

Tops in taste and ambience is this intimate lounge in the Halekulani. Comfy seating around the pillars makes this a great spot for contemporary live jazz, cocktails, and small plates. "Elegant resort attire" required—no T-shirts or flip-flops here. *Halekulani, 2199 Kalia Rd. www.halekulani.com.* ☎ *808/923-2311. Wed–Sat 8pm–midnight. Map p 133.*

★ Murphy's Bar & Grill DOWNTOWN

One of Honolulu's most popular downtown ale houses and

media haunts was once a hotel frequented by Robert Louis Stevenson and King Kalakaua. Now it serves 16 beers on tap, including (of course) Murphy's and Guinness; its casual American menu (steaks, sandwiches, salads) and location make it a popular place for business lunches and dinner, too. *2 Merchant St.* ☎ *808/ 531-0422. www.murphyshawaii.com. Mon–Thurs 11am–8pm, Fri 11am– 9pm. Map p 134.*

★ **Tchin Tchin** CHINATOWN This indoor/outdoor rooftop bar and lounge offers an incomparable wine list and some of the best cocktails in town. The French-leaning small plates and tartines (open-faced sandwiches) are yummy, too. Enter through an unmarked door and up a flight of stairs. *39 N. Hotel St. www.thetchintchinbar.com.* ☎ *808/ 528-1888. Tues–Thurs 5–10pm, Fri– Sat 5pm–midnight. Map p 134.*

Clubs
Bar 35 CHINATOWN If you are looking for a brew, there are more than a hundred craft beers here, plus wine, cocktails (try the lychee martini), pizzas, and small plates (even vegan options). DJs and live

acts get the dancing going around 9pm. You must be at least 21 to enter (strictly enforced). *35 N. Hotel St. www.bar35hawaii.com.* ☎ *808/ 537-3535. Thurs–Fri 4pm–2am, Sat 6pm–2am. Map p 134.*

Scarlet Honolulu CHINATOWN Two dance floors with DJs and the best drag shows in Hawai'i keep this gay bar—an outpost of Scarlet Chicago—hopping into the wee hours. Tables and bottle service available. *80 S. Pauahi St. scarlet honolulu.com.* ☎ *808/200-0910. $20 cover. Fri–Sat 8pm–2am. Map p 134.*

Sky Waikiki WAIKIKI On Friday and Saturday nights, this rooftop restaurant and raw bar pumps up the volume with DJs and dancing. Nineteen stories above the beach, its deck also makes an excellent place for an early happy hour (4–5pm) or sunset cocktails, although be aware it can be quite sunny. If you're more of a morning person (or have a morning hangover), the Sunday mimosa brunch has a restorative Bloody Mary bar. Reservations strongly recommended for meals, but the bar has open seating. *2270 Kalakaua Ave.,*

A Little Night Music & Art

Every Friday and Saturday evening, the **Honolulu Museum of Art** (900 S. Beretania St.) stays open till 9 pm to host HOMA Nights, a lively way to experience the art in its galleries as well as star-gaze in the courtyards, listen to live music, browse pop-up shops, and (till 8:30pm) enjoy nibbles and specialty drinks in the cafe and coffee bar. The Friday version includes free, drop-in art-making sessions for all ages in the Kina'u Courtyard Studio and various galleries. The normal admission fee of $20 adults and free for kids 18 and under applies. For more information, call ☎ **808/ 532-8700** or visit honolulumuseum.org/events. In Chinatown, the first Friday of each month means art galleries stay open till 9pm for the **First Friday Honolulu Art Walk** (www.firstfridayhawaii.com), and revelers pack the nearby nightclubs.

The sun sets behind the 125-year-old banyan tree at the historic Moana Surfrider.

19th floor. www.skywaikiki.com.
☎ 808/979-7590. Sun–Thurs
4–10pm, Fri–Sat 4–11pm. Map p 133.

Film

★ Doris Duke Theatre MAKIKI
At the rear of the Honolulu Museum of Art (with its own entrance from Kina'u St.), this is the largest arthouse film theater in Honolulu, seating 280. Look for special screenings, guest appearances, and cultural performances after its scheduled reopening in early 2023. 900 S. Beretania. www.honolulu museum.org. ☎ 808/532-8703. Most screenings $12; event prices vary. Map p 134.

★★ The Movie Museum
KAIMUKI Film buffs and esoteric movie lovers can enjoy special screenings as they recline comfortably on brown-vinyl stuffed recliners. 3566 Harding Ave. www. kaimukihawaii.com/d/c/movie-museum.html. ☎ 808/735-8771. Tickets $8 (cash only). Reservations required. Map p 134.

Hawaiian Music

★★ The Beach Bar WAIKIKI A
casual gathering place in the beachfront courtyard of the oldest hotel in Hawai'i, this doesn't have the nostalgic elegance of the adjacent Veranda, which now just serves breakfast and a terrific weekend

afternoon tea. But it's still lovely to sip cocktails and watch the sunset in the shade of a banyan tree. Moana Surfrider, 2365 Kalakaua Ave. www.moana-surfrider.com. ☎ 808/922-3111. Map p 133.

★★ Duke's Waikiki WAIKIKI
This popular restaurant's outdoor, beachfront Barefoot Bar is perfect for sipping a tropical drink, watching the waves and sunset, and listening to music. It can get crowded, so get there early, and wear a hat and sunscreen if needed. Hawaiian music is usually from 4 to 6pm daily, and live entertainment (including pop, rock, and "Jawaiian" reggae) occurs nightly from 9:30pm to midnight. Veteran rocker Henry Kapono has been wowing the crowds for decades on Sunday afternoons, inspiring the Jimmy Buffett song "Duke's on Sunday." Outrigger Waikiki Beach Resort, 2335 Kalakaua Ave. www. dukeswaikiki.com. ☎ 808/922-2268. Validated parking available for $6 for 4 hrs. at the Ohana Waikiki East Hotel parking garage, a 5-min. walk. Enter from Kuhio Ave. btw. Walina Ave. & Kanekapolei St. Map p 133.

★★★ House Without a Key
WAIKIKI This iconic outdoor lounge is my favorite place to unwind at sunset, then linger under the stars. From 5:30 to 8:30pm daily, watch elegant Kanoelehua Miller (or another former beautiful Miss Hawai'i) dance graceful hula to the melodies of a Hawaiian music trio with the ocean glowing behind her, the sun setting in the west, and Diamond Head sparkling to the east. Appetizers and cocktails have always been delicious (if pricey) here. Now the menu from the expanded poolside restaurant with a new viewing kitchen also makes this an inviting place to stay for dinner, with delectable entrees such as steamed local snapper in sesame soy ginger sauce and hibachi grilled

Halekulani Hotel's House Without a Key.

chicken with guava chile barbecue sauce. Reserve well in advance. *Halekulani, 2199 Kalia Rd. www. halekulani.com.* ☎ *808/923-2311. Free validated parking. Map p 133.*

★ **Mai Tai Bar** WAIKIKI Named for the cocktail created by "Trader Vic" Bergeron in 1944, and introduced to the islands by the Royal Hawaiian in 1953, this beachfront restaurant with circular bar features live Hawaiian music from 6 to 10pm daily. The biggest throngs in the signature pink seats are at sunset; it's easier to nab a spot after dark. *The Royal Hawaiian, 2259 Kalakaua Ave. www.royal-hawaiian.com/ dining-overview/mai-tai-bar.* ☎ *808/ 923-7311. Free validated parking for 4 hr. with $25 min. purchase. Map p 133.*

Lu'au

★★ **Aha'aina Lu'au at the Royal Hawaiian** WAIKIKI Waikiki's best (and only oceanfront) lu'au traces the history of Helumoa—the Hawaiian name for the area where the Royal Hawaiian now stands—from ancient times through the monarchy, World War II and present day, interpreted in stories, Hawaiian music, and traditional and modern hula. Dinner, currently served as a lavish three-course menu, features Hawaiian and "local" specialties, including spicy ahi poke, saimin (noodle soup with fish cake and

egg), smoked meat, steamed island fish, chicken laulau (steamed with taro leaves) and haupia (coconut pudding) with chocolate dobash (layered) cake. *The Royal Hawaiian, 2259 Kalakaua Ave. www.royal-hawaiian. com.* ☎ *808/921-4600. Mon & Thurs 5:15pm (check-in at 5pm). $225 adults, $135 children 5–12, $20 children 2–4 (seat only; no meal); free for children in laps 0–2. Add $20 for premium seating & lei upgrade. Map p 133.*

Performing Arts Venues

Blue Note Hawai'i WAIKIKI Part of the Blue Note jazz club chain that originated in New York

The Aha'aina Lu'au at the Royal Hawaiian Hotel.

City, this handsome venue does present jazz artists such as the Manhattan Transfer and Dee Bridgewater, but also blues, reggae, R&B, rock, and favorite Hawai'i entertainers of all genres, including ukulele virtuoso Jake Shimabukuro. In recent years, it's added a strong comedy series, with frequent shows by the likes of Chris Redd and Rita Rudner and local comics; the latter are also featured in Sunday brunch shows. Renowned for its excellent acoustics, the club has a wonderful vibe, with intimate booths as well as standing-room tickets by the bar. The restaurant offers hearty bistro fare such as a charcuterie plate, prime rib, and roasted Provençal chicken, plus island favorites such as pork belly bao buns, 'ahi poke, and braised short rib. *Outrigger Waikiki Beach Resort, 2nd floor, 2335 Kalakaua Ave. www.bluenotejazz.com/hawaii.* ☎ *808/777-4890. Ticket prices vary. Map p 133.*

★★★ Hawai'i Theatre Center

CHINATOWN Audiences here have enjoyed performances by nationally renowned acts, including comedians Chelsea Handler and Paula Poundstone, singer-songwriter Norah Jones, and the American Repertory Dance Company. It's also a great place to see home-grown talent, especially the annual May Day Is Lei Day concert, performances by **the Hawai'i Symphony Orchestra** (www.myhso.org; ☎ **808/380-7724**) and **Ballet Hawaii** (www.ballethawaii.org; ☎ **808/521-8600**), and special film screenings. The neoclassical Beaux Arts landmark features a 1922 dome, 1,400 plush seats, a hydraulically elevated organ, and gilt galore. *1130 Bethel St. www.hawaiitheatre.com.* ☎ *808/528-0506. Ticket prices vary. Map p 134.*

★★ Neal Blaisdell Center

WARD This is the state's premier performing arts venue, with a concert hall/exhibition building that can be divided into an intimate 2,175-seat concert hall or an 8,805-seat arena, serving everyone from symphony-goers to punk rockers. From October to April, the highly successful **Hawai'i Opera Theatre** takes to the stage with three mainstage productions (www.hawaiiopera.org; ☎ **808/596-7858**). *Neal Blaisdell Center, 777 Ward Ave. www.blaisdellcenter.com.* ☎ *808/768-5433. Map p 134.*

★★ Waikiki Shell

WAIKIKI This outdoor venue in the middle of

An open-air concert at the Waikiki Shell.

Desperate Measures staged at the Manoa Valley Theatre.

Kapi'olani Park, which includes 1,950 stadium chairs and lawn seating for up to 6,000, allows concertgoers to watch the sunset and see the stars come out before the concert begins. A range of performers, from Hawaiian to jazz musicians, has graced this stage. *2805 Monsarrat Ave. blaisdellcenter.com/venues/tom-moffatt-waikiki-shell.* ☎ *808/768-5433. Map p 133.*

Repertory Theater
★ Diamond Head Theatre
DIAMOND HEAD   The oldest theater in Hawai'i (since 1915), this newly renovated community theater presents a sort of "Broadway of the Pacific," producing a range of popular plays and musicals. *520 Makapu'u Ave. www.diamondheadtheatre.com.* ☎ *808/733-0274. Tickets $15–$45. Map p 134.*

★ Kumu Kahua Theatre
DOWNTOWN   For an intimate glimpse at island life, take in a show at Kumu Kahua. This tiny theater (100 seats) produces plays dealing with today's cultural experience in Hawai'i, by the islands' best and emerging writers. *46 Merchant St. www.kumukahua.org.* ☎ *808/536-4441. Tickets $15–$20. Map p 134.*

Manoa Valley Theatre
MANOA   Honolulu's equivalent of off-Broadway, with performances of well-known shows—anything from *Tick, Tick…Boom!* to *The Mystery of Edwin Drood. 2833 E. Manoa Rd. www.manoavalleytheatre.com.* ☎ *808/988-6131. Tickets $22–$40. Map p 134.* ●

5 The Best **Regional Tours**

The **North Shore**

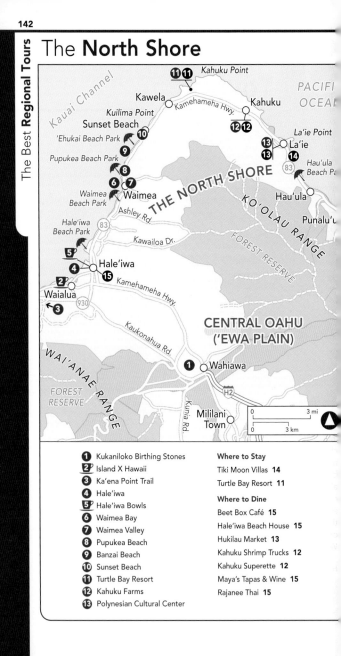

1 Kukaniloko Birthing Stones
2 Island X Hawaii
3 Ka'ena Point Trail
4 Hale'iwa
5 Hale'iwa Bowls
6 Waimea Bay
7 Waimea Valley
8 Pupukea Beach
9 Banzai Beach
10 Sunset Beach
11 Turtle Bay Resort
12 Kahuku Farms
13 Polynesian Cultural Center

Where to Stay

Tiki Moon Villas 14
Turtle Bay Resort 11

Where to Dine

Beet Box Café 15
Hale'iwa Beach House 15
Hukilau Market 13
Kahuku Shrimp Trucks 12
Kahuku Superette 12
Maya's Tapas & Wine 15
Rajanee Thai 15

Previous page: The lookout near the Makapu'u Point Lighthouse.

On O'ahu, don't just stay in Waikiki—get out and see the island. Drive up through the center of O'ahu to the famous North Shore. If you can afford the splurge, rent a bright, shiny convertible—the perfect car for O'ahu, so you can bask in the sun as you go. Suburbs with shopping centers, military compounds, and pineapple fields dot the central plains in place of the original sandalwood forests, cut down for their trade value after Western contact. Beyond them lie the North Shore and the "Surf City" of Hale'iwa, a turn-of-the-20th-century sugar-plantation town that has been designated a historic site. Once a collection of faded clapboard stores, Hale'iwa has evolved into a surfer outpost and major roadside attraction with art galleries, shave ice stands and restaurants, and shops selling aloha wear, beach fashion, and, of course, surfboards.

From Waikiki it's about a 50-min. drive to the North Shore; the drive from resorts and condos in Ko Olina is a few minutes faster. Just be sure to let the morning commuter traffic heading toward downtown or Pearl Harbor ebb before heading out, after 8:30am or so. For a quick hit of Hawaiian culture, make a stop en route in Wahiawa.

1 ★ Kukaniloko Birthstones. This 5-acre site, considered the *piko* (navel) of O'ahu, is one of the most sacred in all Hawai'i. Two rows of 18 lava rocks once flanked a central birthing stone, where women of ancient Hawai'i gave birth to *ali'i* (chiefs or royalty) witnessed by 36 chiefs. Used for generations of births, many of the *pohaku* (rocks) have bowl-like shapes; their positioning also helped teach astronomers and navigators. Look for the interpretive signs explaining the significance of this area and visit www.kukaniloko. org for more details. ◷ 20 min. *Whitmore Ave and Hwy. 80, Wahiawa.*

From Wahiawa, it's another 15-min. drive to Waialua.

2 ★★ Island X Hawai'i. The former sugar plantation town of Waialua has kept more of its funky rough edges than neighboring Hale'iwa. Browse the shops and food outlets in the repurposed Old Waialua Sugar Mill, where coffee and cacao now grow behind the Quonset hut-like buildings, then refresh yourself with an iced coffee or shave ice inside this sprawling store with local crafts and souvenirs. The all-natural fruit syrups are made with local sugar, and you can even adjust the sweetness. ◷ 30–45 min. *67-106 Kealohanui St., Waialua.* www.islandxhawaii.com. ☎ 808/ 637-2624. Mon–Fri 9am–5pm, Sat 8:30am–5pm, Sun 10am–5pm. $.

An 8-mi (12.9km) drive along the rural coastline leads to the trailhead for Ka'ena Point.

Hale'iwa Beach Park.

❸ ★★ **Ka'ena Point Trail.** This long, scenic detour is for avid hikers and wildlife lovers only, but worth the effort. The relatively flat, 5-mile (8k) round-trip dirt trail on an old sugar-cane railroad bed leads past tide-pools, raised limestone reefs, and sandy coves to Ka'ena Point Natural Area Reserve. Laysan albatross (*moli*) nest here in winter, when spouting whales can be seen offshore; the endangered Hawaiian monk seals may snooze on the sand year-round. The view of the Wai'anae Range is also stunning. Bring lots of water and sun protection. ⏱ *2½–3 hr. End of Farrington (Hwy. 930), Mokule'ia. https://dlnr.hawaii.gov/dsp/hiking/oahu/kaena-point-trail. Daily 6am–7pm.*

From the trailhead, it's a 10-mile (16.9km) drive back along the coast and through Waialua to Hale'iwa.

❹ ★★★ **Hale'iwa.** Only 34 miles (55km) from Waikiki lies Hale'iwa, the eclectic ex-sugar-plantation town that's the world capital of big-wave surfing. Officially designated a historic cultural and scenic district, Hale'iwa was founded by sugar baron Benjamin Dillingham in the late 1890s. He opened a Victorian hotel overlooking Kaiaka Bay and named it Hale'iwa, or "house of the *'iwa*," for the great frigate bird often seen here. The hotel is gone, but Hale'iwa, which was rediscovered in the late 1960s by hippies, still resonates with charm. Galleries, boutiques, cafes, and board shops with other beach gear line both sides of the town. There's also a busy fishing harbor full of charter boats. ⏱ *1–2 hr.*

❺ ★ **Hale'iwa Bowls.** Shave ice isn't your only option for cooling down in Hale'iwa. Surfers, locals, and visitors alike love açai bowls: the purple fruit, açai berry, which usually comes frozen from Brazil, is blended and topped with granola,

Waimea Bay.

fresh bananas, and drizzled with honey. This thatched-roof shack with outdoor seating is the best place to try it. Hale'iwa Bowls also dispenses kombucha on tap in fla-vors like liliko'i, ginger, or mango. *66-030 Kamehameha Hwy., Hale'iwa. www.haleiwabowls.com. Daily 7:30am–6:30pm. $.*

Kamehameha Hwy. (Hwy. 83) leads past beaches, famed surf breaks and snorkeling spots, a valley with cul-tural heritage and botanical gardens, a spectacular resort, and farms en route to the Windward Side.

❻ ★★ **Waimea Bay.** From November to March, monstrous waves—some 30 feet (9m) tall—roll into Waimea. When they break on the shore, the ground actually shakes. The best surfers in the world paddle out to challenge these freight trains—it's amazing to see how small they appear in the lip of the giant waves. *See p 170.*

❼ ★ **Waimea Valley.** The 150-acre (61-ha) outdoor cultural center contains 52 themed gardens with more than 5,000 species of tropical plants. Walk on paved paths or dirt trails through the gardens and wind up at 45-foot-high (14m) Waihi Falls (nicknamed Waimea Falls). If condi-tions permit, you're allowed to swim in the cold, somewhat murky 30-foot-deep (9m) pool below, wearing a life vest provided for free. The public is invited to hike the trails and spend a day in this quiet oasis. There are cultural activities, such as lei-making, kapa demonstrations, hula lessons, Hawaiian games and crafts, and music and storytelling. *See p 63,* **7**.

8 ★ Pupukea Beach. This 80-acre (32-ha) beach park, excellent for snorkeling and diving, is a Marine Life Conservation District with strict rules about taking marine life, sand, coral, shells, and rocks. *See p 167.*

9 ★ Banzai Beach. In the winter, this is a very popular beach with surfers, surf fans, curious residents, and visitors; it's less crowded in the summer months. *See p 163.*

10 ★★ Sunset Beach. If it's winter, just people-watch on this sandy beach, as the waves are huge. During the summer, it's usually safe to go swimming. *See p 169.*

11 ★★★ Turtle Bay Resort. The resort is spectacular—an hour's drive from Waikiki but eons away in its country feeling. Sitting on 808 acres (327 ha), it includes 5 miles (8km) of shoreline with secluded white-sand coves. Even if you don't stay here, check out the beach activities, e-bike natural and cultural history tours, golf, horseback riding, tennis, and surf lessons (see chapter 7 for details). It also offers an amazing spa, cowboy-themed barbecue luau, and tours of its 469-acre (190ha) Ku'ilima Farm across the road, where gleaming fresh fruit

Snorkeling at Pupukea Beach.

and crispy banana *lumpia* are for sale. Grab a bite or drink in the Instagram-worthy lobby, where **Off the Lip** lounge offers tasty craft cocktails and small plates, and **Ho'olana** serves excellent espresso drinks and breakfast and lunch fare; both spots have dazzling views. During the wintertime, all the surfers come to **Lei Lei's Bar and Grill** at the golf course for hearty American and local dishes. It's fun to watch wave riders of all abilities on Kawela Bay from poolside **Sunset** restaurant or the more gourmet, farm-centric **Alaia** above it, while **Roy's Beach House** serves dinner by sheltered Ku'ilima Beach with gorgeous sunsets. ⏱ *Depends on your activity. 57–091 Kamehameha Hwy., Kahuku. www.turtlebayresort. com.* ☎ *808/293-6000.*

12 ★ Kahuku Farms. Although its wagon ride tours were still paused at press time (due to the pandemic), you can still learn a lot about tropical fruits like apple banana, liliko'i (passionfruit) and papaya at this working farm by sampling the wares in its cafe, smoothie shack, and new Cocoa House, which features chocolate drinks sourced from its cacao orchard. Don't miss the cafe's grilled banana bread topped with ice cream and *haupia* (coconut) and caramel sauce. ⏱ *30 min. to 1 hr. 56-800 Kamehameha Hwy. www.kahukufarms.com.* ☎ *808/628-0639. Check website for tour availability (previously $16–$32 for adults, $14–$22 for ages 5–12.)*

13 ★★ Ha: Breath of Life at the Polynesian Cultural Center. Catch the evening show at the Polynesian Cultural Center. *See p 17,* **17**.

From the Polynesian Cultural Center, it's a little over an hour's drive back to Waikiki, although it may seem longer at night, when it's very dark much of the way.

Where to **Stay**

Note: For budget accommodations, camping (p 173) and Airbnb are your best options.

★★ **Tiki Moon Villas** LA'IE
This collection of six bungalows (available in multiple configurations) sits on an uncrowded beach across from the Polynesian Cultural Center. Units include handsome island wood furnishings, modern kitchens and baths, air-conditioning, and outdoor gardens and patios steps from the beach. Larger gatherings (up to 36 people) can book the whole compound. *55–367 Kamehameha Hwy., La'ie. www.tiki moonvillas.com.* ☎ *808/800-1137. 6 bungalows. Studio (sleeps 4), from $325; 1-br (sleeps 4), from $344; 2-br/2-bath (sleeps 6), from $365; 3-br/1-bath (sleeps 7), from $405; 3-br/3-bath (sleeps 10) and 4-br/2-bath (sleeps 11), from $690.*

★★★ **Turtle Bay Resort**
KAHUKU   Located in the "country" on 5 miles (8km) of shoreline with secluded white-sand coves, this is the place to stay to get away from everything. The beautifully renovated resort offers excellent dining, adults-only and family swimming pools, tons of outdoor and cultural activities, and 410 serene, beach-chi hotel rooms, all with ocean views and balconies; a separate enclave of 42 bungalows come with private pool and VIP services. It also boasts one of the best spas on the island. The high price tag reflect the level of luxury as well as the North Shore's limited supply of lodgings. *57–091 Kamehameha Hwy., Kahuku. www.turtlebayresort. com.* ☎ *877/482-4857 or 808/293-6000. 452 units. Doubles from $744; suites from $821; bungalows from $1,508.*

Secluded, full-service Turtle Bay Resort.

Where to **Dine**

In addition to the delicious options at Turtle Bay Resort listed in the tour section (p 145), check out these options in Hale'iwa town.

★ **Beet Box Café** HALE'IWA *VEGETARIAN* Warm wood paneling (upcycled, of course) welcomes you into this vegetarian restaurant. Flavors pack a punch in the form of portobello and feta sandwiches, Thai-style tofu tacos, or tortilla soup. At breakfast, açai bowls, burritos, and avocado toast are popular, too. *66-437 Kamehameha Hwy., www.thebeetboxcafe.com.*

☎ *808/637-3000. Entrees $9–$15. Breakfast and lunch daily 9am–3pm.*

★ **Hale'iwa Beach House** HALE'IWA *AMERICAN/LOCAL* When you tire of the North Shore food trucks, come here for a fabulous view of Hale'iwa Beach Park and sunset. Highlights include the grilled catch of the day with ginger scallion beurre blanc and the kalua pork grilled cheese appetizer. *62-540 Kamehameha Hwy., Hale'iwa.* ☎ *808/637-3435. Lunch $18–$29; dinner $33–$51. Lunch 11am to 3pm*

Kahuku & La'ie Food Spots

Kahuku is famous for its shrimp trucks—you can practically smell the garlic wafting in the air as you approach. **Giovanni's Original White Shrimp Truck,** 56-505 Kamehameha Hwy. (www.giovannis shrimptruck.com; ☎ **808/293-1839**), is the most popular, but head north from Giovanni's about a mile, and you'll hit **Romy's Kahuku Prawns & Shrimp,** 56-781 Kamehameha Hwy. (☎ **808/ 232-2202**), a shrimp shack instead of a truck. Here the shrimp actually come from the farm behind it. Garlic lovers will swoon over the Romy's sauce—tons of sautéed and fried diced cloves—over a half-pound of head-on shrimp, plus a container of spicy soy sauce for dipping.

But Kahuku isn't just about shrimp. Head to the back of the nondescript **Kahuku Superette,** 56-505 Kamehameha Hwy. (☎ **808/ 293-9878**) for some of the best poke (raw, seasoned cubes of 'ahi tuna) on the island. The shoyu poke is legendary, infused with ginger, and the limu 'ahi poke, tossed with local Hawaiian seaweed, showcases the fresh fish. Bonus: It's open till 10pm, a rarity out here. For a refreshing variety of food (but no alcohol, due to its Mormon ownership), visit the outdoor **Hukilau Market** at the Polynesian Cultural Center, 55-370 Kamehameha Hwy. in La'ie (☎ **808/293-3142**). Besides the nearly dozen food stalls (Thai, Mexican, New Zealand fish and chips, hot dogs, and shave ice among them) and sit-down restaurant with bakery, the market offers plenty of free parking, clean bathrooms, and free Wi-Fi— great for a pit stop or pre-show dinner.

daily; appetizers 3pm to 5pm and dinner 5 to 8pm Fri–Sun.

★★ Maya's Tapas & Wine

HALE'IWA *SPANISH* Tucked into a corner of North Shore Marketplace, this cozy bistro with a small lanai and popular happy hour fills up quickly—make reservations early. The "small" plates are quite filling, too. At dinner, try the fried brussels sprouts, charred hamachi collar, and lamb empanadas, or feast on the Maya's burger with goat cheese and bacon fig jam. Lunch has a smaller selection of tapas plus delectable flatbreads and sandwiches, including the burger. *66–250 Kamehameha Hwy. www.mayastapasandwine.com.* ☎ *808/200-2964. Lunch tapas $9–$16, entrees $14–$17. Dinner tapas $9–$22; entrees $17–$34. Lunch 11am to 3pm Tues–Sun and dinner 5 to 10pm Tues–Sat.*

★ Rajanee Thai HALE'IWA *THAI*

This cheery little spot serves some of the best Thai food on the island. There are the staples like pad thai and yellow curry, which are solid,

Giovanni's Shrimp Truck.

but also try the zingy pickled ginger salad and the garlicky Bangkok night noodles. *66–111 Kamehameha Hwy. #1001* ☎ *808/784-0023. Entrees $10–$22. Lunch & dinner 12:30 to 8:30pm daily.*

Southern O'ahu & the Windward Coast

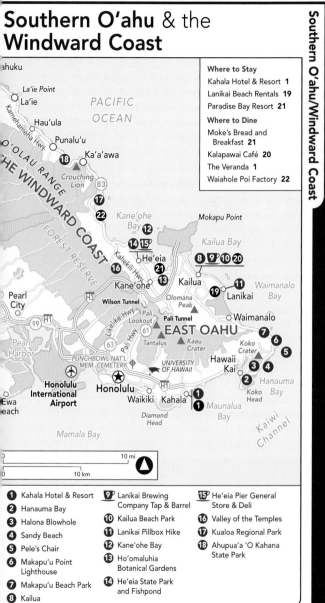

Where to Stay

Kahala Hotel & Resort **1**

Lanikai Beach Rentals **19**

Paradise Bay Resort **21**

Where to Dine

Moke's Bread and
Breakfast **21**

Kalapawai Café **20**

The Veranda **1**

Waiahole Poi Factory **22**

1 Kahala Hotel & Resort

2 Hanauma Bay

3 Halona Blowhole

4 Sandy Beach

5 Pele's Chair

6 Makapu'u Point
Lighthouse

7 Makapu'u Beach Park

8 Kailua

9 Lanikai Brewing
Company Tap & Barrel

10 Kailua Beach Park

11 Lanikai Pillbox Hike

12 Kane'ohe Bay

13 Ho'omaluhia
Botanical Gardens

14 He'eia State Park
and Fishpond

15 He'eia Pier General
Store & Deli

16 Valley of the Temples

17 Kualoa Regional Park

18 Ahupua'a 'O Kahana
State Park

From the high-rises of Waikiki, venture to a very different O'ahu, the arid South Shore and lush Windward Side. The landscape on the south side is like a moonscape, with prickly cactuses on shore and, in winter, spouting whales cavorting in the water. The Kaiwi State Scenic Shoreline shares its name, which means "the bone," with the 26-mile (42k) channel between here and Moloka'i; there are definitely some bone-cracking shorebreaks along this popular coast for bodyboarding. On the Windward Side, lots of rain keeps the vegetation green and growing. A string of white-sand beaches beckon, bracketed by fishponds, taro fields, and other sites revered in Hawaiian culture. From Waikiki, it's a 15-minute drive around either side of Diamond Head to the tony Kahala neighborhood.

1 ★★ Kahala Hotel & Resort.
Stop by this lush, tropical resort where the grounds include a crescent-shaped beach, a lagoon (home to six bottlenose dolphins, sea turtles, and tropical fish), plus a fabulous spa. Start off your day with a splurge on the breakfast buffet ($49 adults, $24 ages 6–12) at the oceanside Plumeria Beach House. ⏱ *1 hr. 5000 Kahala Ave. (next to the Wai'alae Country Club). www.kahalaresort.com.* ☎ *800/367-2525 or 808/369-9480.*

From Kahala, it's about 15 minutes to Hanauma Bay, past shops, neighborhoods and beach parks along busy Kalaniana'ole Hwy. (Hwy. 72).

2 ★★★ Hanauma Bay. This marine preserve is a great place to snorkel, especially early in the morning; visitors need to reserve and pay for entry ($25) in advance. The preserve is closed Mondays and Tuesdays. *See p 164.*

From Hanauma Bay, it's 5 miles (8km) along Kalaniana'ole Hwy. (Hwy. 72) to Makapu'u Beach Park, with a string of sights in quick succession.

3 Halona Blowhole. There are three reasons to pull over at this scenic lookout: You get to watch the ocean waves forced through a hole in the rocks shoot up 30 feet (9m) in the air; you'll see the cove

Aerial view of Hanauma Bay.

The pull-off and observation deck at the Halona Blowhole.

where *From Here to Eternity*'s famous beach tryst was filmed; and there's a great view of Sandy Beach and across the 26-mile (42km) gulf to neighboring Moloka'i, with the faint triangular shadow of Lana'i on the far horizon. Be sure to obey all the signs warning you to stay away from the blowhole. ⏱ *15 min. Kalaniana'ole Hwy. (72) around mile marker 11.*

❹ ★ **Sandy Beach.** This is O'ahu's most dangerous beach—hence an ambulance always standing by to whisk injured wave-catchers to the hospital. Expert bodyboarders love it. I suggest you just sit on the sand and watch. *See p 168.*

❺ **Pele's Chair.** Just after you leave Sandy's, as residents call it, look northwest for this famous formation, which from a distance resembles a mighty throne. Although some today attribute the lava rock outcropping to the volcano goddess Pele, Hawaiians traditionally called it Kapaliokamoa, "the cliff of the chicken," seeing a rooster's comb in its outline.

❻ ★★ **Makapu'u Point Lighthouse.** As you round the bend, ahead lies a 647-foot-high (197m) hill, with a red-roofed lighthouse that once signaled safe passage for steamship passengers arriving from San Francisco. Though closed to visitors, it still lights the south coast for passing tankers, fishing boats,

and sailors. You can take a short hike up here for a spectacular vista. During the winter, you can spot cavorting whales offshore.

❼ ★ **Makapu'u Beach Park.** In summer, the ocean here is as gentle as a Jacuzzi, and swimming and diving are perfect; come winter, however, Makapu'u is hit with big, pounding waves that are ideal for expert bodysurfers but too dangerous for regular swimmers. *See p 166.*

From Makapu'u Beach Park, it's about a 25-minute drive north along Kalaniana'ole Hwy. (Hwy. 72) to Kailua, passing through rural Waimanalo.

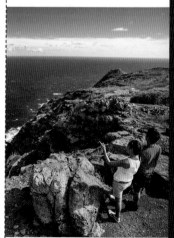

Look for migrating whales on the hike up to the Makapu'u Point Lighthouse.

8 Kailua. This is Hawai'i's biggest beach town, with more than 50,000 residents and two special beaches, Kailua (p 164) and Lanikai (p 165). Funky little Kailua is lined with multimillion-dollar houses next to humble cottages, with a great craft beer and boutique scene, the latter specializing in beachy wear.

9 ★ Lanikai Brewing Company Tap & Barrel. Wash down a wood-fired pizza or Italian-style sandwich with one of many craft beers on tap at this trendy tasting room. The saisons, hazy IPAs and sour beers (to name a few) feature local ingredients such as honey, strawberries, lemongrass, and cacao. *167 Hamakua St., Kailua. www.lanikai brewing.com. Mon–Fri noon–10pm, Sat–Sun 11am–10pm. $$.*

10 ★★ Kailua Beach Park. Windward O'ahu's premier beach is a 2-mile-long (3.2km), wide golden strand with dunes, palm trees, panoramic views, and offshore islets that are home to seabirds and every type of ocean activity you can think of. *See p 164.*

To access Lanikai, it's usually easiest to leave your car at Kailua Beach Park and walk 1 mile (1.6km) to the trailhead at the end of Ka'elepulu Dr.

11 ★ Lanikai Pillbox Hike. This short hike up to the Kaiwi ridge is only about 30 minutes each way up the steep, dirt trail, but the payoff is great: picture-perfect views of Kailua, the Ko'olau mountains, and the twin Mokulua islands. It makes you realize why the pillboxes—created as WWII observation posts, and later abandoned—were built up here in the first place. ⏱ *1 hr. Ka'elepulu Dr.*

Retrace your walking route back to Kailua Beach Park and follow N. Kalaheo Ave. until it becomes Kane'ohe Bay Dr.

12 ★ Kane'ohe Bay. Take an incredibly scenic drive around Kane'ohe Bay, which is spiked with islets and lined with gold-sand beach parks. The bay has a barrier reef and four tiny islets, one of which, Moku o Lo'e, is widely known as Coconut Island. Don't be surprised if it looks familiar—it appeared in *Gilligan's Island.* ⏱ *15 min.*

Lanikai Brewing Company.

Ho'omaluhia Botanical Garden.

⑬ ★ Ho'omaluhia Botanical Garden. If you have had enough time under the hot sun, stop by this 400-acre (162-ha) botanical garden, the perfect place for a picnic or hike. *See p 63, ⑧.*

It's a 10-minute drive from the botanical garden to He'eia State Park. Note Kamehameha Hwy. changes from Hwy. 83 to Hwy. 830 in Kane'ohe.

⑭ He'eia State Park and Fishpond. A gorgeous place to kayak or snorkel (p 189), this beautiful park is also the meeting place for 1-hour tours of He'eia Fishpond, an 88-acre (36ha) rock-walled marvel of Hawaiian aquaculture, under restoration since 2001. The informative, all-ages tour may inspire you to join one of the twice-monthly Saturday morning weekday volunteer sessions. ⓢ *1–2 hr. Fishpond tours by reservation only; $40 for up to 4 people, $10 per person for more. Register online to volunteer 8am–noon, 2nd and 4th Sat of month. paepaeo heeia.org.* ☎ *808/236-6178.*

⑮ ★ He'eia Pier General Store & Deli. At the end of the old He'eia Kea Fishing Pier jutting into Kane'ohe Bay, this simple local-style deli and store is a great place to soak in the views while grabbing a plate lunch, bento box, soft drinks, or other pick-me-ups. *46-499 Kamehameha Hwy., Kane'ohe.* ☎ *808/236-2380. Deli open daily 8am–2pm, store 7am–5pm. $.*

⑯ ★ Valley of the Temples Memorial Park. This famous site

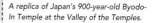

A replica of Japan's 900-year-old Byodo-In Temple at the Valley of the Temples.

is stalked by wild peacocks and about 700 curious people a day, who pay to see the 9-foot (2.7m) meditation Buddha, 2 acres (.8 ha) of ponds full of more than 10,000 Japanese koi fish, and a replica of Japan's 900-year-old Byodo-In Temple. A 3-ton (2,722kg) brass temple bell brings good luck to those who can ring it. ⏱ *1 hr. 47–200 Kahekili Hwy. (Hwy. 83), Kane'ohe. www.byodo-in.com.* ☎ *808/239-8811. $5 adults, $4 seniors 65 & over, $2 ages 2–12. Daily 8:30am–4:30pm.*

It's an 8-mile (13km) drive to Kualoa Regional Park, mostly along the gorgeous, shoreline-hugging Kamehameha Hwy. (which becomes Hwy. 83 again in Kahalu'u).

⑰ ★★ Kualoa Regional Park. This 150-acre (61-ha) coconut palm–fringed peninsula is the biggest beach park on the windward side and one of Hawai'i's most scenic. The long, narrow, white-sand beach is perfect for swimming, walking, beachcombing, kite flying, or just sunbathing. *See p 165.*

Fresh-caught fish in O'ahu.

Continue on Kamehameha Hwy. (Hwy. 83) another 5.3 miles (16km).

⑱ ★★ Ahupua'a 'O Kahana State Park. The white sand, crescent-shaped beach at this culturally oriented enclave has a

A Spa with Suites & Sustainability

The Kahala Hotel & Resort has wowed its spa patrons for years with serenity-inducing massages, facials, and body treatments (from $195) in private spa suites. Formerly garden guest rooms, the personal treatment rooms offer a glass-enclosed shower, private changing area, infinity-edge deep-soaking Jacuzzi tub, and relaxation area. Now the hotel is wooing its guests to support its key sustainability initiative—planting 200,000 native milo trees on the North Shore at Gunstock Ranch (p 183)—by offering a $50 spa credit to those who donate $90 for a tree planting. It must be working: Nearly 14,000 trees have been planted so far. Visit www.kahalaresort.com or call ☎ **808/369-9471** for information.

Hawaiʻi Seafood Primer

The seafood in Hawaiʻi has been described as the best in the world. And why not? Without a doubt, the islands' surrounding waters and a thriving aquaculture industry contribute to the high quality of the seafood here.

Although some menus include the Western description for the fresh fish used, most often the local nomenclature is listed. To help familiarize you with the menu language of Hawaiʻi, here's a basic glossary of island fish:

ʻahi yellowfin or big-eye tuna, important for its use in poke, sashimi, and gourmet entrees, it also appears in fish tacos and burgers

aku skipjack tuna, frequently used in home cooking and poke

ʻehu red snapper, delicate and sumptuous, yet lesser known than ʻopakapaka

hapuʻupuʻu Hawaiian sea bass or grouper, delicate white flesh

hebi spearfish, mildly flavored, and frequently featured as the "catch of the day" in upscale restaurants

kajiki Pacific blue marlin, also called aʻu, with a firm flesh and high fat content that makes it a plausible substitute for tuna

mahimahi dolphinfish (the game fish, not the mammal) or dorado, a classic sweet, white-fleshed fish

monchong big-scale or sickle pomfret, an exotic, tasty fish, but scarce—try it when you see it on a menu

nairagi striped marlin, also called aʻu; good as sashimi and in poke, and often substituted for ʻahi in raw-fish products

onaga ruby snapper, a luxury fish, versatile, moist, and flaky

ono wahoo, firmer and drier than the snappers, often served grilled and in sandwiches; sounds like ʻono, Hawaiian for delicious

opah moonfish, rich and fatty, and versatile—cooked, raw, smoked, and broiled

ʻopakapaka pink snapper, light, flaky, and luxurious, suited for sashimi, poaching, sautéing, and baking

shutome broadbill swordfish, with beefy texture and rich flavor

tombo ʻahi albacore tuna, with a high fat content, suitable for grilling

uhu parrotfish, most often encountered steamed, Chinese style

uku blue-green snapper or grey jobfish, with clear, pale-pink flesh; delicately flavored and moist

picture-perfect backdrop: a huge, jungle-cloaked valley with dramatic, jagged cliffs. The bay's calm water and shallow, sandy bottom make it a safe swimming area for children. See p 174.

From Kahana, it's about a 50-minute drive back to Waikiki. It's an hour to Ko Olina, except during evening rush hour traffic (5–7pm) heading from Honolulu/Pearl Harbor to the West Side.

Where to **Stay**

★★★ Kahala Hotel & Resort

KAHALA   Located in one of O'ahu's most prestigious residential areas, the Kahala offers elegant rooms and serenity away from Waikiki, with the conveniences of central Honolulu just a 10-minute drive away. The lush, tropical grounds include a small beach with a private feel. There's a pool, too, and you can also stay active with kayak, boogieboard or bike rentals; relax in a private spa suite; or learn cultural traditions such as lauhala weaving, bamboo stamping, and hula. *5000 Kahala Ave. (next to the Wai'alae Country Club). www.kahala resort.com. ☎ 808/369-9741. 338 units. Doubles from $595 (ocean-view from $675); suites from $1,225.*

★ Lanikai Beach Rentals

LANIKAI   Due to a crackdown on short-term vacation rentals, this agency only has only two units available for stays under 30 days, but they're both gems, and only 100 yards (91m) to lovely Lanikai Beach. The downstairs, high-ceilinged Garden Studio has a king bed, kitchenette with full-size fridge, and separate dining and seating areas, with lots of island art. The furnishings in the upstairs one-bedroom Tree House (named for its views) are a tad heavy on the rattan, but it also offers a king bed, well-stocked kitchenette, and spacious dining and living rooms. Onsite parking and use of beach gear are included. *1277 Mokulua Dr. (btw. Onekea & 'A'ala drives). www.lanikaibeachrentals. com. ☎ 808/261-7895. Studio from $315, 1-bedroom from $350.*

★ Paradise Bay Resort

KANE'OHE   Nestled in the tranquil, tropical setting on Kane'ohe Bay, with views of the surrounding Ko'olau mountains, this cluster of waterfront cottages and studio suites also has terrific views of the calm waters of the bay and, in the distance, the small islets offshore. All lodgings have a kitchen or kitchenette, and a patio or lanai; choose a cottage or bay-view studio suite for water views. Units are doubles, but one-bedroom suites and cottages can accommodate a third person with a rollaway bed for $30 more a night. *Tip:* Book directly on the hotel's website for deep discounts. *47–039 Lihikai Dr. (off Kamehameha Hwy.). www.paradisebayresorthawaii. com. ☎ 800/735-5071 or 808/239-5711. 20 units. Studio suites $395–$456 ($190–$219 online discount), 1-br suites. $476 ($228 online), 1-br cottage $616 ($296 online).*

A studio apartment from Lanikai Beach Rentals.

Where to **Dine**

★ **Moké's Bread and Breakfast**
KAILUA BREAKFAST/BRUNCH
You can't go wrong with the *liliko'i*
pancakes here, thanks to the sweet
but tangy passionfruit cream sauce
poured over classic fluffy pancakes.
Meat lovers will want to try the loco
moco (available with ribeye steak
instead of a hamburger patty) or
corned beef hash made from whole
brisket. Stuffed hash browns make
a satisfying egg-free alternative to
omelets, although those are top-
notch too. *27 Ho'olai St., Kailua.
www.mokeshawaii.com.* ☎ *808/261-
5565. Entrees $9–$20. Brunch Wed–
Sun 6am–1pm.*

★ **Kalapawai Café** KAILUA
INTERNATIONAL This tiny neighborhood bistro features everything
from gourmet espresso coffee and
breakfast goodies to pizza and
sandwiches for lunch and intriguing
cuisine like fresh fish with lemongrass risotto and red curry aioli for

dinner. Combination deli, market,
and cafe, you can sit inside or on
the garden lanai. **Note:** The original Kalapawai Market, close to the
beach at 306 S. Kalaheo Rd., is
great for breakfast and lunch to go,
open 6am to 8pm daily. *750 Kailua
Rd. (at Kihapai St.). www.kalapawai
market.com.* ☎ *808/262-3354. Dinner entrees $16–$29. Breakfast, lunch
& dinner daily, open Mon–Thurs
6am–8:30pm, Fri 6am–9pm, Sat 7am–
9pm, Sun 7am–8:30pm.*

★★ **The Veranda** KAHALA
INTERNATIONAL Known equally
for its live music in the evening and
sumptuous afternoon tea, this casually elegant lounge within the
Kahala Hotel offers beautiful ocean
views without the sticker shock of
neighboring Hoku's (where prix fixe
dinners start at $124). Graze on
appetizers like truffled deviled eggs
and Kona kampachi rillette, or tuck
into steak frites or salmon in dill

Family run Moké's Bread and Breakfast.

Making Poi at Waiahole Poi Factory.

sauce. There's also a sushi and sashimi menu Friday and Saturday nights. *5000 Kahala Ave. (end of street). www.kahalaresort.com.*

☎ *808/739-8760. Entrees $32–$34, sushi $9–$26, afternoon tea $65. Dinner Tues–Sat 5:30–9pm (live music 6–8pm), afternoon tea Fri–Sat 2–3:30pm.*

★ Waiahole Poi Factory

KANE'OHE *HAWAIIAN* This humble roadside stop in a blink-and-you'll-miss-it hamlet north of Kane'ohe draws lines of patrons for hearty plate lunches with kalua pig, lomi salmon, squid *lu'au*, and other classic Hawaiian dishes. Local farmers provide the taro for freshly pounded poi and *kulolo*, a dense sweet treat served warm with *haupia* (coconut cream) ice cream. The aloha-filled service and setting—a former poi factory more than a century old—are unmistakably Hawaiian, too. *48-140 Kamehameha Hwy. (at Waiahole Valley Rd.),Kane'ohe. Entrees $11–$14. Lunch and dinner daily 10am–6pm.* ●

O'ahu's Best Beaches

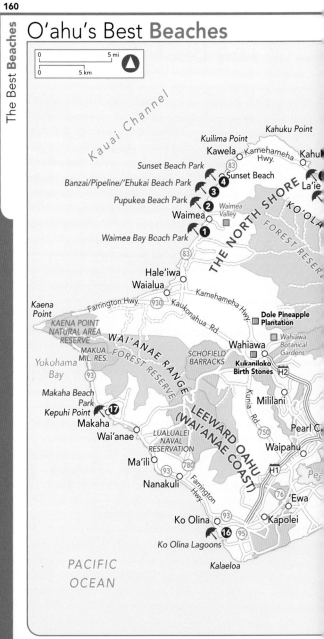

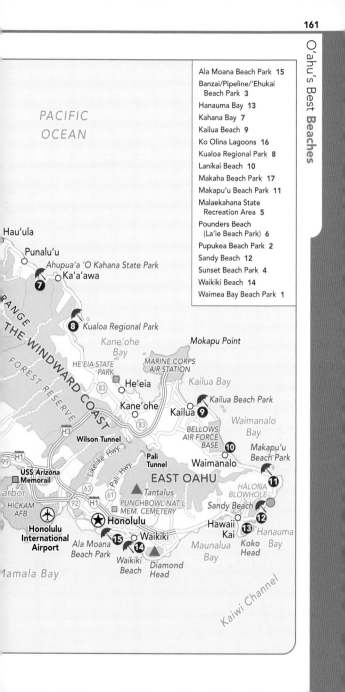

Ala Moana Beach Park **15**
Banzai/Pipeline/'Ehukai
  Beach Park **3**
Hanauma Bay **13**
Kahana Bay **7**
Kailua Beach **9**
Ko Olina Lagoons **16**
Kualoa Regional Park **8**
Lanikai Beach **10**
Makaha Beach Park **17**
Makapu'u Beach Park **11**
Malaekahana State
  Recreation Area **5**
Pounders Beach
  (La'ie Beach Park) **6**
Pupukea Beach Park **2**
Sandy Beach **12**
Sunset Beach Park **4**
Waikiki Beach **14**
Waimea Bay Beach Park **1**

Beaches Best Bets

Best for **Picnic**
★ Ala Moana Beach Park, *1200 Ala Moana Blvd., Honolulu.* (p 163)

Best Place to **"Shoot the Tube"**
★ 'Ehukai Beach Park (Banzai Pipeline), *59–337 Ke Nui Rd., Hale'iwa.* (p 163)

Best **Snorkeling**
★★★ Hanauma Bay Nature Preserve, *7455 Kalaniana'ole Hwy., Honolulu.* (p 164)

Best Place to **Kayak**
★★ Ahupua'a 'O Kahana State Park, *52–222 Kamehameha Hwy., Ka'a'wa.* (p 174)

Best **Windsurfing**
★★★ Kailua Beach, *450 Kawailoa Rd., Kailua.* (p 164)

Best for **Kids**
★ Ko Olina Lagoons, *Ali'inui Dr., Kapolei.* (p 164)

Best **Scenic Beach Park**
★★ Kualoa Regional Park, *49–479 Kamehameha Hwy., Kane'ohe.* (p 165)

Best for **Swimming**
★★ Lanikai Beach, *Mokulua Dr., Kailua.* (p 165)

Best for **Expert Body Surfing**
★ Makapu'u Beach Park, *41–095 Kalaniana'ole Hwy., Waimanalo.* (p 166)

Best **Secluded Beach**
★★ Malaekahana State Recreation Area, *56-020 Kamehameha Hwy., La'ie.* (p 167)

Best **Diving**
★ Pupukea Beach Park, *59–727 Kamehameha Hwy., Pupukea.* (p 167)

Best Beach for **Watching Bodyboarders**
★ Sandy Beach, *8801 Kalaniana'ole Hwy., Honolulu.* (p 168)

Best for **People-Watching**
★★ Sunset Beach Park, *59–100 Kamehameha Hwy., Hale'iwa.* (p 169)

Best for **Sunbathing & Partying**
★★★ Waikiki Beach, *from Ala Wai Yacht Harbor to Kapi'olani Park, Waikiki.* (p 169)

Best for **Big-Wave Watching**
★★★ Waimea Bay Beach Park, *61–031 Kamehameha Hwy., Hale'iwa.* (p 170)

Ala Moana Beach Park has shady lawns, a lagoon, and picnic tables.

O'ahu Beaches A to Z

★ Ala Moana Beach Park

HONOLULU   The gold-sand Ala Moana ("by the sea") stretches for more than a mile along Honolulu's coast between downtown and Waikiki. This 76-acre (31-ha) mid-town beach park, with spreading lawns shaded by banyans and palms, is one of the island's most popular playgrounds, with its own lagoon, yacht harbor, tennis courts, music pavilion, picnic tables, and plenty of wide-open green spaces. The water is calm almost year-round, protected by black lava rocks set offshore. There's a large parking lot as well as metered street parking. *1200 Ala Moana Blvd. (btw. Kamake'e St. & Atkinson Dr.).*

Hanauma Bay is popular for snorkeling and scuba-diving.

★ 'Ehukai Beach Park NORTH

SHORE   There are three separate areas here, but because the sandy beach is continuous, most people think of it as one beach park. Located near Pupukea, **'Ehukai Beach Park** is 1 acre (.4 ha) of grass with a parking lot, great for winter surfing and summer swimming. **Pipeline** is about 100 yards (91m) to the left of 'Ehukai. When the winter surf rolls in and hits the shallow coral shelf, the waves that quickly form are steep—so steep, in fact, that the crest of the wave falls forward, forming a near-perfect tube, or "pipeline." Just west of Pipeline is the area surfers call **"Banzai Beach."** The Japanese word *banzai* means "10,000 years"; it's given as a toast or as a battle charge, meaning "go for it." In the late 1950s,

Pupukea.

filmmaker Bruce Brown was shooting one of the first surf movies ever made, *Surf Safari*, when he saw a bodysurfer ride a huge wave. Brown yelled, "Banzai!" and the name stuck. In the winter, this is a very popular beach with surfers and surf fans. *Access via 'Ehukai Beach Park, 59–337 Ke Nui Rd. (off Kamehameha Hwy.), Pupukea.*

Words of Warning

Wherever you are on O'ahu, remember that you're in an urban area. Never leave valuables in your car. Thefts do occur at O'ahu's beaches, and locked cars are not a deterrent. Also, alcohol and smoking are prohibited at all public beaches.

★★★ Hanauma Bay Nature Preserve KOKO HEAD

One of the most popular attractions on the island, the small, curved, 2,000-foot (610m) gold-sand beach at this preserve is not the draw as much as the bay's shallow shoreline water and abundant marine life; the deeper water outside the bay is great for scuba diving. It's a marine conservation district; don't touch any marine life, stand on the living coral reef, or feed the fish here (or anywhere else in the state, really). Before walking or taking the free tram down to the bay, visitors are required to watch a 9-minute video about reef safety in the education center's theater. Online paid reservations ($25 ages 13 and older, free for younger) are essentially required, as only a handful of walk-up entries are reserved for those without Internet access; they're available up to 48 hours in advance. Parking costs another $3, cash only, paid in person. Facilities include restrooms, lifeguards, picnic tables, and food concessions. *7455 Kalaniana'ole Hwy. (at Hanauma Bay Rd.). www.honolulu.gov/parkshbay/home.html. Closed Mon–Tues.*

Open 6:45am–4pm (last entry 1:30pm, beach cleared at 3:30pm).

★★ Kahana Bay (Ahupua'a o Kahana State Park) WINDWARD

This white-sand, crescent-shaped beach is backed by a huge, jungle-cloaked valley with dramatic, jagged cliffs and is protected by ironwood and kamani trees. The bay's calm water and shallow, sandy bottom make it a safe swimming area for children. The surrounding park has picnic areas, camping, and hiking trails. The wide sand-bottom channel that runs through the park and out to Kahana Bay is one of the largest on O'ahu, perfect for kayakers, who can also head inland via Kahana Stream. *52–222 Kamehameha Hwy., Kahana.*

★★★ Kailua Beach WINDWARD

Windward O'ahu's premier beach is a 2-mile-long (3.2km), wide golden strand with dunes, palm trees, panoramic views, and offshore islets that are home to seabirds. The swimming is excellent, and the warm, azure waters are usually decorated with bright sails; this is O'ahu's premier windsurfing beach as well. It's also a favorite spot to sail catamarans, bodysurf the gentle waves, or paddle a kayak. Water conditions are quite safe, especially at the mouth of Ka'elepulu Stream, where toddlers play in the freshwater shallows at the middle of the beach park. Facilities include lifeguards, picnic tables, barbecues, restrooms, a volleyball court, a public boat ramp, and free parking. *450 Kawailoa Rd., Kailua.*

★ Ko Olina Lagoons LEEWARD

The developer of the 640-acre (259-ha) Ko Olina Resort created four golden sand lagoons to make the rocky shoreline more attractive and accessible. (The resort also offers access to the smaller, natural lagoons in front of Lanikuhonua Cultural Institute and the Paradise

Windsurfing at Kailua Beach.

Cove Luau, with more limited parking.) The artificial lagoons—three with adjacent hotels or condos—offer calm, shallow waters and a powdery beach bordered by a broad, grassy lawn. No lifeguards are present, but the generally tranquil waters are great for swimming, are perfect for kids, and offer some snorkeling opportunities around the boulders at the ocean entrance, roped off for safety. Each lagoon has restrooms and showers; arrive early for parking, especially on weekends (Lagoon 4, next to the Ko Olina Marina, has the most spaces). The resort prohibits beach umbrellas, Frisbees, fishing, or ball-playing, among other restrictions; see koolina.com/destination/lagoons. *Off Ali'inui Dr. (btw. Olani & Mauloa places), Ko Olina Resort, Kapolei.*

★★ Kualoa Regional Park
WINDWARD This 150-acre (61-ha) coconut palm–fringed peninsula is one of the largest and most scenic on the Windward Side. The park has a broad lawn and a long, narrow, cream-colored beach ideal for swimming, walking, beachcombing, kite flying, or sunbathing; picnic and camping areas are available.

The waters are shallow and safe for swimming year-round, and at low tide, you can swim or wade out to the islet of Mokoli'i (formerly nicknamed "Chinaman's Hat"), but be aware of possible jellyfish. There's a small sandy beach and steep trail; be aware of stiff currents on the islet's ocean side. *49–600 Kamehameha Hwy., Kualoa.*

★★ Lanikai Beach WINDWARD
One of Hawai'i's best spots for swimming, gold-sand Lanikai's crystal-clear lagoon is like a giant saltwater swimming pool. The beach is a mile (1.6km) long and very thin in places, but the sand is soft, and onshore trade winds make this an excellent place for sailing and windsurfing. Kayakers often paddle out to the two tiny offshore Mokulua islands, which are seabird sanctuaries. Access is only via marked paths between private residences. Arrive early in the morning to find parking and enjoy the sun; the Ko'olau Mountains block the afternoon rays. *Mokulua Dr., Kailua.*

★★★ Makaha Beach Park
LEEWARD When surf's up here, it's spectacular: Monstrous waves

Calm summer waters at Makaha Beach give way to big waves in the winter.

Makapu'u Beach Park.

pound the beach from October to April. Nearly a mile (1.6km) long, this half-moon gold-sand beach is tucked between 231-foot (70m) Lahilahi Point, which locals call Black Rock, and Kepuhi Point, a toe of the Wai'anae mountain range. Summer is the best time for swimming. Children hug the shore on the north side of the beach, near the lifeguard stand, while surfers dodge the rocks and divers seek an offshore channel full of big fish. It's a local favorite, so please be gracious in sharing the beach. Facilities include restrooms, lifeguards, and parking. *84–369 Farrington Hwy. (near Kili Dr.), Waianae.*

★ **Makapu'u Beach Park** WIND-WARD Hawaii's most famous bodysurfing beach is a beautiful 1,000-foot-long (305m) gold-sand beach cupped in stark black cliffs. Summertime waters are perfect for swimming and diving, but in winter, Makapu'u is hit with big, pounding waves that are ideal for expert bodysurfers. Small boards—no longer than 3 feet (.9m) and without skeg (bottom fin)—are permitted; regular board surfing is banned. Facilities include restrooms, lifeguards, barbecue grills, picnic tables, and parking. *41–095 Kalaniana'ole Hwy. (across the street from Sea Life Park), Waimanalo.*

Staying Safe in the Water

Whether from existing health concerns or unfamiliarity with the ocean and its changing conditions, every year visitors drown or become in need of rescue. For daily surf conditions and general advisories, check hawaiibeachsafety.com before heading out. Then keep these tips in mind when swimming in Hawaii's gorgeous waters:

Never swim alone.

Always supervise children in the water.

Always swim at beaches with lifeguards.

Know your limits—don't swim out farther than you know you can swim back.

Novice snorkelers should practice in a pool first.

Read the posted warning signs before you enter the water.

Call a lifeguard or 911 if you see someone in distress.

★★ Malaekahana State Recreation Area

NORTH SHORE   This almost mile-long white-sand crescent lives up to just about everyone's image of the perfect Hawaiian beach: It's excellent for swimming, and at low tide you can wade offshore to Goat Island (*Mokuauia*), a sanctuary for seabirds and turtles (no goats). Facilities include restrooms, barbecue grills, picnic tables, outdoor showers, and parking. *Kamehameha Hwy. 83 (2 miles/3.2km north of the Polynesian Cultural Center).*

★ Pounders Beach (La'ie Beach Park)

NORTH SHORE The beach park that includes Pounders, named for its strong shorebreak, extends a quarter-mile (.4km) between two points, is easily accessed from the highway and very popular on weekends. At the west end of the beach, the waters usually are calm and safe for swimming (during May–Sept). However, at the opposite end, near the limestone cliffs, the shorebreak can be dangerous for inexperienced

The roiling waves of Sandy Beach at Koko Head are for experienced bodysurfers only.

bodysurfers; the bottom drops off abruptly, causing rip currents. Go on a weekday morning to have the beach to yourself. *Kamehameha Hwy. (about ½ mile/.8km south of Polynesian Cultural Center), La'ie.*

★ Pupukea Beach Park

NORTH SHORE   This 80-acre (32-ha) beach park, very popular for snorkeling

Pupukea Beach Park, a Marine Life Conservation District.

Protecting Your Skin and the Reef

Hawai'i's white population has one of the highest incidences of malignant melanoma (deadly skin cancer) in the world. And nobody is completely safe from the sun's harmful rays: All skin types can burn, with children and infants especially vulnerable. But scientists have found several chemicals found in many sunscreens are harmful to coral reefs and their marine life. Hawai'i has already banned sales of sunscreen with two such ingredients, oxybenzone and octinoxate, and lawmakers are hoping to ban two more, avobenzone and octocrylene. So only bring or buy mineral-based sunscreens, i.e., zinc oxide or titanium dioxide. With tinted, powdered, and sprayable versions now available, you won't sport a thick patch of white paste. Other tips:

- **Use mineral sunscreen with high SPF ratings and reapply often.** Start with SPF 30 at a minimum, apply it liberally and reapply every 2 hours—more if you've been perspiring a lot.
- **Wear a hat and sunglasses on land and rash guards in water.** The hat should have a brim all the way around to cover not only your face but also the sensitive back of your neck. Make sure your sunglasses have UV filters. You won't have to use so much sunscreen swimming or snorkeling if you don a lightweight, long-sleeved rash guard.
- **If it's too late.** The best remedy for a sunburn is to stay out of the sun until all the redness is gone. Aloe vera, cool compresses, cold baths, and anesthetic benzocaine also help with the pain of sunburn.

and diving, is a Marine Life Conservation District. Locals divide the area into two: **Shark's Cove** (which is *not* named for an abundance of sharks), great for snorkeling and, outside the cove, good diving; and at the southern end, **Three Tables** (named for the three flat sections of reef visible at low tide), also great for snorkeling, where the water is about 15 feet (4.6m) deep, and diving outside the tables, where the water is 30 to 45 feet (9.1–14m) deep. It's packed May to October, when swimming, diving, and snorkeling are best; the water is usually calm, but watch out for surges. In the winter, when currents form and waves roll in, this area is very dangerous, even in the tide pools, and also much less crowded. No lifeguards. *59–727 Kamehameha Hwy., Pupukea.*

★ **Sandy Beach** KOKO HEAD Sandy Beach is one of the best bodysurfing beaches on O'ahu. It's also one of the most dangerous. The 1,200-foot-long (366m) goldsand beach is pounded by wild waves and haunted by a dangerous shore break and strong backwash; the experienced bodysurfers make wave riding look easy, but it's best just to watch the daredevils risking their necks. Weak swimmers and children should definitely stay out of the water here—Sandy Beach's heroic lifeguards make more rescues in a year than at any other beach on O'ahu. Lifeguards post flags to alert beachgoers to the day's surf: Green means safe, yellow means caution, and red indicates very dangerous water conditions; always check the flags before heading in. Facilities include restrooms and parking. Go weekdays to avoid the crowds and weekends to catch the bodysurfers in action. *8800 Kalaniana'ole Hwy. (about 2 miles/3.2km east of Hanauma Bay), Honolulu.*

★★ Sunset Beach Park NORTH SHORE

Surfers around the world know this famous site for its spectacular winter surf—the huge thundering waves can reach 15 to 20 feet (4.5–6m). During the winter surf season (Oct–Apr), swimming is very dangerous here, due to the powerful rip currents. The only safe time to swim is during the calm summer months. The wide sandy beach is a great place to people-watch, but don't go too close to the water when the lifeguards have posted the red warning flags. Parking and

Windsurfing at Kailua Beach.

restrooms are across the highway in Sunset Beach Support Park. *59–100 Kamehameha Hwy. (near Paumalu Place), Hale'iwa.*

★★★ Waikiki Beach WAIKIKI

No beach anywhere is so widely known or so universally sought after as this narrow, 1½-mile-long (2.4km) crescent of

Waikiki Beach attracts nearly 5 million visitors each year.

sand (now imported from Moloka'i or dredged from offshore) at the foot of a string of high-rise hotels. Home to the world's longest-running beach party, Waikiki attracts nearly 5 million visitors a year from every corner of the planet. Waikiki is actually a string of beaches that extends from **Sans Souci/Kaimana Beach** near Diamond Head to the east, to **Duke Kahanamoku Beach,** in front of the Hilton Hawaiian Village Beach Resort & Spa to the west. Great stretches along Waikiki include **Kuhio Beach,** next to the Westin Moana Surfrider, which provides the quickest access to the Waikiki shoreline; the stretch in front of the Royal Hawaiian Hotel known as **Grey's Beach,** which is

canted so that it catches the rays perfectly; and **Sans Souci (Kaimana Beach),** the small, popular beach in front of Kaimana Beach Hotel that's locally known as "Dig Me" Beach because of all the gorgeous bods strutting their stuff here. Waikiki is fabulous for swimming, board and bodysurfing, outrigger canoeing, diving, sailing, snorkeling, and pole fishing. Every imaginable type of marine equipment is available for rent here. Facilities include showers, lifeguards, restrooms, grills, picnic tables, and pavilions at the **Queen's Surf** end of the beach (at Kapi'olani Park). *From Ala Wai Yacht Harbor to Kapi'olani Park.*

★★★ Waimea Bay Beach Park

NORTH SHORE   This deep, sandy bowl has gentle summer waves that are excellent for swimming, snorkeling, and bodysurfing. To one side of the bay is a huge rock that local kids like to climb up and dive from. The scene is much different in winter, when waves pound the narrow bay, sometimes rising to 50 feet (15m) high. When the surf's really up, very strong currents and shore breaks sweep the bay—and it seems like everyone on O'ahu drives out to Waimea to get a look at the monster waves and those who ride them; to avoid the crowds, go on weekdays. Facilities include lifeguards, restrooms, showers, parking, and nearby restaurants and shops in Hale'iwa town. *61–031 Kamehameha Hwy., Hale'iwa.* ●

Waimea Bay Beach Park.

The Great Outdoors

O'ahu's Best Hiking & Camping

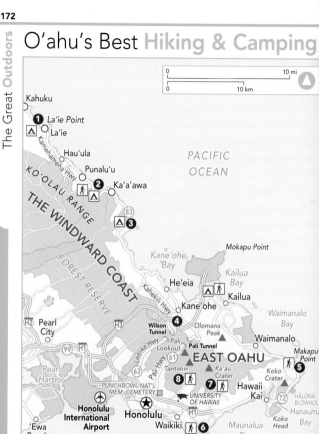

0   10 mi
0   10 km

Kahuku

1 *La'ie Point*

🏕 La'ie

Hau'ula

Punalu'u

🏕🥾 **2** Ka'a'awa

🏕 **3**

Kamehameha Hwy.

KO'OLAU RANGE

THE WINDWARD COAST

FOREST RESERVE

PACIFIC OCEAN

Mokapu Point

Kane'ohe Bay

Kailua Bay

He'eia

🏕🥾 Kailua

Kanehili Hwy.

Kane'ohe **4**

Waimanalo Bay

Pearl City

H2

H3

99

Kamehameha Hwy.

Likelike Hwy.

Wilson Tunnel

Pali Lookout

Olomana Peak

Pali Tunnel

EAST OAHU

Waimanalo

Makapu Point

🥾 **5**

Pearl Harbor

63

61

Pali Hwy.

Tantalus

8 🥾

Ka'au Crater

7 🥾

Hawaii Kai

Koko Crater

PUNCHBOWL NAT'L MEM. CEMETERY

UNIVERSITY OF HAWAII

Koko Head

72

HĀLONA BLOWHOLE

Honolulu International Airport

⭐ **Honolulu**

H1

Maunalua Bay

Hanauma Bay

'Ewa Beach

Waikiki

🥾 **6**

Diamond Head

Kaiwi Channel

Mamala Bay

Hiking 🥾

Ahupua'a 'O Kahana State Park **2**

Diamond Head Crater **6**

Honolulu Mauka Trails **8**

Ho'omaluhia Botanical Gardens **4**

Makapu'u Lighthouse Trail **5**

Manoa Falls Trail **7**

Camping 🏕

Ahupua'a 'O Kahana State Park **2**

Ho'omaluhia Botanical Gardens **4**

Kualoa Regional Park **3**

Malaekahana State Recreation Area **1**

Previous page: Surfing in O'ahu.

On O'ahu you can camp by the ocean, hike in a tropical rainforest, and take in scenic views that will imprint themselves on your memory forever. If you plan to camp, bring your own gear or rent through Hawai'i Camp Life (hawaiicamplife.com), one of very few places on the island that rents camping equipment. Enter the dates you're interested in (minimum 24 hours in advance) and the website will show you the gear available for tent or car camping. You'll then book pickup and drop-off times with owner Allysa Lapine at a location about 20 minutes from the airport. If you plan to go hiking, take plenty of water, sun protection, and a fully charged smartphone—good for photos as well as emergency calls.

★★★ Diamond Head State Monument

Hiking This is a short but steep walk to the summit of the 750-foot (229m) volcanic cone, O'ahu's most famous landmark, with a reward of a 360-degree view of the island. The 1.4-mile (2.3km) round-trip takes about 1½ hours. The entry fee is $5 for visitors and parking is $10, with reservations required for both. You might want to put all your gear in a pack to leave your hands free for the climb. Reserve an early slot, preferably just after the 6am opening, before the midday sun starts beating down. Gates lock at 6pm; the last hiker is allowed in at 4pm (daily). *Monsarrat & 18th aves. gostateparks. hawaii.gov/diamondhead. Daily 6am–6pm. Fee $5 per person and $10 per car, by reservation only.*

Safety Tip

When planning sunset activities, be aware that Hawai'i, like other places close to the equator, has a very short (25 min.) twilight period after the sun sets. After that, it's dark. If you hike out to watch the sunset, be sure you can make it back quickly, or take a flashlight.

★ Ho'omaluhia Botanical Gardens

Hiking & Camping This relatively unknown windward-side

Downtown Honolulu and Waikiki from the rim of Diamond Head Crater.

camping area, outside Kane'ohe, is a real find. *Ho'omaluhia* means "peace and tranquility," an apt description for this 400-acre (162-ha) lush botanical garden. Standing among the rare plants, with craggy cliffs in the background, it's hard to believe you're just a half-hour from downtown Honolulu. A 32-acre (13-ha) lake sits in the middle of the scenic park (no swimming or boating is allowed), and there are numerous hiking trails. Facilities include three tent-camp areas with 28 sites total, restrooms, cold showers, picnic tables, grills, and water. Camping permits are $32, good for up to 10 people for up to 3 nights (Fri–Sun only); they're issued online at camping.honolulu.gov. You can obtain a permit up to two Fridays in advance. *Ho'omaluhia Botanical Gardens, 45–680 Luluku Rd. (at Kamehameha Hwy.), Kane'ohe. https:// www.honolulu.gov/parks/hbg.*

Ahupua'a 'O Kahana State Park.

html?id=569:ho. ☎ 808/233-7323. Daily 9am–4pm. Call ahead for information on guided hikes.

★★ Ahupua'a 'O Kahana State Park

Camping   Under jungle cliffs, with a beautiful, gold-sand crescent beach framed by casuarina trees, this 5,300-acre state park is close to the road but still a place of beauty, as well as a "living park" where 31 families maintain and share Hawaiian traditions. You can swim in Kahana Bay, bodysurf, fish, hike, picnic, help restore a fishpond, or just sit and listen to the trade winds whistle through the beach pines. Both tent and vehicle camping are allowed, but permits must be obtained online from camping.ehawaii.gov. There is a $30 fee per campsite per night, Friday through Tuesday nights only. Facilities include restrooms, picnic tables, drinking water, public phones, and a boat-launching ramp.

Hiking   Spectacular views of this verdant valley and a few swimming holes are the rewards of the 5-mile (8km) Nakoa loop trail above the beach. The downsides to this 2- to 3-hour, often muddy adventure are mosquitoes (clouds of them) and some thrashing about in dense forest along the not-always-marked trail. Follow the main road up the valley to the trailhead; an easier 1-mile loop with Kahana Bay views starts at the park's Orientation Center. *52–222 Kamehameha Hwy. (Hwy. 83), Kahana. dlnr.hawaii.gov/dsp/parks/oahu/ahupuaa-o-kahana-state-park. Open during daylight hours only. Bus: 55.*

★★ Kualoa Regional Park

Camping   Located on a peninsula in Kane'ohe Bay, this park has a spectacular setting right on a gold-sand beach, with a great view of Mokoli'i Island. Facilities include restrooms, showers, picnic tables, drinking fountains, and a public phone. One set of 7 campsites

Camping Permits

You must get a permit for all camping in all parks on O'ahu. For the 17 Honolulu County Parks with campsites, such as Kualoa Regional Park, contact Honolulu Department of Parks and Recreation (camping.honolulu.gov; ☎ **808/523-4525**) for information and permits. County parks charge $32 for a 3-day permit and $52 for a 5-day permit. For state parks, permits cost $30 for nonresidents, per campsite per night. Permits are limited to 5 nights and can only be obtained at camping.ehawaii.gov/camping. County and state parks do not allow camping Wednesdays or Thursdays.

Hiking to Makapu'u Point Lighthouse.

closes during summer for park programs, but the other set of 14, next to scenic fishponds, are open year-round, with permits required for both. They cost $52 for stays of up to 5 days (Fri–Tues only) for up to 10 people. *49–479 Kamehameha Hwy., across from Mokoli'i Island (btw. Waikane & Ka'a'awa). camping. honolulu.gov/campsites/search?park_id=6 and https://camping.honolulu. gov/campsites/search?park_id=7.*

★ Makapu'u Lighthouse Trail

Hiking This easy 45-minute (one-way) hike winds around the 646-foot-high (197m) sea bluff overlooking the red-roofed lighthouse, built in 1909. Although the beacon is off limits, the views of Koko Head, the Windward Coast, blue Pacific and islets are rewarding. Look for spouting whales in winter. *Kalaniana'ole Hwy. (½ mile/.8km down the road from the Hawai'i Kai Golf Course), past Sandy Beach. dlnr. hawaii.gov/dsp/hiking/oahu/ makapuu-point-lighthouse-trail.*

Water Safety

Water might be everywhere in Hawai'i, but it likely isn't safe to drink. Stream water is often contaminated with leptospirosis bacteria, which produce flulike symptoms and can be fatal. So boil your drinking water, or, if boiling isn't an option, use tablets with tetraglycine hydroperiodide; portable water filters will not prevent leptospirosis.

★★ Honolulu Mauka Trails

Hiking The slopes of Makiki Valley are the starting place for some of O'ahu's best hiking trails, often less than a mile (1.6km) in length. The Makiki Valley, Maunalaha, Kanealole, Moleka and Ualaka'a and Nahuina trails all converge in this area, featuring breathtaking views, historic remains, and incredible vegetation. Download a trail map at dlnr.hawaii.gov/recreation/nah/oahu or stop by the Division of Forestry and Wildlife branch office on Makiki Heights Drive for information. *2135 Makiki Heights Dr. ☎ 808/973-9778. Mon–Fri 7:45am–4:30pm.*

★★★ Malaekahana State Recreation Area

Camping A mile-long (1.6km) gold-sand beach with woods offers 37 tent campsites. Permits are required; they're available at camping.ehawaii.gov for $30 per night for up to 10 persons, Friday through Tuesday nights. Facilities include picnic tables, restrooms, showers, sinks, drinking water, and a phone. *Kamehameha Hwy 83 (btw. La'ie & Kahuku). dlnr.hawaii.gov/ dsp/parks/oahu/malaekahana-state-recreation-area. ☎ 808/293-1736.*

★★ Manoa Falls Trail

Hiking This easy, .8-mile (1.3km) hike (one-way) is terrific for families; it takes less than an hour to reach idyllic Manoa Falls. The often-muddy trail follows Waihi Stream and meanders through the forest reserve past guavas, mountain apples, and wild ginger. The forest is moist and humid and is inhabited by giant bloodthirsty mosquitoes, so bring repellent. If it has rained recently, stay on the trail and step carefully, as it can be very slippery. The trail head is marked by a footbridge. *End of Manoa Rd., past Lyon Arboretum. hawaiitrails.hawaii.gov/ trails/#/trail/manoa-falls-trail/225.*

O'ahu's Best Golf Courses

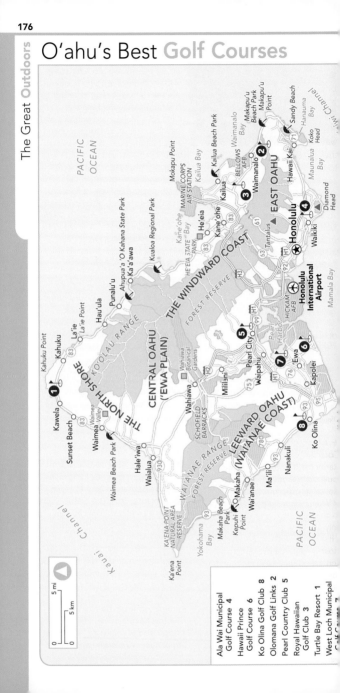

Ala Wai Municipal Golf Course **4**

Hawaii Prince Golf Course **6**

Ko Olina Golf Club **8**

Olomana Golf Links **2**

Pearl Country Club **5**

Royal Hawaiian Golf Club **3**

Turtle Bay Resort **1**

West Loch Municipal

'ahu offers 40 golf courses, ranging from bare-bones municipal links to exclusive country club courses with membership
fees of up to six figures a year. Below are the best of a great
bunch. As you play O'ahu's courses, you'll come to know that the
windward courses play much differently than the leeward courses.
On the windward side, the prevailing winds blow from the ocean to
shore, and the grain direction of the greens tends to run the same
way—from the ocean to the mountains. Leeward golf courses have
the opposite tendency: The winds usually blow from the mountains
to the ocean, with the grain direction of the greens corresponding.

Olomana Golf Links.

★ Ala Wai Municipal Golf
Course This is O'ahu's most popular course. Duffers play some 500
rounds a day on this 18-hole municipal course, within walking distance
of Waikiki's hotels. It is a challenge
to get a tee time (you can book
only 3 days in advance). Ala Wai has
a flat layout and is less windy than
most O'ahu courses, but pay attention: Some holes are not as easy as
you may think. **Note:** Club and pull
cart rentals may be limited if the
pro shop remains under construction. *404 Kapahulu Ave., Waikiki.
www.honolulu.gov/des/golf/alawai.
html.* ☎ *808/207-6856 (reservations), (808) 733-7387 (office). Greens
fees $86, twilight rate $43.*

★★ Hawaii Prince Golf Club
Designed by Arnold Palmer and Ed
Seay, this 27-hole course affiliated
with the Prince Waikiki hotel sits on
270 acres in Honolulu's sunny western suburb of Ewa Beach. Ten lakes
dot its long fairways framed by
Wai'anae Mountain views, while its
three interchangeable nines make
it suitable for all skill levels. A new
driving range and Sunday brunch at
its Bird of Paradise restaurant are
other reasons to make the drive
from Waikiki. *91-1200 Fort Weaver
Rd., Ewa Beach. www.hawaiiprince
golf.com.* ☎ *808/944-4567. Greens
fees $152.*

★★★ Ko Olina Golf Club

Golf Digest once named this one of "America's Top 75 Resort Courses." The Ted Robinson–designed course (6,867-yard/6,279m, par 72) has rolling fairways and elevated tee and water features. The signature hole—the 12th, a par 3—has an elevated tee that sits on a rock garden with a cascading waterfall. At the 18th hole, water's all around—seven pools begin on the right side of the fairway, sloping down to a lake. Book in advance; this course is crowded all the time. Facilities include a driving range, locker rooms, a Jacuzzi, steam rooms, and a restaurant and bar. Lessons are available. *92–1220 Ali'inui Dr., Kapolei. www.koolinagolf.com.* ☎ *808/676-5300. Greens fees (include cart) $245 ($215 for Ko Olina Resort guests), twilight rates $180. Golf attire (no T-shirts, tank tops, or cutoffs) required. $40 roundtrip shuttle from Waikiki or Kahala available with 24-hr. advance booking.*

★★ Olomana Golf Links

This par-72, 6,326-yard (5,784m) course is popular with locals and visitors alike, with gorgeous views of the Ko'olau Mountains, including Olomana Peak. The course starts off a bit hilly on the front 9 but flattens out by the back 9, where there are some tricky water hazards; it's also very, very green, thanks to frequent if brief passing showers. You can spot the regular players here—they all carry umbrellas. Facilities include a driving range with beer garden, practice greens, club rental, pro shop, and restaurant. *41–1801 Kalaniana'ole Hwy., Waimanalo. www.olomanalinks.com.* ☎ *808/259-7926. Greens fees $90–$130, twilight $70–$90.*

★★ Pearl Country Club

Looking for a challenge? Sure, the 6,230-yard (5,697m), par-72 course looks harmless enough, and the views of Pearl Harbor and the USS *Arizona* Memorial are gorgeous, but around the 5th hole, you'll start to see what you're in for: water hazards, forest, and doglegs that allow only a small margin of error between the tee and the steep out-of-bounds hillside. O'ahu residents can't get enough of it, so don't even try to get a tee time on weekends. Facilities include a driving range, practice greens, pro shop, and restaurant. *98–535 Kaonohi St., Aiea. www.pearlcc.com.* ☎ *808/487-3802. Greens fees $160, twilight $95.*

★★ Royal Hawaiian Golf Club

Here's another gorgeous course, often referred to as the Jurassic Park of golf courses, both for the breathtaking scenery and because it's not for the faint hearted. Designed by Perry and Pete Dye

Hole 13 at Pearl Country Club, with view of Pearl Harbor.

Turtle Bay Resort, home to two top golf courses.

1993, it was redeveloped two decades later by hall-of-fame golfer Greg Norman. Switchback trails lead you up to wide vistas that help take the sting out of losing so many balls. Facilities include a pro shop, driving range (closed at press time), putting and chipping greens, and restaurant. *770 Auloa Rd., Kailua. www.royalhawaiiangc.com.* ☎ *808/262-2139. Greens fees $165.*

★★★ **Turtle Bay Resort** This North Shore resort is home to two of Hawai'i's top golf courses: the 18-hole Arnold Palmer Course, designed by Arnold Palmer and Ed Seay, and the par-71, 6,200-yard (5,669m) George Fazio Course, temporarily closed at press time. Palmer's is the more challenging, with the front 9 playing like a British Isles course (rolling terrain, only a few trees, and lots of wind). The back 9 has narrower, tree-lined fairways and water. Fazio is a more forgiving course, without all the water hazards and bunkers. Facilities

include a pro shop, driving range, putting and chipping green, and restaurant. Weekdays are best for tee times. *57–049 Kamehameha Hwy., Kahuku. www.turtlebayresort. com/things-to-do/golf.* ☎ *808/293-8574. Greens fees $179 resort guests, $209 visitors, twilight $139.*

★ **West Loch Municipal Golf Course** This par-72, 6,615-yard (6,049m) course located just 30 minutes from Waikiki, in Ewa Beach, offers golfers a challenge at bargain rates. The difficulties on this unusual municipal course, designed by Robin Nelson and Rodney Wright, are water (lots of hazards), constant trade winds, and narrow fairways. Facilities include a driving range and practice greens, but currently no pro shop or rentals. *91–1126 Okupe St., Ewa Beach. www. honolulu.gov/des/golf/westloch.html.* ☎ *808/207-6720 (reservations), 808/675-6076 (office). Greens fees $86 for 18 holes, twilight $43 for 9 holes.*

Adventures on & Above Land

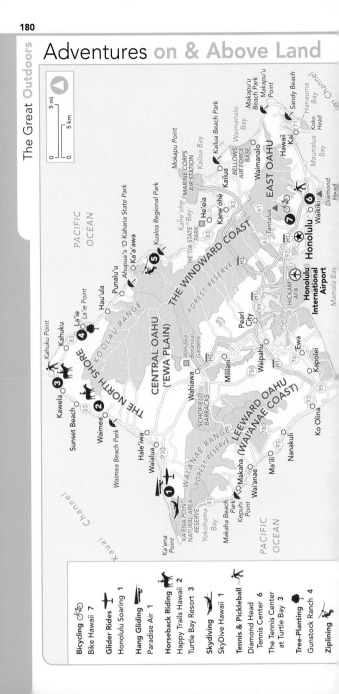

Bicycling 🚲
Bike Hawaii 7

Glider Rides ✈
Honolulu Soaring 1

Hang Gliding 🪂
Paradise Air 1

Horseback Riding 🐎
Happy Trails Hawaii 2
Turtle Bay Resort 3

Skydiving 🪂
SkyDive Hawaii 1

Tennis & Pickleball 🎾
Diamond Head
Tennis Center 6
The Tennis Center
at Turtle Bay 3

Tree-Planting 🌳
Gunstock Ranch 4

Ziplining 🪢

O'ahu isn't just sparkling ocean water and rainbow-colored fish; it's also the land of adventure—you can cycle through rainforest; soar through the air in a glider; gallop by a deserted sandy beach; ride a zipline through a spectacular valley; or go off-roading on an eco-tour that includes planting native trees.

Aerial Activities

Formerly known as Dillingham Airfield, Kawaihapai Airfield on the rural North Shore is the launchpad for all sorts of adventures in the air. With the breathtaking **glider rides** from **Honolulu Soaring** (www.honolulusoaring.com; ☎ **808/637-0207**), a plane tows you to the right altitude before your captain and you soar buoyed by thermals; rides start at $85 for 10 minutes. You can also try **hang gliding** with **Paradise Air** (www.paradiseairhawaii.com; ☎ **808/497-6033**); after instruction, tandem rides begin at $225 for 30 minutes in the air. Daredevils will enjoy **parachuting,** strapped to an instructor who actually pulls the ripcord, with **SkyDive Hawaii** (www.skydivehawaii.com; ☎ **808/637-9700**); online prices start at $270 for a jump from 12,000 feet (3,658m), including a $20 fuel surcharge. *Kawaihapai (Dillingham) Airfield, 69-415 Farrington Hwy., Waialua.*

Bicycling

Whether you prefer to coast downhill on a comfy cruiser bike or use an electric-assisted mountain bike to head uphill, the friendly nature guides at **Bike Hawaii** will lead you through lush rainforest on paved roads with scenic viewpoints. The 5-mile, 3-hour, family-friendly Downhill Bike Adventure can be combined with a guided hike to Manoa Falls or snorkeling adventure; round-trip shuttle from Kahala, Waikiki and the Aloha Tower is included. The 10-mile E-Bike Tour, for ages 14 and older, harnesses the power of the 250-watt motor (and 500-watt battery) to climb 1,600 feet on quiet roads in the forested mountains above Honolulu; an optional shuttle from Waikiki costs $25. *www.bikehawaii.com.* ☎ *808/734-4214. Downhill ride $81 adults, children 14 & under $62; fee includes cruiser bike, van transportation, helmet, & guide. E-bike ride*

Hang gliding with Paradise Air.

Bike tour with Bike Hawaii.

$115 ages 14 and older; fee includes e-bike, helmet, & guide.

Horseback Riding

★ **Happy Trails Hawaii** NORTH SHORE   This small operation welcomes families (kids may be as young as 6) on these guided trail rides on a hilltop above Pupukea Beach and overlooking Waimea Valley, on the North Shore. *59–231 Pupukea Rd. www.happytrailshawaii. com.* ☎ *808/638-RIDE (7433). From $109 for 1½-hr. rides.*

★★ **Turtle Bay Resort** NORTH SHORE   Riders ages 7 and up can trot along a deserted North Shore beach with spectacular ocean views and through a forest of ironwood trees or take a romantic evening ride at sunset with your sweetheart. *57–091 Kamehameha Hwy., Kahuku. www.turtlebayresort.com.* ☎ *808/293-8811. Trail ride (45 min.) $95; sunset ride (75 min.) $145.*

Tennis & Pickleball

Free Courts   O'ahu has 202 free public tennis courts and 163 pickleball courts (although only 10 or so of the latter are dedicated striped courts with permanent nets). Courts are available on a first-come, first-served basis; playing time is limited

Bike Around Town on a Biki

O'ahu is not the most bike-friendly place, thanks to heavy urban traffic, rural roads with narrow shoulders, and a strong car and truck culture. But the 2017 launch of Biki (gobiki.org), Honolulu's non-profit-managed bike-sharing program, has brought 1,300 bikes, 130 stations, and even a few protected bike lanes to Waikiki and other busy Honolulu locations. Modeled after other systems in cities such as Paris and New York, it requires an email address and is best used via an app. A one-way, 30-minute ride costs $4.50; a pass for 300 minutes, good for up to a year, costs $25. Since Biki users must be 16 years or older, helmets are not required by law, but are highly recommended—in most cases, you'll still be sharing the road. Biki operator Bikeshare Hawai'i (☎ **888/340-2454**) may have helmets available for a $20 donation at its office, 529 Ko'ula St., Honolulu, open weekdays 8am to 5pm.

Glide by the Sea on a Segway

A fun way to tour Waikiki, downtown Honolulu, and the trendy Kaka'ako neighborhood is on a Segway Personal Transporter, one of those two-wheeled machines you stand on while it reads the motion of your body to turn, go forward or reverse. They only take a few minutes to get used to and are a lot of fun. Family-owned **Segway of Hawaii** (www.segwayofhawaii.com; ☎ 808/591-2100), offers tours for ages 10 and up that include a half-hour introduction ($99); 90-minute to 2-hour rides around Kapi'olani Park, historic Honolulu, Magic Island, Kaka'ako's waterfront and vibrant murals, or Waikiki and Diamond Head ($160–$195); and a 3-hour tour from Magic Island to Diamond Head ($249). Feel more comfortable seated? The company also leads several e-bike tours, including 2½-hour rides in Waikiki/Diamond Head or historic Honolulu ($199) and a 2½-hour bike-and-hike to Manoa Falls ($225). Private e-bike tours are available for a $30 per person surcharge.

to 45 minutes if others are waiting. The closest courts of either kind to Waikiki are the **Diamond Head Tennis Center.** *3908 Paki Ave. (across from Kapi'olani Park), Waikiki. For a list of all public tennis courts:* www.honolulu.gov/cms-dpr-menu/site-dpr-sitearticles/44119-tennis-courts.html. *For pickleball courts:* www.honolulu.gov/parks/default/park-locations/182-site-dpr-cat/27199-pickle-ball-courts.html.

Tree-Planting

Gunstock Ranch At this 900-acre North Shore cattle ranch and reforestation project, you can help restore native ecosystem by planting a monarch milo tree, treasured by Hawaiians for its many uses and beautiful blooms. Getting to the planting site is half the fun, via horseback or off-road vehicles on private tours, some of which also reveal the ranch's World War II sites, a hidden cave, horses, and ocean views. *56-250 Kamehameha Hwy., Kahuku.* gunstockranch.com. ☎ *808/341-3995. 2-hr. Off-Road Planters Experience, ages 3 and older, $125 (includes lunch); all-ages 1-hr Planters Experience, $52; 2-hr. Horseback Planters Experience, ages 7 and older, $179 (includes lunch).*

Ziplining

Kualoa Ranch WINDWARD SIDE The backdrop for 200-plus movies and TV shows, including *Jurassic World* and *Lost,* Kualoa Ranch hosts all kinds of tours in stunning Ka'a'awa Valley. The most exhilarating, though, is the 3-hour Jurassic Valley Zipline tour, which includes seven tandem lines, two suspension bridges, and five nature trails. You'll also learn about Hawaiian traditions, flora, and fauna en route. Book well in advance—it's understandably popular. *49-560 Kamehameha Hwy., Kane'ohe.* www.kualoa.com/jurassic-valley-zipline. ☎ *808/237-7321, toll-free 800/231-7321. $180 adults, $140 ages 10–12.*

O'ahu's Best Snorkeling

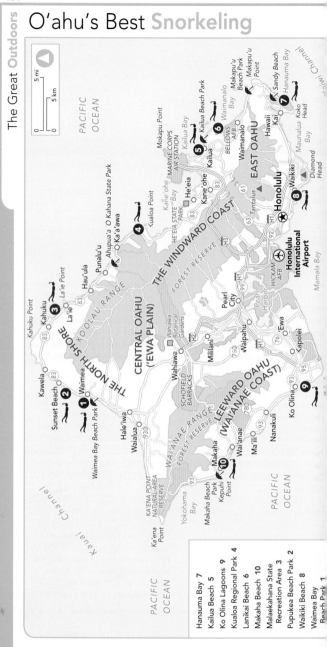

Snorkeling is a huge attraction on O'ahu—just relax as you float over underwater worlds populated with colorful clouds of tropical fish. If you've never snorkeled before, most resorts and excursion boats offer instruction, but it's easy to figure it out for yourself. All you need are a mask, a snorkel, fins, and some basic swimming skills; practice in a pool first if unsure. In many places, all you have to do is wade into the water and look down. Below are O'ahu's best snorkeling beaches.

★★★ Hanauma Bay Nature Preserve KOKO HEAD

One of the most popular attractions on the island, this curved bay in a volcanic crater boasting shallow shoreline water and abundant marine life is a marine conservation district; don't touch any marine life, stand on the living coral reef, or feed the fish here (or anywhere else in the state, really). Before walking or taking the free tram down to the bay, visitors are required to watch a 9-minute video about reef safety in the education center's theater. Online paid reservations ($25 ages 13 and older, free for younger) are essentially required, as only a handful of walk-up entries are reserved for those without Internet access; they're available up to 48 hours in advance. Parking costs another $3, cash only, paid in person. Facilities include restrooms, lifeguards, picnic tables, snorkel gear rentals (pricey at $20), and concessions. *7455 Kalaniana'ole Hwy. (at Hanauma Bay Rd. www.honolulu.gov/parks-hbay/home.html. Closed Mon–Tues. Open 6:45am–4pm (last entry 1:30pm, beach cleared at 3:30pm).*

★★★ Kailua Beach WINDWARD

This 2-mile-long (3.2km) golden strand (with dunes, palm trees, panoramic views, and offshore islets) offers great snorkeling (along with a host of other ocean activities) with safe water conditions most of the year. *Kailua Beach Park, 526 Kawailoa Rd., Kailua.*

★ Ko Olina Lagoons LEEWARD

When the developer of the 640-acre (259-ha) Ko Olina Resort blasted four white-sand lagoons out of the shoreline to make the rocky shoreline more attractive and accessible, he created a great snorkeling area around the boulders at the entrance to each lagoon. The artificial lagoons offer calm, shallow waters and a powdery white-sand beach bordered by a broad, grassy lawn. No lifeguards are present, but the generally tranquil waters are safe. Snorkeling in the shallow, natural lagoons at adjacent Lanikuhonua Cultural Center is possible, too; see koolina.com/destination/lagoons/ for details on public access. *Off Ali'inui Dr., Ko Olina Resort, Kapolei.*

Snorkeling in Hanauma Bay, which was formed in a volcanic crater.

There are plenty of shallow beaches for novice snorkelers.

★★ Kualoa Regional Park

WINDWARD This 150-acre (61-ha) coconut palm–fringed peninsula is the biggest beach park on the windward side and one of the most scenic in Hawai'i. The sandy waters offshore are generally safe and have snorkeling areas. Just 500 yards (457m) offshore is the tiny islet Mokoli'i Island, which has a small sandy beach and is a bird preserve—so don't spook the red-footed boobies. Check for jellyfish warnings. *49–600 Kamehameha Hwy., Kualoa.*

★★ Lanikai Beach WINDWARD

One of best spots for snorkeling in Hawai'i is off the gold-sand Lani-kai's crystal-clear lagoon (there are so many fish it feels like a giant saltwater aquarium). The reef extends out for about a half mile (.8km), with snorkeling along the entire length. Arrive early to search for limited neighborhood parking near the marked public-access paths. *Off Mokulua Dr., Kailua.*

★ Makaha Beach LEEWARD

During the summer, the waters here are clear and filled with a range of sea life (from green sea turtles to schools of tropical fish to an occasional manta ray). Plus the underwater landscape has arches and tunnels just 40 feet (12m) down, great habitats for reef fish. Weekends see heavy local use. *84–369 Farrington Hwy., Makaha.*

★★★ Malaekahana State Recreation Area NORTH SHORE

This almost mile-long (1.6km) white-sand crescent lives up to just about everyone's image of the perfect Hawaiian beach. In summer, head for the rocky areas around either of

Where to Rent Beach Equipment

If you want to rent beach toys and gear, Waikiki has plenty of vendors, although the best prices aren't necessarily found on the beach. For snorkel gear and boogie boards, go to **Snorkel Bob's** at 700 Kapahulu Ave. (www.snorkelbob.com; ☎ 808/735-7944). For surfboard, stand-up paddleboard, and boogie board rentals, visit **Aloha Beach Services** at the Moana Surfrider, 2365 Kalakaua Ave. (www.alohabeachservices.com; ☎ **808/922-3111,** ext. 2341) or Moku Hawai'i, 2446 Koa Ave. (www.mokuhawaii.surf; ☎ **808/926-6658**).

On O'ahu's windward side, rent kayaks, snorkel sets, and other gear at Kailua Beach Adventures, 130 Kailua Rd., near Kailua Beach Park (www.kailuabeachadventures.com; ☎ **808/262-2555**). On the North Shore, rent all kinds of boards and snorkel gear from Surf-N-Sea, 62–595 Kamehameha Hwy., Hale'iwa (www.surfnsea.com; ☎ **808/637-9887**).

Pupukea Beach Park.

the two points (Makahoa Point and Kalanai Point) that define this bay. *Kamehameha Hwy. (2 miles/3.2km north of the Polynesian Cultural Center).*

★ **Pupukea Beach Park** NORTH SHORE   This North Shore beach is great for snorkeling (May–Oct) not only because of the lush marine life but also because it is a marine life conservation district (sort of like an underwater park), which means that it's illegal to take anything from this park (fish, marine critters, even coral); thus the fish are not only plentiful but also very friendly. As you face the ocean, the northern end is known as Shark's Cove (don't let the name deter you); the southern end is called Three Tables (from the shore, you can see the three flat "tables" and fairly shallow water). Summer snorkeling is normally great in both areas. In the winter, when the big waves roll into

the North Shore, this area can be very dangerous. *59–727 Kamehameha Hwy., Pupukea.*

★★★ **Waikiki Beach** WAIKIKI   This famous 1½-mile-long (2.4km) crescent of sand (much of it imported from Moloka'i or dredged offshore) has great snorkeling spots along nearly the entire length of the beach, but my favorite is Queen's Beach or Queen's Surf Beach, between the Natatorium and the Waikiki Aquarium. It's less crowded here, the waters are calm, and the fish are plentiful. *Stretching from Ala Wai Small Boat Harbor to Kaimana Beach (near Diamond Head).*

★★ **Waimea Beach Park** NORTH SHORE   In summer, this deep, sandy bowl has gentle waves that allow access to great snorkeling around the rocks and reef. Snorkeling isn't an option in the winter, when huge waves pummel the shoreline. *51–031 Kamehameha Hwy., Waimea.*

Snorkelers and sunbathers take to the waters of Hanauma Bay.

Adventures in the Ocean

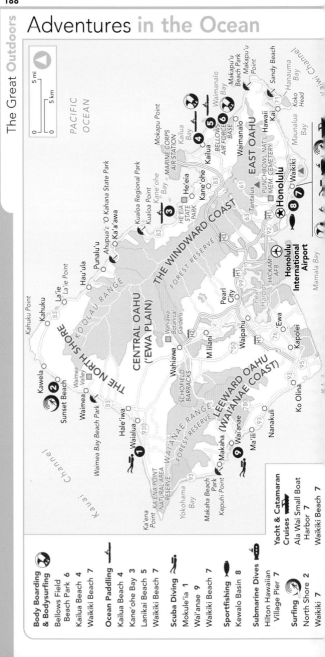

Body Boarding & Bodysurfing
Bellows Field Beach Park 6
Kailua Beach 4
Waikiki Beach 7

Ocean Paddling
Kailua Beach 4
Kane'ohe Bay 3
Lanikai Beach 5
Waikiki Beach 7

Scuba Diving
Mokule'ia 1
Wai'anae 9
Waikiki Beach 7

Sportfishing
Kewalo Basin 8

Submarine Dives
Hilton Hawaiian Village Pier 7

Surfing
North Shore 2
Waikiki 7

Yacht & Catamaran Cruises
Ala Wai Small Boat Harbor 7
Waikiki Beach 7

To really appreciate O'ahu, you need to get off the land. Strap on some scuba gear and plunge beneath the ocean, skip across the water in a sailing charter, go sportfishing and battle a 1,000-pound (454kg) marlin, glide over the water in a kayak or stand-up paddleboard, or ride the waves bodysurfing, board surfing or in an outrigger canoe. Whichever ocean adventure thrills you, you will find it here.

Bodyboarding (Boogie Boarding) & Bodysurfing

Riding the waves without a board, becoming one with the rolling water, is a way of life in Hawai'i. Some bodysurfers just rely on their hands to ride the waves; others use hand boards, a boogie board, or a bodyboard. Both bodysurfing and bodyboarding require a pair of open-heeled swim fins to help propel you through the water. Good places to learn to bodyboard are in the small waves of **Waikiki Beach** and **Kailua Beach** (both reviewed in chapter 6), and Bellows Field Beach Park, off Kalaniana'ole Hwy. 72 in Waimanalo, which is open to the public only noon to 7:45pm Friday, 6am to 7:45pm Saturday and Sunday.

Ocean Paddling

Seeing O'ahu from the sea the way the early Hawaiians did—that's what outrigger canoeing, ocean kayaking and stand-up paddling (SUP) is all about. Early mornings are always best, because the wind comes up around 11am, making seas choppy and paddling difficult. The whole family can surf the waves of Waikiki in an **outrigger canoe** with an experienced "beach boy" as captain; **Waikiki Beach Vendors** (www.waikikibeachservices.com; ☎ 808/927-7441) offers the best value at $35 per rider. For a wonderful adventure, rent a **kayak** or **SUP,** drive to **Lanikai Beach** just as the sun is appearing (the rental places will give you straps for your car), and paddle across the emerald lagoon to the pyramid-shaped islands called Mokulua—it's an experience you won't forget. A second favorite launching area is **Kailua Beach.** Kayak rentals start at $49 half-day for a single kayak ($65 for a double kayak) and SUP rentals start at $55 half-day. See the box "Where to Rent Beach Equipment" on p 186.

★★ **Kama'aina Kayak and Snorkel Eco-Ventures** Revel in amazing views both above and

A bodyboarder takes on some waves.

Waikiki from the Waves

One of the most fun and effortless ways to get in the water is a sail or cruise off Waikiki. Many catamarans launch from Waikiki, but the **Holokai Catamaran** (www.sailholokai.com; ☎ 808/922-2210) is one of the best "booze cruises." It's the least crowded and rowdy, and the drink selection is the best. The 90-minute **Sunset Sail** ($70, ages 21 and up only) is the most popular and festive, with an open bar, while the 90-minute **Tradewind Sail** ($50), which pushes off in the afternoon, is mellower. The most romantic? The **Friday Fireworks Cruise,** an hourlong, adults-only excursion ($70 with open bar) illuminated by the pyrotechnics of the weekly fireworks show. Swim near green sea turtles and other unique marine life on Holokai's twice-daily, 2½-hour **Turtle Canyon Snorkel Sail** ($95).

My favorite non-sailing cruises are offered by the luxury yacht **Vida Mia** (www.thevidamia.com; ☎ 808/746-8342), departing from Ala Wai Small Boat Harbor and heading toward Diamond Head. The 90-minute **Coffee Cruise** ($89 adults, $69 12 and younger) sets off at 7am and features fresh Kona coffee, fruit, and pastries from Honolulu Coffee Company. Two-hour **Sunset Cruises** offer live music and cocktails with appetizers ($129) or chef-made dinner ($189), with fireworks and open bar on Friday nights ($299).

below the water on the Windward Coast by renting a kayak and optional snorkel gear to explore almost-always calm Kane'ohe Bay in the shadow of the majestic Ko'olau Range. After giving advice on the best snorkel sites, the outfitters will set you up right in the water (no lugging it across a beach). As you head to Coconut Island (aka Gilligan's Island), you'll stop to snorkel and admire the fish and turtles. Proceeds go to Kama'aina Kids, which runs environmental education programs for children, and improving He'eia State Park. *46-465 Kamehameha Hwy., Kane'ohe, at He'eia State Park. www.kamaainakidskayaking.org.* ☎ *808/781-4773. Single kayaks half-day $69, full-day $89; $20 extra for snorkel gear. Double kayaks half-day $89, full-day $109; $30 extra for snorkel gear.*

★ Kailua Beach Adventures

First-time kayakers can learn a lot on a 2-hour guided tour, designed for the novice. The fee ($179 adults, $159 kids 8–12) covers lunch, all equipment, lessons, 2 hours of kayaking in Kailua Bay to Popoi'a islet (and bird refuge), plus beach gear

The shallow waters at Pupukea Beach Park are ideal for first-time snorkelers.

Kayaking on the windward coast.

to enjoy for another 2 hours after the tour. Self-guided ($119) and 5-hour tours for experienced kayakers ($249, ages 13 and up) are also available. Two-hour **SUP group lessons** include paddle to Popoi'a and snacks ($179, ages 13 and up); all-day **self-guided SUP tours** include lunch and beach gear ($119 adults, $89 ages 8–12). *130 Kailua Rd., Kailua. www.kailuabeachadventures.com.* ☎ *808/262-2555.*

Scuba Diving

O'ahu is a wonderful place to scuba dive, especially for those interested in wreck diving. One of the more famous wrecks in Hawaii is the *Mahi,* a 185-foot (56m) former minesweeper easily accessible just south of Wai'anae. Abundant marine life makes this a great place to shoot photos—schools of lemon butterfly fish and ta'ape (blue-lined snapper) are so comfortable with divers and photographers that they practically pose. Eagle rays, green sea turtles, manta rays, and white-tipped sharks occasionally cruise by as well, and eels peer out from the wreck.

For non-wreck diving, one of the best dive spots in summer is **Kahuna Canyon,** a massive amphitheater located near Mokule'ia. Walls rising from the ocean floor create the illusion of an underwater Grand Canyon. Inside the amphitheater, crabs, octopuses, slippers,

and spiny lobsters abound (be aware that taking them in summer is illegal), and giant trevally, parrotfish, and unicorn fish congregate as well. Outside the amphitheater, you're likely to see an occasional shark in the distance.

Because O'ahu's greatest dives are offshore, your best bet is to book a two-tank dive from a dive boat. Hawaii's oldest and largest outfitter is **Aaron's Dive Shop,** 307 Hahani St., Kailua (www.aaronsdiveshop. com; ☎ **808/262-2333**). A two-tank boat dive costs $150, including transportation from the Kailua shop and certified divers. Dives start at $100 per person. **Kaimana Divers,** 930 McCully St., Honolulu (waikiki scuba.com; ☎ **808/772-1795**), founded in 2006, offers two-tank dives in Waikiki and sites around the island for $129 for boat charters and $109 for shore dives.

Sportfishing

Marlin (as big as 1,200 lb./544kg), tuna, ono, and mahimahi await the baited hook in Hawaii's coastal and channel waters. No license is required; just book a sportfishing vessel out of Kewalo Basin, on Ala Moana Boulevard (at Ward Ave.), the main location for charter fishing boats on O'ahu, located between the Honolulu International Airport and Waikiki, or contact **Sportfish Hawaii.** This sportfishing booking agency helps match you with the best fishing boat; every vessel it books has been inspected and must meet rigorous criteria to guarantee that you will have a great time. *Note:* Family-friendly, 3-hour in-shore fishing trips are also available for $83 per person. *www.sportfishhawaii.com.* ☎ *877/388-1376 or 808/295-8355. Private charters for 6 passengers start at $1,050 for four hours ($1,600 for up to 12 passengers), full-day charters $1,250 to $2,600.*

Atlantis Adventures submarine, for those who want to go underwater without getting wet.

Submarine Dives

Atlantis* Submarine** will take you on an adventure 100 feet (30.5m) below the surface in high-tech comfort, narrating your 45-minute tour as large portholes reveal tropical fish and sunken ships just outside the sub; if swimming's not your thing, this is a great way to see Hawai'i's sea life. ***Warning: Skip this if you suffer from claustrophobia. *Shuttle boats to the sub (45 min. round-trip) leave from Hilton Hawaiian Village Pier. www.atlantis adventures.com/Waikiki.* ☎ *800/ 381-0237 or 808/973-9800. $143 for adults, $66 for kids 12 & under (who must be at least 36 in. tall).*

Surfing

The ancient Hawaiian sport of *he'e nalu* (wave sliding) is probably the sport most people picture when they think of the islands. In summer, when the water's warm and there's a soft breeze in the air, the south swell comes up. It's surf season in Waikiki, the best place on O'ahu to learn how to surf. For lessons, find **Hans Hedemann Surf School** (www.hhsurf.com; ☎ **808/ 924-7778**) at the Queen Kapi'olani Hotel in Waikiki (and, if you're on the North Shore, there's also an outpost in Hale'iwa). Hans Hedemann, a champion surfer for 18

O'ahu is the perfect place to learn to hang ten.

Sea Life Primer

You're likely to spot one or more of the following fish while underwater:

- **Angelfish** can be distinguished by the spine, located low on the gill plate; some change genders and vibrant hues as they age. They're very shy (perhaps why the five species here have no Hawaiian names); scan closely for them in clear waters above coral reefs, especially the orange-and-blue Potter's angelfish.
- **Butterflyfish** (*kikikapu, lauhau,* etc.), among the most colorful of the reef fish, are usually seen in pairs (scientists believe they mate for life) and appear to spend most of their day feeding. Most butterflyfish have a dark band through the eye and a spot near the tail resembling an eye, meant to confuse their predators (moray eels love to lunch on them).
- **Moray** and **conger eels** (*puhi*) are the most common eels seen in Hawai'i. Morays are usually docile except when provoked or when there's food around. Although morays may look menacing, conger eels look downright happy, with big lips and pectoral fins (looking like big ears) that give them the appearance of a perpetually smiling face.
- **Parrotfish** (*uhu*), one of the largest and most colorful of the reef fish, can grow up to 40 inches (102cm) long. They're easy to spot and even hear underwater—their front teeth are fused together, protruding like buck teeth that allow them to feed by scraping algae from rocks and coral. Native parrotfish species include yellowbar, regal, and spectacled.
- **Scorpion fish** (*nohu*) are what scientists call "ambush predators." They hide under camouflaged exteriors and ambush their prey. Several of the 28 species in Hawai'i sport a venomous dorsal spine. These fish don't have a gas bladder, so when they stop swimming, they sink—that's why you usually find them "resting" on ledges and on the ocean bottom. They're not aggressive, but be very careful where you put your hands and feet in the water so as to avoid those venomous spines.
- **Surgeonfish,** sometimes called tang, get their name from the scalpel-like spines located on each side of the body near the base of the tail. Several surgeonfish, such as the brightly colored yellow tang (*lau'ipala*), are boldly colored; others are adorned in more conservative shades of gray, brown, or black. The convict tang (*manini*) takes its name from its bold, vertical black stripes on a silver background, mimicking prison bars.
- **Wrasses** (*hinalea*) are a very diverse family of fish, ranging in length from 2 to 15 inches (5–38cm). Wrasses can change gender from female to male. Some have brilliant coloration that transforms as they age.

Experiencing *Jaws:* Up Close & Personal

Ocean Ramsey and her crew at **One Ocean Diving** ★★★ (www. oneoceandiving.com; ☎ **808/649-0018**) are on a first-name basis with some of the sharks they swim with. That's right, *swim with,* cage free. And you can join them, with little more than a snorkel, mask, and fins on your feet (this is a snorkeling trip, not scuba diving). As you ride the boat out, about 3 miles offshore from Hale'iwa, where sharks are known to congregate, the crew educates you about shark behavior. For one, they're really not that interested in humans. Two, most of the sharks you'll see are sandbar and Galapagos sharks, which are not considered dangerous. And three, if you should see a potentially more threatening shark, such as a tiger shark, they teach you how to conjure your alpha shark: Stay at the top of the ocean, and don't turn your back on them. Your guides are always alert and nearby; only eight people are allowed in the water at a time. One Ocean Diving hopes to change misconceptions about sharks and bring awareness to their plight as their numbers dwindle. A dive with them is as educational as it is exciting. Rates are $150 a person ($105 if you just want to ride along), and a snorkel mask and fins are provided; you must be 4 feet or taller to enter the water.

years, gives private lessons—at $400 for a 2-hour session (celebrity clients have included Cameron Diaz and Adam Sandler). If the expenditure is beyond your budget, go for a $90, 2-hour group lesson (maximum four people, ages 14 and up) taught by other friendly instructors.

Surf's Up!

To get a free, 5-day forecast of where the waves are, join Surf News Network (www.surfnewsnetwork. com). Or visit hawaiibeachsafety. com for the latest surf and ocean conditions. ●

The Savvy Traveler

Before You Go

Government Tourist Offices

The **Hawai'i Visitors and Convention Bureau (HVCB)** has an office at 2270 Kalakaua Ave., Ste. 801, Honolulu, HI 96815 (www.gohawaii.com; ☎ 800/GO-HAWAII [464-2924] or 808/923-1811). The **O'ahu Visitors Bureau** is at 2270 Kalakaua Ave., Ste. 801, Honolulu, HI 96815 (www. gohawaii.com/oahu; ☎ 877/525-OAHU [6248] or 808/524-0722).

The Best Time to Go

Most visitors don't come to Honolulu when the weather's best in the islands; rather, they come when it's at its worst everywhere else. Thus, the **high season**—when prices are up and resorts are booked to capacity—generally runs from late November to March or mid-April (depending on when Easter falls). The last 2 weeks of December in particular are the prime time for travel. If you're planning a holiday trip, make your reservations as early as possible, count on holiday crowds, and expect to pay top dollar for accommodations, car rentals, and airfare. Whale-watching season begins in January and continues through the rest of winter, sometimes lasting into May.

The **off seasons,** when the best bargain rates are available, are spring (mid-Apr to mid-June) and fall (Sept to mid-November)—a paradox, because these are the best seasons in terms of reliably great weather. If you're looking to save money, or if you just want to avoid the crowds, this is the time to visit. Hotel rates tend to be significantly lower during these off seasons. Airfares also tend to be lower—again, sometimes substantially—and good packages and special deals are often available.

Note: If you plan to come to Honolulu between the last week in April and the first week in May, be sure to book your accommodations, air reservations, and car rental in advance. In Japan, the last week of April is called **Golden Week** because three Japanese holidays take place one after the other. Honolulu is typically busy with Japanese tourists during this time.

Due to the large number of families traveling in **summer** (June–Aug), you won't get the fantastic bargains of spring and fall. A note for surfers: In summer (roughly Jun to the beginning of Sept), the surf comes from the south, Waikiki. During this time, the other side of the island, the North Shore, is calm. During winter (roughly Nov–Feb), big waves roll into the North Shore and Waikiki's water is placid.

Festivals & Special Events

WINTER At the Van's **Triple Crown of Surfing,** the world's top professional surfers compete in events for more than $1 million in prize money. Competition takes place on the North Shore whenever the surf's up, from mid-November through December. Visit www.vanstriplecrownofsurfing.com. The second Sunday in December is the **Honolulu Marathon,** one of the largest marathons in the world, with more than 30,000 competitors. Visit www.honolulumarathon.org. In late January or early February (depending on the lunar calendar), the red carpet is rolled out for **Chinese New Year** with a traditional lion dance, fireworks, food booths, and a host of activities. Call ☎ 808/533-3181 (www.chinesechamber.com). Depending on surf conditions,

February or March brings the **Buffalo's Big Board Classic** at Makaha Beach. You'll see traditional Hawaiian surfing, long boarding, and canoe surfing. Visit www.hoomaa.org/bbbsc.

SPRING The **Annual Easter Sunrise Service** is celebrated with the century-old sunrise services at the National Cemetery of the Pacific, Punchbowl Crater, Honolulu. Call ☎ 808/532-3720 (www.cem.va.gov/cems/nchp/nmcp.asp). In late April, the world's best slack key guitarists perform at the all-day **Waimanalo Kanikapila**, a free concert in Waimanalo Beach Park on the island's windward side. The concert also honors the late Gabby and Cyril Pahinui, who helped preserve this distinctive style of music that began with the arrival of Mexican cowboys in the 1800s. Visit www.cyrilpahinui.com. The **Waikiki Spam Jam Festival** celebrates the locally beloved canned meat with free festivities at shopping malls and special dishes at restaurants. Visit spamjamhawaii.com. May 1 means Lei Day in Hawai'i. On O'ahu, lei-making contests and other activities are organized by the parks department (www.honolulu.gov/parks). Mid-May brings the **World Fireknife Championships** and **We Are Samoa Festival,**

Polynesian Cultural Center, La'ie, where junior and adult fire-knife dancers from around the world converge for one of the most amazing performances you'll ever see. Authentic Samoan food and cultural festivities round out the fun. Call ☎ 808/293-3333 (www.worldfireknife.com).

SUMMER In June, the **King Kamehameha Celebration,** a state holiday on or near June 11, features a massive floral parade, *ho'olaulea* (party), and much more. Call ☎ 808/586-0300 (ags.hawaii.gov/Kamehameha). Late July is the annual **Queen Lili'uokalani Keiki Hula Competition** at the Neal Blaisdell Center, Honolulu. More than 500 *keiki* (children) representing 22 *halau* (hula schools) from the islands compete in this dancefest. Call ☎ 808/521-6905 (www.keikihula.org).

FALL The statewide **Aloha Festivals,** with parades and other events celebrating Hawaiian culture and friendliness throughout the state, take place in September and October. Call ☎ 808/923-1094 (www.alohafestivals.com) for a schedule of events. The annual **Hawai'i International Film Festival** takes place the first 2 weeks in November. This cinema festival with a cross-cultural spin features

Useful Websites

- **www.gohawaii.com**: An excellent, all-around guide to activities, tours, lodging, and events put together by the Hawai'i Visitors and Convention Bureau.
- **www.gohawaii.com/oahu**: The O'ahu chapter of the state visitors' bureau lists activities, dining, lodging, parks, shopping, and more.
- **www.hawaiian105.com**: Hawaiian music plays around the clock at this radio station, with local events listed on the website.
- **www.staradvertiser.com**: Honolulu's daily newspaper includes a section on entertainment.
- **www.weather.com**: Up-to-the-minute worldwide weather reports are available here.

HONOLULU'S AVERAGE TEMPERATURES & RAINFALL

	JAN	FEB	MAR	APR	MAY	JUNE
High (F/C)	80/27	81/27	82/28	83/28	85/29	87/31
Low (F/C)	66/19	65/18	67/19	68/20	70/21	72/22
Water temp (F/C)	75/24	75/24	76/24	77/25	79/26	81/27
Rain (in/cm)	3.5/9	2.5/6.5	2.5/6.5	1.5/4	1/2.5	0.5/1.5

	JULY	AUG	SEPT	OCT	NOV	DEC
High (F/C)	88/31	89/32	89/32	87/31	84/29	82/28
Low (F/C)	74/23	75/24	74/23	73/23	71/22	68/20
Water temp (F/C)	81/27	81/27	81/27	81/27	79/26	76/24
Rain (in/cm)	0.5/1.5	0.5/1.5	1/2.5	2.5/6.5	3/7.5	4/10

filmmakers from Asia, the Pacific Islands, and the United States. Call ☎ 808/792-1577 (www.hiff.org).

The Weather

Because Honolulu lies at the edge of the tropical zone, it technically has only two seasons, both of them warm. The dry season corresponds to summer, and the rainy season generally runs during the winter, from November to March. It rains every day somewhere in the islands at any time of the year, but the rainy season can be more overcast and cooler. Honolulu and Waikiki generally may have a brief rain shower, followed by bright sunshine and maybe a rainbow. The **year-round temperature** usually varies no more than about 10°, but it depends on where you are. Honolulu's **leeward** sides (the west and south, where Waikiki and Honolulu are located) are usually hot and dry, whereas the **windward** sides (east and north) are generally cooler and moist. If you want arid, sunbaked, desertlike weather, go leeward. If you want lush, often wet, junglelike weather, go windward. If you want to know how to pack just before you go, check CNN's online 5-day forecast at www.cnn.com/weather. You can also get the local weather by calling ☎ 808/973-4380.

Restaurant & Activity Reservations

I can't say it enough: Book well in advance if you're determined to eat at a particular spot or participate in a certain activity. For popular restaurants, if you didn't call in advance, try asking for early or late hours—often tables are available before 6:30pm and after 9pm. You could also call the day before or first thing in the morning, when you may be able to take advantage of a cancellation.

Cell (Mobile) Phones

In general, it's a good bet that your phone will work in Honolulu, although coverage may not be as good as in your hometown.

Getting **There**

By Plane

Fly directly to Honolulu. **United Airlines** (www.united.com; ☎ 800/864-8331) offers the most frequent service from the U.S. mainland. **Alaska Airlines** (www.alaskaair.com; ☎ 800/252-7522) has flights from the West Coast, Salt Lake City and

Boise. **American Airlines** (www.aa.com; ☎ 800/433-7300) offers flights from Dallas, Chicago, Phoenix, and Los Angeles. **Delta Air Lines** (www.delta.com; ☎ 800/221-1212) flies nonstop from Seattle, Los Angeles, Atlanta, New York City, and Minneapolis, among other cities. **Hawaiian Airlines** (www.hawaiianairlines.com; ☎ 800/367-5320) offers nonstop flights to Honolulu from many West Coast cities as well as Austin, Boston, Orlando, and New York City. It also flies nonstop from a variety of Asia Pacific hubs. Bargain hunters will want to check **Southwest Airlines** (www.southwest.com; ☎ 800/435-9792) for flights from the West Coast, Las Vegas, and (seasonally) Phoenix.

Among airlines typically serving Honolulu from places other than the U.S. mainland are **Air Canada** (www.aircanada.com; ☎ 800/776-3000); **Air New Zealand** (www.airnewzealand.com; ☎ 0800/737-000 in New Zealand, 800/262-1234 in the U.S.); **Qantas** (www.qantas.com; ☎ 13 13 13 in Australia, 800/227-4500 in the U.S.); **Japan Air Lines** (www.jal.co.jp/jp/en; ☎ 0570 025 121 worldwide, 800/525-3663 in the U.S.); **Jetstar** (www.jetstar.com; ☎ 866/397-8170) from Sydney; **All Nippon Airways** (**ANA**; www.ana.co.jp; ☎ 310 782 3011 worldwide, 800/235-9262 in the U.S.); **Asiana Airlines** (www.flyasiana.com; ☎ 1588-8000 within Korea, 800/227-5118 in the U.S.); **Korean Air** (www.koreanair.com; ☎ 1588 2001 in Seoul, 800/438-5000 in the U.S.); and **Philippine Airlines** (www.philippineairlines.com; ☎ 632 8855 8888 in Manila, 800/435-9725 in the U.S.).

Getting Around

The best way to sightsee around the entire island is to rent a car. There is bus service ideal for short trips in and around Waikiki, as are ride-share apps like **Uber** (www.uber.com), **Lyft** (www.lyft.com) and their local rival **Holoholo** (www.rideholoholo.com). However, **The Bus** (www.thebus.org; ☎ 808/848-5555) requires riders to put all luggage under the seat (no surfboards or golf clubs), plus timetables and routes are primarily set up for commuters; many visitor attractions do not have direct routes from Waikiki. Book online for the best rates. Until Covid forced massive fleet sell-offs, Honolulu had one of the least expensive car-rental rates in the country; prices are expected to drop once demand has leveled off but be prepared to pay a minimum of $70 a day (including all state taxes and fees). Cars are usually plentiful, but book well ahead for the holidays, which in Hawai'i also means King Kamehameha Day (June 11 or the closest weekend), Prince Kuhio Day (Mar 26), and Admission Day (third weekend in Aug). All the major car-rental agencies have offices in Honolulu: **Alamo** (www.goalamo.com; ☎ 800/327-9633), **Avis** (www.avis.com; ☎ 800/321-3712), **Budget** (www.budget.com; ☎ 800/218-7992), **Dollar** (www.dollar.com; ☎ 800/800-4000), **Enterprise** (www.enterprise.com; ☎ 800/325-8007), **Hertz** (www.hertz.com; ☎ 800/654-3011), **National** (www.nationalcar.com; ☎ 800/227-7368), and **Thrifty** (www.thrifty.com; ☎ 800/367-2277). It's almost always cheaper to rent a car at the airport than in Waikiki or through your hotel (unless there's one already included in your package deal). Many locals make their cars available via **Turo** (www.turo.com), the automobile version of Airbnb, but be aware owners are not allowed to park their cars at the airport, so you'll have to negotiate how to pick up your vehicle.

To rent a car in Hawai'i, you must be at least 25 years old and have a valid driver's license and a credit card. Hawai'i is a no-fault state, which means that if you don't have collision-damage insurance, you are required to pay for all damages before you leave the state, regardless of whether the accident was your fault. Your personal car insurance back home may provide rental-car coverage; read your policy or call your insurer before you leave home. Bring your insurance identification card if you decline the optional insurance, which usually costs from $20 to $42 a day, and obtain the name of your company's local claim representative before you go. Some credit card companies also provide collision-damage insurance for their customers; check with yours before you rent.

Fast **Facts**

ATMS Hawaii pioneered the use of **ATMs** nearly 3 decades ago, and now they're everywhere. You'll find them at most banks, in supermarkets, at Longs Drugs, and in most resorts and shopping centers.

BABYSITTING The first place to check is with your hotel. Many hotels have babysitting services or will provide you with lists of reliable sitters. If this doesn't pan out, call **People Attentive to Children** (PATCH; www.patchhawaii.org; ☎ 808/839-1988), which will refer you to individuals who have taken its childcare training courses.

BANKING HOURS Banks usually open at 8 or 8:30am and close between 4 and 6pm Monday through Friday. Weekend hours, if any, are typically 9am to 1pm Saturday; nearly all are closed Sunday.

BED & BREAKFAST, CONDOMINIUM & VACATION RENTALS While true bed-and-breakfasts are scarce these days, you'll find plenty of rental rooms and homes on airbnb.com and vrbo.com. Make sure to check the reviews to know what you're getting into and look for TAT and TMK numbers to ensure they're legal listings; local authorities have stepped up enforcement efforts.

BUSINESS HOURS Most offices are open from 8am to 5pm. Most shopping centers are open Monday through Friday from 10am to 9pm (although staffing shortages may mean earlier closures), Saturday from 10am to 5:30pm, and Sunday from 10am to 5 or 6pm.

CLIMATE See "The Weather" on p 198.

CONSULATES & EMBASSIES Honolulu hosts several European consulates and many Asia-Pacific consulates, among them: **Australia,** 1000 Bishop St., Penthouse Ste. (https://usa.embassy.gov.au/honolulu; ☎ 808/529-8100); **Federated States of Micronesia,** 3049 Ualena St., Ste. 908 (www.tsmgov.org; ☎ 808/836-4775); **Japan,** 1742 Nuuanu Ave. (www.honolulu.us.emb-japan.go.jp; ☎ 808/543-3111); **Korea,** 2756 Pali Hwy. (https://overseas.mofa.go.kr/us-honolulu-ko; ☎ 808/595-6109); **Republic of the Marshall Islands,** 1888 Lusitana St., Ste. 301 (www.rmiembassyus.org; ☎ 808/545-7767); **Philippines,** 2433 Pali Hwy. (https://honolulupcg.dfa.gov.ph; ☎ 808/595-6316).

CUSTOMS Depending on the city of your departure, some countries (such as Canada) clear customs at the city of departure, while other countries clear customs in Honolulu.

DENTISTS If you need dental attention on O'ahu, find a dentist near you through the website of the **Hawai'i Dental Association** (www.hawaiidentalassociation.net).

DINING With a few exceptions at the high end of the scale, dining attire is fairly casual. It's a good idea to make reservations well in advance if you plan on eating between 6 and 9pm.

DOCTORS Straub Doctors on Call (www.hawaiipacifichealth.org/straub/patient-visitors/doctors-on-call) can dispatch a van if you need help getting to its clinics at Hilton Hawaiian Village (☎ 808/973-5250) and the Sheraton Waikiki (☎ 808/971-6000); it accepts most insurance plans.

ELECTRICITY Like Canada, the United States uses 110–120 volts AC (60 cycles), compared to 220–240 volts AC (50 cycles) in most of Europe, Australia, and New Zealand. If your small appliances use 220 to 240 volts, you'll need a 110-volt transformer and a plug adapter with two flat parallel pins to operate them here. Downward converters that change 220–240 volts to 110–120 volts are difficult to find in the United States, so bring one with you.

EMBASSIES See "Consulates & Embassies," above.

EMERGENCIES Dial ☎ **911** for the police, an ambulance, or the fire department. For the **Poison Control Center,** call ☎ **800/222-1222.**

EVENT LISTINGS The best sources for listings are the Friday edition of the local daily newspaper, *Honolulu Star-Advertiser* (www.staradvertiser. com); and the weekly shopper, *Mid-Week* (www.midweek.com). There are also several tourist publications, such as *This Week on Oahu* (www. thisweekhawaii.com/oahu).

INTERNET ACCESS Every hotel and vacation rental has Internet access, typically high-speed and free (or bundled into the ubiquitous "resort" fees charged by hotels). Hotels may charge for premium streaming services. If you're not staying someplace with service and can't get online via your smartphone, head to the **public libraries** for free Wi-Fi and, if needed, computer access to the Internet for up to four 1-hour sessions per day.

LGBT TRAVELERS The **International Gay & Lesbian Travel Association** (IGLTA; www.iglta.org; ☎ 954/630-1637) is the trade association for the gay and lesbian travel industry and offers an online directory of gay- and lesbian-friendly travel businesses.

MAIL & POSTAGE To find the nearest post office, call ☎ 800/ASK-USPS (275-8777) or visit www.usps. com. The Waikiki post office is at 330 Saratoga Rd. (open 9am to 4:30pm Mon–Fri and 9am to 1pm Sat).

PASSPORTS Always keep a photocopy of your passport with you when you're traveling. If your passport is lost or stolen, having a copy significantly facilitates the reissuing process at your consulate. Keep your passport and other valuables in your room's safe.

PHARMACIES CVS operates the island drugstores known as **Longs Drugs** (www.cvs.com for locations). Longs has six 24-hour pharmacies on O'ahu. The closest to Waikiki are at 2470 S. King St. (☎ 808/947-2651), and 1330 Pali Hwy., near Vineyard Boulevard (☎ 808/536-5542).

RIDESHARING Uber (www.uber. com), Lyft (www.lyft.com) and their local rival **Holoholo** (www.ride holoholo.com) all offer rides on O'ahu for rates that are often higher than taxis during times of peak demand; also, service outside of Waikiki and the airport can mean significantly longer wait times.

SAFETY Although Hawai'i is generally a safe tourist destination, visitors have been crime victims, so stay alert. The most common crime against tourists is rental-car break-ins. Never leave any valuables in your car, not even in your trunk. Be especially careful in high-risk areas, such as beaches and resorts. Never carry large amounts of cash with you. Stay in well-lighted areas after dark. Don't hike on deserted trails or swim in the ocean alone. If you are a victim of crime, first contact the **Honolulu Police Department** (www.honolulu pd.org; ☎ 808/529-3111). For emotional and short-term logistical support, contact **Visitor Aloha Society of Hawaii (VASH),** Waikiki Shopping Plaza, 2250 Kalakaua Ave., Ste. 403–3 (www.visitoralohasociety ofhawaii.org; ☎ 808/926-8274).

SPECTATOR SPORTS Each January, you've got the **Sony Open,** the pro-golf tournament at the tony Waialae Country Club (www.sonyopenin hawaii.com); from May to September, watch for **Hawaiian outrigger canoe races** (www.ohcra.com); in December and January, **surfing contests** like the Triple Crown (www.triplecrownofsurfing.com) draw crowds to the North Shore.

SUNSCREEN Anyone can get a sunburn, but people with lighter skin should be especially mindful of strong UV rays, even on overcast days. Hawai'i forbids the sale of sunscreens with oxybenzone and octinoxate, two chemicals harmful to coral reefs, but do marine life a favor by using only mineral-based sunscreens. Minimize the amount needed by wearing a long-sleeved rash guard in the water and a broad hat and lightweight coverups.

TAXIS Taxis are easy to hail at the airport; go to the center median outside of baggage claim and a uniformed taxi dispatcher (look for their bright yellow shirt) will flag one down for you. Fares are standard for all taxi firms; from the airport, expect to pay about $35 to $40 to Waikiki and about $25 to downtown Honolulu (plus tip). To hail in town, try **The Cab** (www.the cabhawaii.com; ☎ 808/422-2222).

TELEPHONE For directory assistance, dial ☎ **411;** for long-distance

information, dial 1, then the appropriate area code and 555-1212. Pay phones cost 50¢ for local calls (all calls on the island of O'ahu are local calls). The area code for all of Hawaii is 808. Calls to other islands are considered long distance, so you have to dial 1 + 808 + the seven-digit phone number.

TIPPING Tipping is ingrained in the American way of life. Here are some rules of thumb: In hotels, tip bellhops at least $3 for one bag, $5 for two, $10 to $20 if you have three or more pieces of luggage, and tip housekeeping $5 per day ($10 for a suite), and more if you've left a disaster area to clean up, or if you're traveling with kids and/or pets. Tip the doorman or concierge only if he or she has provided you with some specific service (such as calling a cab). In restaurants, bars, and nightclubs, tip service staff 20% of the check before tax and tip bartenders 10% to 15% and please round up—no one wants coins. Tipping is not expected in cafeterias and fast-food restaurants. Tip cab drivers 15% of the fare and tip skycaps at airports at least $3 per bag, more if you have a lot or very bulky luggage.

TOILETS Your best bet is Starbucks or a fast-food restaurant. You can also head to hotel lobbies and shopping centers. Parks have restrooms, but generally they are not very clean and are in need of major repairs.

TOURIST OFFICES See "Government Tourist Offices" on p 196.

TRAVELERS WITH DISABILITIES Travelers with disabilities are made to feel very welcome in Hawaii. Hotels are required to offer wheelchair-accessible rooms, and tour companies provide many special services.

Soderholm Bus & Mobility (www.soderholmbus.com; ☎ 808/834-1417) has two wheelchair-accessible vans for rent for $245 a day, plus airport and hotel pickup/dropoff charges ($50 and $100 respectively, each way).

Wheelchair Transportation (☎ 808/723-9055) is a private company offering wheelchair taxi services in air-conditioned vehicles that are specially equipped with ramps and wheelchair lockdowns. To rent hand-controlled cars, contact **Avis** (www.avis.com; ☎ 800/331-1212) and **Hertz** (www.hertz.com; ☎ 800/654-3131). The number of hand-controlled cars in Hawaii is limited, so be sure to book well in advance. Vision-impaired travelers and others with service dogs will need to make sure their airline allows animals on flights and complete paperwork in advance that includes proof of rabies vaccination and microchipping, among other requirements. For detailed regulations and information, visit hdoa.hawaii.gov/ai/aqs/aqs-info, the animal quarantine page of the State of Hawaii Animal Industry Division (☎ 808/483-7151). Without the right paperwork, animals may be quarantined at a state-run facility for up to 30 days at your expense.

Hawai'i: **A Brief History**

AROUND 500 OR EARLIER Paddling outrigger canoes, the first ancestors of today's Hawaiians follow the stars, currents, and birds across the sea to Hawai'i from the Marquesas and Society islands of modern French Polynesia.

AROUND 1300 The voyages to and from Tahiti end for some reason, and Hawai'i begins to develop its own culture in earnest. The settlers build temples, fishponds, and aqueducts to irrigate taro plantations. Sailors become farmers and fishermen. Each island is a separate kingdom. The *ali'i* (royalty) create a caste system and establish taboos. Violators risk severe punishment, including death. High priests ask the gods Lono, Kane, Kanaloa, and Ku for divine guidance. Ritual human sacrifices are common.

1778 Captain James Cook, trying to find the mythical Northwest Passage to link the Pacific and Atlantic oceans, sails into Waimea Bay on Kaua'i, arriving at a time and manner associated with the god Lono. Overnight, Stone Age Hawai'i enters the age of iron.

Nails are traded for fresh water, pigs, and other goods. The sailors bring syphilis, measles, and other diseases to which the Hawaiians have no natural immunity, thereby unwittingly wreaking havoc on the native population.

FEB 14, 1779 In a skirmish provoked by theft, kidnapping, and cultural misunderstanding, Hawaiians kill Cook and four of his crew in Kealakekua Bay on the island of Hawai'i.

1782 Kamehameha, a warrior born into a chiefly family on Hawai'i Island, begins battling for control first of his home island, then the rest.

1795 Now a king, Kamehameha conquers O'ahu in a bloody battle fought the length of Nu'uanu Valley.

1804 King Kamehameha moves his court from the island of Hawai'i to Waikiki and 5 years later relocates to what is now downtown Honolulu, next to Nimitz Highway at Queen and Bethel streets.

1810 Also known as Kamehameha the Great, the king finally unites the Hawaiian Islands under a single leader, avoiding bloodshed on Kaua'i and Ni'ihau

1819 This year brings events that change the Hawaiian Islands forever: Kamehameha I dies, his son Liholiho is proclaimed Kamehameha II, and, under the influence of Queen Ka'ahumanu, Kamehameha II orders the destruction of *heiau* (temples) and an end to the *kapu* (taboo) system, thus overthrowing the traditional Hawaiian religion. The first whaling ship, *Bellina,* drops anchor in Lahaina.

1820 Missionaries arrive from New England, bent on converting the pagans. Intent on instilling their brand of Christianity in the islanders, the missionaries clothe the natives, ban them from dancing the hula, and nearly dismantle their ancient culture. They also bring literacy and Western musical traditions, creating a written language to translate the Bible and hymns into Hawaiian. They try to keep the whalers and sailors out of the bawdy houses, where a flood of whiskey quenches fleet-size thirsts and venereal diseases spread into the local population.

1845 King Kamehameha III moves the capital of Hawai'i from Lahaina to Honolulu, where more commerce can be accommodated due to the natural harbor there. Honolulu is still the capital and dominant city today.

1848 The Great Mahele is signed by King Kamehameha III, which allows commoners and foreigners to own land outright or in "fee simple," inadvertently leading to the dispossession of many traditional caretakers of the land and generational poverty that continues today.

1882 'Iolani Palace is built in Honolulu, the only royal residence and seat of government in the U.S.

1885 The first contract laborers from Japan arrive to work on sugarcane plantations.

JAN 17, 1893 A group of American sugar planters and missionary descendants, with the support of U.S. Marines, imprisons Queen Lili'uokalani in 'Iolani Palace and illegally overthrows the Hawaiian government.

1898 Despite a massive petition drive by Native Hawaiians against it, Hawai'i is annexed to the United States.

1900 Hawai'i becomes a U.S. territory. The Great Chinatown Fire leaves 7,000 people homeless in Honolulu.

1922 Prince Jonah Kuhio Kalaniana'ole, the last powerful member of the royal Hawaiian family, dies.

1927 First nonstop air flight is made from the mainland to Honolulu.

DEC 7, 1941 Japanese Zeros bomb American warships based at Pearl Harbor, plunging the United States into World War II.

MAR 18, 1959 Hawai'i becomes the last star on the Stars and Stripes, the 50th state of the Union. This year also sees the arrival of the first jet airliners, which bring 250,000 tourists to the fledgling state.

1967 The state of Hawai'i hosts one million tourists, almost all heading to Waikiki.

1990s Hawai'i's state economy goes into a tailspin following a series of events: First, the Gulf War severely curtails air travel to the island; then Hurricane 'Iniki slams into Kaua'i, crippling its infrastructure; and, finally, sugar-cane companies across the state begin shutting down, laying off thousands of workers.

2008 One of the biggest booms to Hawai'i's tourism comes from a son of Hawai'i, Barack Obama, when he is elected the 44th president of the United States.

2019 A record 10.4 million visitors arrive in Hawai'i, heightening concerns throughout the state about overtourism, illegal vacation rentals, and related issues.

2020 The coronavirus pandemic prompts a virtual lockdown on tourism for 7 months due to a mandatory 2-week quarantine. While case numbers and deaths are among the lowest in the U.S., widespread unemployment and business closures result. Tourism is slowly reintroduced later through a pre-arrival testing program.

2022 In March, the state removes all restrictions on incoming domestic travelers and lifts statewide masking rules. Many businesses remain short-staffed. Newly aware of Hawai'i's relative safety as well as beauty, mainlanders snap up condos and houses, and hotel and rental car prices surge due to renewed demand.

The Hawaiian **Language**

The official languages of Hawai'i are English and Hawaiian. From the 1830s to the 1950s, the language was in danger of extinction as the number of native speakers of Hawaiian steeply declined. But since the late 20th century, the Hawaiian language has been experiencing a revival, fueled by an interest in preserving Native Hawaiian culture.

These days, all visitors will hear the words *aloha* (hello, goodbye, love) and *mahalo* (thank you). If you've just arrived, you're a *malihini*. Someone who's been here a long time is a *kama'aina*. When you finish a job or your meal, you are *pau* (finished). On Friday it's *pau hana*, work finished. You eat *pupu* (Hawaii's version of hors d'oeuvres) when it's *pau hana* time.

The Hawaiian alphabet, created by the New England missionaries, has only 12 of the letters used in English, plus a glottal stop, called *'okina*, that serves as a consonant—it's the audible pause between vowels made in English words like "uh-oh." The vowels are a, e, i, o, and u; if there is a macron (*kahakō*) over them, they are lengthened. The vowels are pronounced in the Roman fashion, that is, *ah, ay, ee, oh,* and *oo* (as in "too")—not *ay,* *ee, eye, oh,* and *you,* as in English. For example, *huhu* (to pet) is pronounced *who-who*; *huhu* (anger) is *who-whoo*. The consonants are h, k, l, m, n, p, and w; the 'okina is represented by the '. Although they're becoming more common in signage and print, you may not always see the macron and 'okina in written language. Still, be aware they affect meaning as well as pronunciation. For typographical reasons, this guidebook only uses the 'okina.

Useful Words & Phrases

Here are some basic Hawaiian words that you'll often hear in Hawai'i and see throughout this book; the plurals of most nouns are the same as the singular form. For dictionaries of Hawaiian words, including place names, see www.wehewehe.org.

The Savvy Traveler

ali'i Hawaiian royalty
aloha greeting or farewell
halau canoe shed, meeting house, or hula school
hale house or building
heiau Hawaiian temple or place of worship
kahuna priest or expert
kama'aina "child of the land," non-Native Hawaiian longtime residents
kapa tapa, bark cloth
kapu taboo, forbidden
keiki child
lanai porch or veranda
lomilomi traditional massage or style of salmon poke
mahalo thank you
makai toward the sea (used in directions)
mana spiritual power
mauka toward the mountains (used in directions)
mu'umu'u loose-fitting gown or dress
'ono delicious (ono without an 'okina is a kind of mackerel)
pali cliff
paniolo Hawaiian cowboy
wikiwiki very quickly

Hawaiian Pidgin

A creole language, Hawaiian Pidgin is spoken throughout the islands and cherished as a living, evolving legacy of the plantation era, when workers from different cultures needed to communicate. It's based on English but with some distinctly Hawaiian syntax and a vocabulary that draws from English, Hawaiian, Ilocano, Tagalog, Japanese, Chinese, and Portuguese. Visitors shouldn't try to speak it, but it helps to recognize words and phrases in common use, like the following.

aurite all right
bumbye later, eventually
grinds or grindz food
howzit how's it going?
kaukau to eat, or food and drink
lua bathroom or outhouse
shishi to urinate
slippahs flip-flops (thonged sandals)
talk story have a conversation

Eating in **Honolulu**

In the mid-1980s, Hawai'i Regional Cuisine (HRC) ignited a culinary revolution, showcasing the rich bounty of the islands' farms, ranches, and fishing boats with a mix of European and Asian cooking techniques. Reflecting waves of immigration, local produce now includes fruits and vegetables traditional to Vietnamese, Filipino, Thai, Japanese, Chinese, and Polynesian cuisines; the seafood menu has expanded to include delicious farmed shrimp, abalone, lobster, and even oysters.

Today's top chefs delve freely into the islands' multicultural plantation heritage as well as gastronomic trends from the mainland, leading to exciting new interpretations of "local food." By that I mean plate lunches and poke, shave ice and saimin, bento lunches and *manapua* (steamed buns)— cultural hybrids all. A **plate lunch** consists of a hearty protein such as fried mahimahi, teriyaki beef, kalbi ribs, kalua pork, or shoyu chicken, plus "two scoops rice," macaroni salad, and a few leaves of green— typically julienned cabbage. Heavy gravy is often the condiment of choice, accompanied by a soft drink in a paper cup or straight out of the can. Another favorite is **saimin**—the local version of noodles in broth topped with egg, green onions, fish cake, and sometimes pork.

The **bento,** another popular quick meal available throughout Hawai'i, is a compact, boxed assortment of picnic fare usually consisting of neatly arranged sections of rice, pickled vegetables, and fried chicken, beef, or pork. From the plantations come **manapua,** a bready, doughy sphere filled with tasty fillings of sweetened pork or sweet beans. The daintier Chinese delicacy **dim sum** is made of translucent wrappers filled with fresh seafood, pork hash, and vegetables, served for breakfast and lunch. For dessert or a snack, the prevailing choice is **shave ice,** the island version of a snow cone. The local twist on Japanese sweets, *mochi* (pillowy confections made with rice flour) and *manju* (miniturnovers made with pie crust) may be filled with sweet beans, peanut butter, or fruit and are also worth seeking out. For a savory hit, try a Spam *musubi*—a grilled slab of the canned meat with rice in a *nori* seaweed wrap.

Recommended **Reading**

Fiction

The first book people often think about is James A. Michener's *Hawaii.* Published in 1959, and made into an equally epic movie in 1966, this novel traces the islands' pre-statehood history beginning with their volcanic formation. Although dated, it's generally empathetic to the struggles of Hawaiians in the wake of Western contact, and to the Chinese and Japanese immigrants who followed them. For a more contemporary look at life in Hawai'i, one of the best novels is 1995's *Shark Dialogues,* by Kiana Davenport, which tells the story of Pono, a larger-than-life matriarch, and her four daughters of mixed races. Lois-Ann Yamanaka uses a very "local" voice (including Hawaiian Pidgin) and stark depictions of life in the islands in fabulous novels such as 1996's *Blu's Hanging.* Kaui Hart Hemming's 2007 novel *The Descendants* provides keen insights into the lifestyle of the islands' elite class, with a protagonist memorably played by George Clooney in the 2011 film version.

History & Memoir

Mark Twain's writing on Hawai'i in the 1860s offers a wonderful introduction to Hawai'i in the first century after Capt. Cook's arrival in 1778, especially *Mark Twain in Hawaii: Roughing It in the Sandwich Islands.* Another great depiction of the Hawaii of 1889 is *Travels in Hawaii* by Robert Louis Stevenson.

There are many great books on Hawai'i's history, but one of the best places to start is with the formation of the Hawaiian Islands, vividly described in David E. Eyre's *By Wind, By Wave: An Introduction to Hawaii's Natural History* (2000). In addition to chronicling the natural history of Hawai'i, Eyre describes the complex interrelationships among the plants, animals, ocean, and people.

For a history of "precontact" Hawai'i, David Malo's *Hawaiian Antiquities* is the preeminent source. Malo was born around 1793 and wrote about Hawaii at that time as well as the beliefs and religion of his people. Bishop Museum's 1976 edition is an excellent reference book, but not a fast read. For more readable books on old Hawaii, try *Stories of Old Hawaii*, a 1997 collection of myths and legends by Roy Kakulu Alameida; the 1998 Thomas G. Thrum's anthology *Hawaiian Folk Tales*; and *The Legends and Myths of Hawaii*, a 1992 reissue of stories collected by King David Kalakaua.

The best story of the 1893 overthrow of the Hawaiian monarchy is told by Queen Lili'uokalani, in her book *Hawaii's Story by Hawaii's Queen Liliuokalani*. When it was written in 1898, it was an international plea for justice for her people, but it is a poignant read even today. It's also a "must read" for people interested in current events

and the recent rally in the 50th state for sovereignty. Two more recent books on the question of Hawai'i's sovereignty are Tom Coffman's 1998 *Nation Within—The Story of America's Annexation of the Nation of Hawaii* and Julia Flynn Siler's 2012 *Lost Kingdom: Hawaii's Last Queen, the Sugar Kings, and America's First Imperial Adventure*.

Lawrence H. Fuchs's 1991 *Hawaii Pono* is a carefully researched tome on the contributions of each of Hawai'i's main immigrant communities (Chinese, Japanese, and Filipino) between 1893 and 1959. An insightful look at history and its effect on the Hawaiian culture is *Waikiki, a History of Forgetting and Remembering*, by Andrea Feeser (2006). A beautiful art book (designed by Gaye Chan), this is not your normal coffee-table tome but a different look at the cultural and environmental history of Waikiki. Using historical texts, photos, government documents, and interviews, this book lays out the story of how Waikiki went from a self-sufficient agricultural area to a tourism mecca.

Another great cultural book is Davianna Pomaikai McGreggor's *Na Kua'aina, Living Hawaiian Culture* (2007). McGregor, a professor of ethnic studies at University of Hawai'i, examines how people lived in rural lands and how they kept the Hawaiian traditions alive. ●

Index

See also Accommodations and Restaurant indexes, below.

Photo **Credits**